Game Theory for Applied Economists

Game Theory for Applied Economists

Robert Gibbons

Princeton University Press
Princeton, New Jersey

Library of Congress Cataloging-in-Publication Data

Gibbons, R. 1958–
    Game theory for applied economists / Robert Gibbons.
       p.   cm.
    Includes bibliographical references and index.
    ISBN 0-691-04308-6 (CL)
    ISBN ISBN 0-691-00395-5 (PB)
    1. Game theory. 2. Economics, Mathematical. 3. Economics–Mathematical
Models. I. Title.
  HB144.G49   1992
  330′.01′5193–dc20   92-2788
                                              CIP

This book was composed with L#T_EX by Archetype Publishing Inc., P.O. Box 6567,
Champaign, IL 61821.

Printed in the United States

10 9 8 7 6 5 4 3 2

Outside of the United States and Canada, this book is available through Harvester
Wheatsheaf under the title *A Primer in Game Theory*.

for Margaret

Contents

Preface

Game theory is the study of multiperson decision problems. Such problems arise frequently in economics. As is widely appreciated, for example, oligopolies present multiperson problems — each firm must consider what the others will do. But many other applications of game theory arise in fields of economics other than industrial organization. At the micro level, models of trading processes (such as bargaining and auction models) involve game theory. At an intermediate level of aggregation, labor and financial economics include game-theoretic models of the behavior of a firm in its input markets (rather than its output market, as in an oligopoly). There also are multiperson problems within a firm: many workers may vie for one promotion; several divisions may compete for the corporation's investment capital. Finally, at a high level of aggregation, international economics includes models in which countries compete (or collude) in choosing tariffs and other trade policies, and macroeconomics includes models in which the monetary authority and wage or price setters interact strategically to determine the effects of monetary policy.

This book is designed to introduce game theory to those who will later construct (or at least consume) game-theoretic models in applied fields within economics. The exposition emphasizes the economic applications of the theory at least as much as the pure theory itself, for three reasons. First, the applications help teach the theory; formal arguments about abstract games also appear but play a lesser role. Second, the applications illustrate the process of model building — the process of translating an informal description of a multiperson decision situation into a formal, game-theoretic problem to be analyzed. Third, the variety of applications shows that similar issues arise in different areas of economics, and that the same game-theoretic tools can be applied in each setting. In order to emphasize the broad potential scope of the theory, conventional applications from industrial organization largely have been replaced by applications from labor, macro, and other applied fields in economics.[1]

We will discuss four classes of games: static games of complete information, dynamic games of complete information, static games of incomplete information, and dynamic games of incomplete information. (A game has incomplete information if one player does not know another player's payoff, such as in an auction when one bidder does not know how much another bidder is willing to pay for the good being sold.) Corresponding to these four classes of games will be four notions of equilibrium in games: Nash equilibrium, subgame-perfect Nash equilibrium, Bayesian Nash equilibrium, and perfect Bayesian equilibrium.

Two (related) ways to organize one's thinking about these equilibrium concepts are as follows. First, one could construct sequences of equilibrium concepts of increasing strength, where stronger (i.e., more restrictive) concepts are attempts to eliminate implausible equilibria allowed by weaker notions of equilibrium. We will see, for example, that subgame-perfect Nash equilibrium is stronger than Nash equilibrium and that perfect Bayesian equilibrium in turn is stronger than subgame-perfect Nash equilibrium. Second, one could say that the equilibrium concept of interest is always perfect Bayesian equilibrium (or perhaps an even stronger equilibrium concept), but that it is equivalent to Nash equilibrium in static games of complete information, equivalent to subgame-perfection in dynamic games of complete (and perfect) information, and equivalent to Bayesian Nash equilibrium in static games of incomplete information.

The book can be used in two ways. For first-year graduate students in economics, many of the applications will already be familiar, so the game theory can be covered in a half-semester course, leaving many of the applications to be studied outside of class. For undergraduates, a full-semester course can present the theory a bit more slowly, as well as cover virtually all the applications in class. The main mathematical prerequisite is single-variable calculus; the rudiments of probability and analysis are introduced as needed.

---

[1] A good source for applications of game theory in industrial organization is Tirole's *The Theory of Industrial Organization* (MIT Press, 1988).

I learned game theory from David Kreps, John Roberts, and Bob Wilson in graduate school, and from Adam Brandenburger, Drew Fudenberg, and Jean Tirole afterward. I owe the theoretical perspective in this book to them. The focus on applications and other aspects of the pedagogical style, however, are largely due to the students in the MIT Economics Department from 1985 to 1990, who inspired and rewarded the courses that led to this book. I am very grateful for the insights and encouragement all these friends have provided, as well as for the many helpful comments on the manuscript I received from Joe Farrell, Milt Harris, George Mailath, Matthew Rabin, Andy Weiss, and several anonymous reviewers. Finally, I am glad to acknowledge the advice and encouragement of Jack Repcheck of Princeton University Press and financial support from an Olin Fellowship in Economics at the National Bureau of Economic Research.

Game Theory for Applied Economists

Chapter 1

Static Games of Complete Information

In this chapter we consider games of the following simple form: first the players simultaneously choose actions; then the players receive payoffs that depend on the combination of actions just chosen. Within the class of such static (or simultaneous-move) games, we restrict attention to games of *complete information*. That is, each player's payoff function (the function that determines the player's payoff from the combination of actions chosen by the players) is common knowledge among all the players. We consider dynamic (or sequential-move) games in Chapters 2 and 4, and games of incomplete information (games in which some player is uncertain about another player's payoff function—as in an auction where each bidder's willingness to pay for the good being sold is unknown to the other bidders) in Chapters 3 and 4.

In Section 1.1 we take a first pass at the two basic issues in game theory: how to describe a game and how to solve the resulting game-theoretic problem. We develop the tools we will use in analyzing static games of complete information, and also the foundations of the theory we will use to analyze richer games in later chapters. We define the *normal-form representation* of a game and the notion of a *strictly dominated strategy*. We show that some games can be solved by applying the idea that rational players do not play strictly dominated strategies, but also that in other games this approach produces a very imprecise prediction about the play of the game (sometimes as imprecise as "anything could happen"). We then motivate and define *Nash equilibrium*—a solution concept that produces much tighter predictions in a very broad class of games.

In Section 1.2 we analyze four applications, using the tools developed in the previous section: Cournot's (1838) model of imperfect competition, Bertrand's (1883) model of imperfect competition, Farber's (1980) model of final-offer arbitration, and the problem of the commons (discussed by Hume [1739] and others). In each application we first translate an informal statement of the problem into a normal-form representation of the game and then solve for the game's Nash equilibrium. (Each of these applications has a unique Nash equilibrium, but we discuss examples in which this is not true.)

In Section 1.3 we return to theory. We first define the notion of a *mixed strategy*, which we will interpret in terms of one player's uncertainty about what another player will do. We then state and discuss Nash's (1950) Theorem, which guarantees that a Nash equilibrium (possibly involving mixed strategies) exists in a broad class of games. Since we present first basic theory in Section 1.1, then applications in Section 1.2, and finally more theory in Section 1.3, it should be apparent that mastering the additional theory in Section 1.3 is not a prerequisite for understanding the applications in Section 1.2. On the other hand, the ideas of a mixed strategy and the existence of equilibrium do appear (occasionally) in later chapters.

This and each subsequent chapter concludes with problems, suggestions for further reading, and references.

1.1   Basic Theory: Normal-Form Games and Nash Equilibrium

1.1.A   Normal-Form Representation of Games

In the normal-form representation of a game, each player simultaneously chooses a strategy, and the combination of strategies chosen by the players determines a payoff for each player. We illustrate the normal-form representation with a classic example — *The Prisoners' Dilemma*. Two suspects are arrested and charged with a crime. The police lack sufficient evidence to convict the suspects, unless at least one confesses. The police hold the suspects in separate cells and explain the consequences that will follow from the actions they could take. If neither confesses then both will be convicted of a minor offense and sentenced to one month in jail. If both confess then both will be sentenced to jail for six months. Finally, if one confesses but the other does not, then the confessor will be released immediately but the other will be sentenced to nine months in jail—six for the crime and a further three for obstructing justice.

The prisoners' problem can be represented in the accompanying bi-matrix. (Like a matrix, a bi-matrix can have an arbitrary number or rows and columns; "bi" refers to the fact that, in a two-player game, there are two numbers in each cell—the payoffs to the two players.)

Prisoner 2

		Mum	Fink
Prisoner 1	Mum	$-1, -1$	$-9, \ \ 0$
	Fink	$0, -9$	$-6, -6$

The Prisoners' Dilemma

In this game, each player has two strategies available: confess (or fink) and not confess (or be mum). The payoffs to the two players when a particular pair of strategies is chosen are given in the appropriate cell of the bi-matrix. By convention, the payoff to the so-called row player (here, Prisoner 1) is the first payoff given, followed by the payoff to the column player (here, Prisoner 2). Thus, if Prisoner 1 chooses Mum and Prisoner 2 chooses Fink, for example, then Prisoner 1 receives the payoff -9 (representing nine months in jail) and Prisoner 2 receives the payoff 0 (representing immediate release).

We now turn to the general case. The *normal-form representation* of a game specifies: (1) the players in the game, (2) the strategies available to each player, and (3) the payoff received by each player for each combination of strategies that could be chosen by the players. We will often discuss an n-player game in which the players are numbered from 1 to n and an arbitrary player is called player i. Let S_i denote the set of strategies available to player i (called i's *strategy space*), and let s_i denote an arbitrary member of this set. (We will occasionally write $s_i \in S_i$ to indicate that the strategy s_i is a member of the set of strategies S_i.) Let $(s_1, \ldots, s_n)$ denote a combination of strategies, one for each player, and let u_i denote player i's *payoff function*: $u_i(s_1, \ldots, s_n)$ is the payoff to player i if the players choose the strategies $(s_1, \ldots, s_n)$. Collecting all of this information together, we have:

Definition *The **normal-form representation** of an n-player game specifies the players' strategy spaces $S_1, \ldots, S_n$ and their payoff functions $u_1, \ldots, u_n$. We denote this game by $G = \{S_1, \ldots, S_n; u_1, \ldots, u_n\}$.*

Although we stated that in a normal-form game the players choose their strategies simultaneously, this does not imply that the parties necessarily *act* simultaneously: it suffices that each choose his or her action without knowledge of the others' choices, as would be the case here if the prisoners reached decisions at arbitrary times while in their separate cells. Furthermore, although in this chapter we use normal-form games to represent only static games in which the players all move without knowing the other players' choices, we will see in Chapter 2 that normal-form representations can be given for sequential-move games, but also that an alternative—the *extensive-form* representation of the game—is often a more convenient framework for analyzing dynamic issues.

1.1.B   Iterated Elimination of Strictly Dominated Strategies

Having described one way to represent a game, we now take a first pass at describing how to solve a game-theoretic problem. We start with the Prisoners' Dilemma because it is easy to solve, using only the idea that a rational player will not play a strictly dominated strategy.

In the Prisoners' Dilemma, if one suspect is going to play Fink, then the other would prefer to play Fink and so be in jail for six months rather than play Mum and so be in jail for nine months. Similarly, if one suspect is going to play Mum, then the other would prefer to play Fink and so be released immediately rather than play Mum and so be in jail for one month. Thus, for prisoner i, playing Mum is dominated by playing Fink—for each strategy that prisoner j could choose, the payoff to prisoner i from playing Mum is less than the payoff to i from playing Fink. (The same would be true in any bi-matrix in which the payoffs 0, -1, -6, and -9 above were replaced with payoffs T, R, P, and S, respectively, provided that $T > R > P > S$ so as to capture the ideas of temptation, reward, punishment, and sucker payoffs.) More generally:

Definition *In the normal-form game $G = \{S_1, \ldots, S_n; u_1, \ldots, u_n\}$, let s_i' and s_i'' be feasible strategies for player i (i.e., s_i' and s_i'' are members of S_i). Strategy s_i' is **strictly dominated** by strategy s_i'' if for each feasible combination of the other players' strategies, i's payoff from playing s_i' is strictly less than i's payoff from playing s_i'':*

$$u_i(s_1, \ldots, s_{i-1}, s_i', s_{i+1}, \ldots, s_n) < u_i(s_1, \ldots, s_{i-1}, s_i'', s_{i+1}, \ldots, s_n) \quad \text{(DS)}$$

for each $(s_1, \ldots, s_{i-1}, s_{i+1}, \ldots, s_n)$ that can be constructed from the other players' strategy spaces $S_1, \ldots, S_{i-1}, S_{i+1}, \ldots, S_n$.

Rational players do not play strictly dominated strategies, because there is no belief that a player could hold (about the strategies the other players will choose) such that it would be optimal to play such a strategy.[1] Thus, in the Prisoners' Dilemma, a rational player will choose Fink, so (Fink, Fink) will be the outcome reached by two rational players, even though (Fink, Fink) results in worse payoffs for both players than would (Mum, Mum). Because the Prisoners' Dilemma has many applications (including the arms race and the free-rider problem in the provision of public goods), we will return to variants of the game in Chapters 2 and 4. For now, we focus instead on whether the idea that rational players do not play strictly dominated strategies can lead to the solution of other games.

Consider the abstract game in Figure 1.1.1.[2] Player 1 has two strategies and player 2 has three: $S_1 = \{\text{Up}, \text{Down}\}$ and $S_2 = \{\text{Left}, \text{Middle}, \text{Right}\}$. For player 1, neither Up nor Down is strictly

---

[1] A complementary question is also of interest: if there is no belief that player i could hold (about the strategies the other players will choose) such that it would be optimal to play the strategy s_i, can we conclude that there must be another strategy that strictly dominates s_i? The answer is "yes," *provided* that we adopt appropriate definitions of "belief" and "another strategy," both of which involve the idea of mixed strategies to be introduced in Section 1.3.A.

[2] Most of this book considers economic applications rather than abstract examples, both because the applications are of interest in their own right and because, for many readers, the applications are often a useful way to explain the underlying theory. When introducing some of the basic theoretical ideas, however, we will sometimes resort to abstract examples that have no natural economic interpretation.

Player 2

		Left	Middle	Right
Player 1	Up	1, 0	1, 2	0, 1
	Down	0, 3	0, 1	2, 0

Figure 1.1.1.

dominated: Up is better than Down if 2 plays Left (because $1 > 0$), but Down is better than Up if 2 plays Right (because $2 > 0$). For player 2, however, Right is strictly dominated by Middle (because $2 > 1$ and $1 > 0$), so a rational player 2 will not play Right. Thus, if player 1 knows that player 2 is rational then player 1 can eliminate Right from player 2's strategy space. That is, if player 1 knows that player 2 is rational then player 1 can play the game in Figure 1.1.1 *as if* it were the game in Figure 1.1.2.

Player 2

		Left	Middle
Player 1	Up	1, 0	1, 2
	Down	0, 3	0, 1

Figure 1.1.2.

In Figure 1.1.2, Down is now strictly dominated by Up for player 1, so if player 1 is rational (and player 1 knows that player 2 is rational, so that the game in Figure 1.1.2 applies) then player 1 will not play Down. Thus, if player 2 knows that player 1 is rational, *and* player 2 knows that player 1 knows that player 2 is rational (so that player 2 knows that Figure 1.1.2 applies), then player 2 can eliminate Down from player 1's strategy space, leaving the game in Figure 1.1.3. But now Left is strictly dominated by Middle for player 2, leaving (Up, Middle) as the outcome of the game.

This process is called *iterated elimination of strictly dominated strategies*. Although it is based on the appealing idea that rational players do not play strictly dominated strategies, the process has two drawbacks. First, each step requires a further assumption

Player 2

		Left	Middle
Player 1	Up	1,0	1,2

Figure 1.1.3.

about what the players know about each other's rationality. If we want to be able to apply the process for an arbitrary number of steps, we need to assume that it is *common knowledge* that the players are rational. That is, we need to assume not only that all the players are rational, but also that all the players know that all the players are rational, and that all the players know that all the players know that all the players are rational, and so on, *ad infinitum*. (See Aumann [1976] for the formal definition of common knowledge.)

The second drawback of iterated elimination of strictly dominated strategies is that the process often produces a very imprecise prediction about the play of the game. Consider the game in Figure 1.1.4, for example. In this game there are no strictly dominated strategies to be eliminated. (Since we have not motivated this game in the slightest, it may appear arbitrary, or even pathological. See the case of three or more firms in the Cournot model in Section 1.2.A for an economic application in the same spirit.) Since all the strategies in the game survive iterated elimination of strictly dominated strategies, the process produces no prediction whatsoever about the play of the game.

	L	C	R
T	0,4	4,0	5,3
M	4,0	0,4	5,3
B	3,5	3,5	6,6

no prediction from domination

Figure 1.1.4.

We turn next to Nash equilibrium—a solution concept that produces much tighter predictions in a very broad class of games. We show that Nash equilibrium is a stronger solution concept

NE gives tighter predictions than domination

than iterated elimination of strictly dominated strategies, in the sense that the players' strategies in a Nash equilibrium always survive iterated elimination of strictly dominated strategies, but the converse is not true. In subsequent chapters we will argue that in richer games even Nash equilibrium produces too imprecise a prediction about the play of the game, so we will define still-stronger notions of equilibrium that are better suited for these richer games.

1.1.C Motivation and Definition of Nash Equilibrium

One way to motivate the definition of Nash equilibrium is to argue that if game theory is to provide a unique solution to a game-theoretic problem then the solution must be a Nash equilibrium, in the following sense. Suppose that game theory makes a unique prediction about the strategy each player will choose. In order for this prediction to be correct, it is necessary that each player be willing to choose the strategy predicted by the theory. Thus, each player's predicted strategy must be that player's best response to the predicted strategies of the other players. Such a prediction could be called *strategically stable* or *self-enforcing*, because no single player wants to deviate from his or her predicted strategy. We will call such a prediction a Nash equilibrium:

Definition *In the n-player normal-form game* $G = \{S_1, \ldots, S_n; u_1, \ldots, u_n\}$, *the strategies* $(s_1^*, \ldots, s_n^*)$ *are a **Nash equilibrium** if, for each player* i, s_i^* *is (at least tied for) player i's best response to the strategies specified for the* $n-1$ *other players,* $(s_1^*, \ldots, s_{i-1}^*, s_{i+1}^*, \ldots, s_n^*)$:

$$u_i(s_1^*, \ldots, s_{i-1}^*, s_i^*, s_{i+1}^*, \ldots, s_n^*)$$
$$\geq u_i(s_1^*, \ldots, s_{i-1}^*, s_i, s_{i+1}^*, \ldots, s_n^*) \qquad (NE)$$

for every feasible strategy s_i *in* S_i; *that is,* s_i^* *solves*

$$\max_{s_i \in S_i} u_i(s_1^*, \ldots, s_{i-1}^*, s_i, s_{i+1}^*, \ldots, s_n^*).$$

To relate this definition to its motivation, suppose game theory offers the strategies $(s_1', \ldots, s_n')$ as the solution to the normal-form game $G = \{S_1, \ldots, S_n; u_1, \ldots, u_n\}$. Saying that $(s_1', \ldots, s_n')$ is *not* a Nash equilibrium of G is equivalent to saying that there exists some player i such that s_i' is *not* a best response to $(s_1', \ldots, s_{i-1}', s_{i+1}', \ldots, s_n')$. That is, there exists some s_i'' in S_i such that

$$u_i(s_1', \ldots, s_{i-1}', s_i', s_{i+1}', \ldots, s_n') < u_i(s_1', \ldots, s_{i-1}', s_i'', s_{i+1}', \ldots, s_n').$$

Thus, if the theory offers the strategies $(s_1', \ldots, s_n')$ as the solution but these strategies are not a Nash equilibrium, then at least one player will have an incentive to deviate from the theory's prediction, so the theory will be falsified by the actual play of the game. A closely related motivation for Nash equilibrium involves the idea of convention: if a convention is to develop about how to play a given game then the strategies prescribed by the convention must be a Nash equilibrium, else at least one player will not abide by the convention. <!-- marginalia: Convention -->

To be more concrete, we now solve a few examples. Consider the three normal-form games already described—the Prisoners' Dilemma and Figures 1.1.1 and 1.1.4. A brute-force approach to finding a game's Nash equilibria is simply to check whether each possible combination of strategies satisfies condition (NE) in the definition.[3] In a two-player game, this approach begins as follows: for each player, and for each feasible strategy for that player, determine the other player's best response to that strategy. Figure 1.1.5 does this for the game in Figure 1.1.4 by underlining the payoff to player j's best response to each of player i's feasible strategies. If the column player were to play L, for instance, then the row player's best response would be M, since 4 exceeds 3 and 0, so the row player's payoff of 4 in the (M, L) cell of the bi-matrix is underlined.

A pair of strategies satisfies condition (NE) if each player's strategy is a best response to the other's—that is, if both payoffs are underlined in the corresponding cell of the bi-matrix. Thus, (B, R) is the only strategy pair that satisfies (NE); likewise for (Fink, Fink) in the Prisoners' Dilemma and (Up, Middle) in

---

[3]In Section 1.3.A we will distinguish between pure and mixed strategies. We will then see that the definition given here describes *pure-strategy* Nash equilibria, but that there can also be *mixed-strategy* Nash equilibria. Unless explicitly noted otherwise, all references to Nash equilibria in this section are to pure-strategy Nash equilibria.

	L	C	R
T	0,$\underline{4}$	$\underline{4}$,0	5,3
M	$\underline{4}$,0	0,$\underline{4}$	5,3
B	3,5	3,5	$\underline{6},\underline{6}$

Figure 1.1.5.

Figure 1.1.1. These strategy pairs are the unique Nash equilibria of these games.[4]

We next address the relation between Nash equilibrium and iterated elimination of strictly dominated strategies. Recall that the Nash equilibrium strategies in the Prisoners' Dilemma and Figure 1.1.1—(Fink, Fink) and (Up, Middle), respectively—are the only strategies that survive iterated elimination of strictly dominated strategies. This result can be generalized: if iterated elimination of strictly dominated strategies eliminates all but the strategies $(s_1^*, \ldots, s_n^*)$, then these strategies are the unique Nash equilibrium of the game. (See Appendix 1.1.C for a proof of this claim.) Since iterated elimination of strictly dominated strategies frequently does *not* eliminate all but a single combination of strategies, however, it is of more interest that Nash equilibrium is a stronger solution concept than iterated elimination of strictly dominated strategies, in the following sense. If the strategies $(s_1^*, \ldots, s_n^*)$ are a Nash equilibrium then they survive iterated elimination of strictly dominated strategies (again, see the Appendix for a proof), but there can be strategies that survive iterated elimination of strictly dominated strategies but are not part of any Nash equilibrium. To see the latter, recall that in Figure 1.1.4 Nash equilibrium gives the unique prediction (B, R), whereas iterated elimination of strictly dominated strategies gives the maximally imprecise prediction: no strategies are eliminated; anything could happen.

Having shown that Nash equilibrium is a stronger solution concept than iterated elimination of strictly dominated strategies, we must now ask whether Nash equilibrium is too strong a solution concept. That is, can we be sure that a Nash equilibrium

---

[4]This statement is correct even if we do not restrict attention to pure-strategy Nash equilibrium, because no mixed-strategy Nash equilibria exist in these three games. See Problem 1.10.

exists? Nash (1950) showed that in any finite game (i.e., a game in ~~exists~~ which the number of players n and the strategy sets $S_1, \ldots, S_n$ are all finite) there exists at least one Nash equilibrium. (This equilibrium may involve mixed strategies, which we will discuss in Section 1.3.A; see Section 1.3.B for a precise statement of Nash's Theorem.) Cournot (1838) proposed the same notion of equilibrium in the context of a particular model of duopoly and demonstrated (by construction) that an equilibrium exists in that model; see Section 1.2.A. In every application analyzed in this book, we will follow Cournot's lead: we will demonstrate that a Nash (or stronger) equilibrium exists by constructing one. In some of the theoretical sections, however, we will rely on Nash's Theorem (or its analog for stronger equilibrium concepts) and simply assert that an equilibrium exists.

We conclude this section with another classic example—*The Battle of the Sexes*. This example shows that a game can have multiple Nash equilibria, and also will be useful in the discussions of mixed strategies in Sections 1.3.B and 3.2.A. In the traditional exposition of the game (which, it will be clear, dates from the 1950s), a man and a woman are trying to decide on an evening's entertainment; we analyze a gender-neutral version of the game. While at separate workplaces, Pat and Chris must choose to attend either the opera or a prize fight. Both players would rather spend the evening together than apart, but Pat would rather they be together at the prize fight while Chris would rather they be together at the opera, as represented in the accompanying bi-matrix.

Pat

		Opera	Fight
Chris	Opera	2, 1	0, 0
	Fight	0, 0	1, 2

The Battle of the Sexes

Both (Opera, Opera) and (Fight, Fight) are Nash equilibria.

We argued above that if game theory is to provide a unique solution to a game then the solution must be a Nash equilibrium. This argument ignores the possibility of games in which game theory does not provide a unique solution. We also argued that if a convention is to develop about how to play a given game, then the strategies prescribed by the convention must be a Nash equilibrium, but this argument similarly ignores the possibility of games for which a convention will not develop. In some games with multiple Nash equilibria one equilibrium stands out as the compelling solution to the game. (Much of the theory in later chapters is an effort to identify such a compelling equilibrium in different classes of games.) Thus, the existence of multiple Nash equilibria is not a problem in and of itself. In the Battle of the Sexes, however, (Opera, Opera) and (Fight, Fight) seem equally compelling, which suggests that there may be games for which game theory does not provide a unique solution and no convention will develop.[5] In such games, Nash equilibrium loses much of its appeal as a prediction of play.

Appendix 1.1.C

This appendix contains proofs of the following two Propositions, which were stated informally in Section 1.1.C. Skipping these proofs will not substantially hamper one's understanding of later material. For readers not accustomed to manipulating formal definitions and constructing proofs, however, mastering these proofs will be a valuable exercise.

Proposition A *In the n-player normal-form game* $G = \{S_1, \ldots, S_n; u_1, \ldots, u_n\}$, *if iterated elimination of strictly dominated strategies eliminates all but the strategies* $(s_1^*, \ldots, s_n^*)$, *then these strategies are the unique Nash equilibrium of the game.*

Proposition B *In the n-player normal-form game* $G = \{S_1, \ldots, S_n; u_1, \ldots, u_n\}$, *if the strategies* $(s_1^*, \ldots, s_n^*)$ *are a Nash equilibrium, then they survive iterated elimination of strictly dominated strategies.*

---

[5]In Section 1.3.B we describe a third Nash equilibrium of the Battle of the Sexes (involving mixed strategies). Unlike (Opera, Opera) and (Fight, Fight), this third equilibrium has symmetric payoffs, as one might expect from the unique solution to a symmetric game; on the other hand, the third equilibrium is also inefficient, which may work against its development as a convention. Whatever one's judgment about the Nash equilibria in the Battle of the Sexes, however, the broader point remains: there may be games in which game theory does not provide a unique solution and no convention will develop.

Since Proposition B is simpler to prove, we begin with it, to warm up. The argument is by contradiction. That is, we will assume that one of the strategies in a Nash equilibrium is eliminated by iterated elimination of strictly dominated strategies, and then we will show that a contradiction would result if this assumption were true, thereby proving that the assumption must be false.

Suppose that the strategies $(s_1^*, \ldots, s_n^*)$ are a Nash equilibrium of the normal-form game $G = \{S_1, \ldots, S_n; u_1, \ldots, u_n\}$, but suppose also that (perhaps after some strategies other than $(s_1^*, \ldots, s_n^*)$ have been eliminated) s_i^* is the first of the strategies $(s_1^*, \ldots, s_n^*)$ to be eliminated for being strictly dominated. Then there must exist a strategy s_i'' that has not yet been eliminated from S_i that strictly dominates s_i^*. Adapting (DS), we have

$$u_i(s_1, \ldots, s_{i-1}, s_i^*, s_{i+1}, \ldots, s_n)$$
$$< u_i(s_1, \ldots, s_{i-1}, s_i'', s_{i+1}, \ldots, s_n) \qquad (1.1.1)$$

for each $(s_1, \ldots, s_{i-1}, s_{i+1}, \ldots, s_n)$ that can be constructed from the strategies that have not yet been eliminated from the other players' strategy spaces. Since s_i^* is the first of the equilibrium strategies to be eliminated, the other players' equilibrium strategies have not yet been eliminated, so one of the implications of (1.1.1) is

$$u_i(s_1^*, \ldots, s_{i-1}^*, s_i^*, s_{i+1}^*, \ldots, s_n^*)$$
$$< u_i(s_1^*, \ldots, s_{i-1}^*, s_i'', s_{i+1}^*, \ldots, s_n^*). \qquad (1.1.2)$$

But (1.1.2) is contradicted by (NE): s_i^* must be a best response to $(s_1^*, \ldots, s_{i-1}^*, s_{i+1}^*, \ldots, s_n^*)$, so there cannot exist a strategy s_i'' that strictly dominates s_i^*. This contradiction completes the proof.

Having proved Proposition B, we have already proved part of Proposition A: all we need to show is that if iterated elimination of dominated strategies eliminates all but the strategies $(s_1^*, \ldots, s_n^*)$ then these strategies are a Nash equilibrium; by Proposition B, any other Nash equilibria would also have survived, so this equilibrium must be unique. We assume that G is finite.

The argument is again by contradiction. Suppose that iterated elimination of dominated strategies eliminates all but the strategies $(s_1^*, \ldots, s_n^*)$ but these strategies are not a Nash equilibrium. Then there must exist some player i and some feasible strategy s_i in S_i such that (NE) fails, but s_i must have been strictly dominated by some other strategy s_i' at some stage of the process. The formal statements of these two observations are: there exists s_i in S_i such that

$$u_i(s_1^*, \ldots, s_{i-1}^*, s_i^*, s_{i+1}^*, \ldots, s_n^*)$$
$$< u_i(s_1^*, \ldots, s_{i-1}^*, s_i, s_{i+1}^*, \ldots, s_n^*); \qquad (1.1.3)$$

and there exists s_i' in the set of player i's strategies remaining at some stage of the process such that

$$u_i(s_1, \ldots, s_{i-1}, s_i, s_{i+1}, \ldots, s_n)$$
$$< u_i(s_1, \ldots, s_{i-1}, s_i', s_{i+1}, \ldots, s_n) \qquad (1.1.4)$$

for each $(s_1, \ldots, s_{i-1}, s_{i+1}, \ldots, s_n)$ that can be constructed from the strategies remaining in the other players' strategy spaces at that stage of the process. Since the other players' strategies $(s_1^*, \ldots, s_{i-1}^*, s_{i+1}^*, \ldots, s_n^*)$ are never eliminated, one of the implications of (1.1.4) is

$$u_i(s_1^*, \ldots, s_{i-1}^*, s_i, s_{i+1}^*, \ldots, s_n^*)$$
$$< u_i(s_1^*, \ldots, s_{i-1}^*, s_i', s_{i+1}^*, \ldots, s_n^*). \qquad (1.1.5)$$

If $s_i' = s_i^*$ (that is, if s_i^* is the strategy that strictly dominates s_i) then (1.1.5) contradicts (1.1.3), in which case the proof is complete. If $s_i' \neq s_i^*$ then some other strategy s_i'' must later strictly dominate s_i', since s_i' does not survive the process. Thus, inequalities analogous to (1.1.4) and (1.1.5) hold with s_i' and s_i'' replacing s_i and s_i', respectively. Once again, if $s_i'' = s_i^*$ then the proof is complete; otherwise, two more analogous inequalities can be constructed. Since s_i^* is the only strategy from S_i to survive the process, repeating this argument (in a finite game) eventually completes the proof.

1.2   Applications

1.2.A   Cournot Model of Duopoly

As noted in the previous section, Cournot (1838) anticipated Nash's definition of equilibrium by over a century (but only in the context of a particular model of duopoly). Not surprisingly, Cournot's work is one of the classics of game theory; it is also one of the cornerstones of the theory of industrial organization. We consider a very simple version of Cournot's model here, and return to variations on the model in each subsequent chapter. In this section we use the model to illustrate: (a) the translation of an informal statement of a problem into a normal-form representation of a game; (b) the computations involved in solving for the game's Nash equilibrium; and (c) iterated elimination of strictly dominated strategies.

Let q_1 and q_2 denote the quantities (of a homogeneous product) produced by firms 1 and 2, respectively. Let $P(Q) = a - Q$ be the market-clearing price when the aggregate quantity on the market is $Q = q_1 + q_2$. (More precisely, $P(Q) = a - Q$ for $Q < a$, and $P(Q) = 0$ for $Q \geq a$.) Assume that the total cost to firm i of producing quantity q_i is $C_i(q_i) = cq_i$. That is, there are no fixed costs and the marginal cost is constant at c, where we assume $c < a$. Following Cournot, suppose that the firms choose their quantities simultaneously.[6]

In order to find the Nash equilibrium of the Cournot game, we first translate the problem into a normal-form game. Recall from the previous section that the normal-form representation of a game specifies: (1) the players in the game, (2) the strategies available to each player, and (3) the payoff received by each player for each combination of strategies that could be chosen by the players. There are of course two players in any duopoly game—the two firms. In the Cournot model, the strategies available to each firm are the different quantities it might produce. We will assume that output is continuously divisible. Naturally, negative outputs are not feasible. Thus, each firm's strategy space can be represented as $S_i = [0, \infty)$, the nonnegative real numbers, in which case a typical strategy s_i is a quantity choice, $q_i \geq 0$. One could argue that extremely large quantities are not feasible and so should not be included in a firm's strategy space. Because $P(Q) = 0$ for $Q \geq a$, however, neither firm will produce a quantity $q_i > a$.

It remains to specify the payoff to firm i as a function of the strategies chosen by it and by the other firm, and to define and

---

[6]We discuss Bertrand's (1883) model, in which firms choose prices rather than quantities, in Section 1.2.B, and Stackelberg's (1934) model, in which firms choose quantities but one firm chooses before (and is observed by) the other, in Section 2.1.B. Finally, we discuss Friedman's (1971) model, in which the interaction described in Cournot's model occurs repeatedly over time, in Section 2.3.C.

solve for equilibrium. We assume that the firm's payoff is simply
its profit. Thus, the payoff $u_i(s_i, s_j)$ in a general two-player game
in normal form can be written here as[7]

$$\pi_i(q_i, q_j) = q_i[P(q_i + q_j) - c] = q_i[a - (q_i + q_j) - c].$$

Recall from the previous section that in a two-player game in normal form, the strategy pair (s_1^*, s_2^*) is a Nash equilibrium if, for
each player i,

$$u_i(s_i^*, s_j^*) \geq u_i(s_i, s_j^*) \qquad \text{(NE)}$$

for every feasible strategy s_i in S_i. Equivalently, for each player i,
s_i^* must solve the optimization problem

$$\max_{s_i \in S_i} u_i(s_i, s_j^*).$$

In the Cournot duopoly model, the analogous statement is that
the quantity pair (q_1^*, q_2^*) is a Nash equilibrium if, for each firm i,
q_i^* solves

$$\max_{0 \leq q_i < \infty} \pi_i(q_i, q_j^*) = \max_{0 \leq q_i < \infty} q_i[a - (q_i + q_j^*) - c].$$

Assuming $q_j^* < a - c$ (as will be shown to be true), the first-order
condition for firm i's optimization problem is both necessary and
sufficient; it yields

$$q_i = \frac{1}{2}(a - q_j^* - c). \qquad (1.2.1)$$

Thus, if the quantity pair (q_1^*, q_2^*) is to be a Nash equilibrium, the
firms' quantity choices must satisfy

$$q_1^* = \frac{1}{2}(a - q_2^* - c)$$

and

$$q_2^* = \frac{1}{2}(a - q_1^* - c).$$

---

[7]Note that we have changed the notation slightly by writing $u_i(s_i, s_j)$ rather
than $u_i(s_1, s_2)$. Both expressions represent the payoff to player i as a function of
the strategies chosen by all the players. We will use these expressions (and their
n-player analogs) interchangeably.

Solving this pair of equations yields

$$q_1^* = q_2^* = \frac{a-c}{3},$$

which is indeed less than $a - c$, as assumed.

The intuition behind this equilibrium is simple. Each firm would of course like to be a monopolist in this market, in which case it would choose q_i to maximize $\pi_i(q_i, 0)$—it would produce the monopoly quantity $q_m = (a - c)/2$ and earn the monopoly profit $\pi_i(q_m, 0) = (a - c)^2/4$. Given that there are two firms, aggregate profits for the duopoly would be maximized by setting the aggregate quantity $q_1 + q_2$ equal to the monopoly quantity q_m, as would occur if $q_i = q_m/2$ for each i, for example. The problem with this arrangement is that each firm has an incentive to deviate: because the monopoly quantity is low, the associated price $P(q_m)$ is high, and at this price each firm would like to increase its quantity, in spite of the fact that such an increase in production drives down the market-clearing price. (To see this formally, use (1.2.1) to check that $q_m/2$ is *not* firm 2's best response to the choice of $q_m/2$ by firm 1.) In the Cournot equilibrium, in contrast, the aggregate quantity is higher, so the associated price is lower, so the temptation to increase output is reduced—reduced by just enough that each firm is just deterred from increasing its output by the realization that the market-clearing price will fall. See Problem 1.4 for an analysis of how the presence of n oligopolists affects this equilibrium trade-off between the temptation to increase output and the reluctance to reduce the market-clearing price.

Rather than solving for the Nash equilibrium in the Cournot game algebraically, one could instead proceed graphically, as follows. Equation (1.2.1) gives firm i's best response to firm j's *equilibrium* strategy, q_j^*. Analogous reasoning leads to firm 2's best response to an *arbitrary* strategy by firm 1 and firm 1's best response to an arbitrary strategy by firm 2. Assuming that firm 1's strategy satisfies $q_1 < a - c$, firm 2's best response is

$$R_2(q_1) = \frac{1}{2}(a - q_1 - c);$$

likewise, if $q_2 < a - c$ then firm 1's best response is

$$R_1(q_2) = \frac{1}{2}(a - q_2 - c).$$

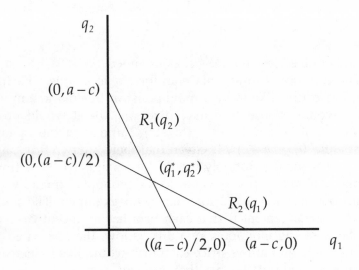

Figure 1.2.1.

As shown in Figure 1.2.1, these two best-response functions intersect only once, at the equilibrium quantity pair (q_1^*, q_2^*).

A third way to solve for this Nash equilibrium is to apply the process of iterated elimination of strictly dominated strategies. This process yields a unique solution—which, by Proposition A in Appendix 1.1.C, must be the Nash equilibrium (q_1^*, q_2^*). The complete process requires an infinite number of steps, each of which eliminates a fraction of the quantities remaining in each firm's strategy space; we discuss only the first two steps. First, the monopoly quantity $q_m = (a - c)/2$ strictly dominates any higher quantity. That is, for any $x > 0$, $\pi_i(q_m, q_j) > \pi_i(q_m + x, q_j)$ for all $q_j \geq 0$. To see this, note that if $Q = q_m + x + q_j < a$, then

$$\pi_i(q_m, q_j) = \frac{a - c}{2} \left[\frac{a - c}{2} - q_j \right]$$

and

$$\pi_i(q_m + x, q_j) = \left[\frac{a - c}{2} + x \right] \left[\frac{a - c}{2} - x - q_j \right] = \pi_i(q_m, q_j) - x(x + q_j),$$

and if $Q = q_m + x + q_j \geq a$, then $P(Q) = 0$, so producing a smaller quantity raises profit. Second, given that quantities exceeding q_m have been eliminated, the quantity $(a - c)/4$ strictly dominates any lower quantity. That is, for any x between zero and $(a - c)/4$, $\pi_i[(a - c)/4, q_j] > \pi_i[(a - c)/4 - x, q_j]$ for all q_j between zero and $(a - c)/2$. To see this, note that

$$\pi_i \left(\frac{a - c}{4}, q_j \right) = \frac{a - c}{4} \left[\frac{3(a - c)}{4} - q_j \right]$$

and

$$\pi_i \left(\frac{a - c}{4} - x, q_j \right) = \left[\frac{a - c}{4} - x \right] \left[\frac{3(a - c)}{4} + x - q_j \right]$$

$$= \pi_i(q_m, q_j) - x \left[\frac{a - c}{2} + x - q_j \right].$$

After these two steps, the quantities remaining in each firm's strategy space are those in the interval between $(a - c)/4$ and $(a - c)/2$. Repeating these arguments leads to ever-smaller intervals of remaining quantities. In the limit, these intervals converge to the single point $q_i^* = (a - c)/3$.

Iterated elimination of strictly dominated strategies can also be described graphically, by using the observation (from footnote 1; see also the discussion in Section 1.3.A) that a strategy is strictly dominated if and only if there is no belief about the other players' choices for which the strategy is a best response. Since there are only two firms in this model, we can restate this observation as: a quantity q_i is strictly dominated if and only if there is no belief about q_j such that q_i is firm i's best response. We again discuss only the first two steps of the iterative process. First, it is never a best response for firm i to produce more than the monopoly quantity, $q_m = (a - c)/2$. To see this, consider firm 2's best-response function, for example: in Figure 1.2.1, $R_2(q_1)$ equals q_m when $q_1 = 0$ and declines as q_1 increases. Thus, for any $q_j \geq 0$, if firm i believes that firm j will choose q_j, then firm i's best response is less than or equal to q_m; there is no q_j such that firm i's best response exceeds q_m. Second, given this upper bound on firm j's quantity, we can derive a lower bound on firm i's best response: if $q_j \leq (a - c)/2$, then $R_i(q_j) \geq (a - c)/4$, as shown for firm 2's best response in Figure 1.2.2.[8]

---

[8]These two arguments are slightly incomplete because we have not analyzed

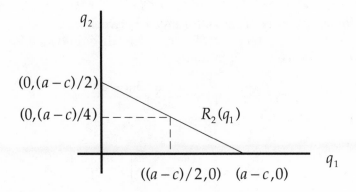

Figure 1.2.2.

As before, repeating these arguments leads to the single quantity $q_i^* = (a - c)/3$.

We conclude this section by changing the Cournot model so that iterated elimination of strictly dominated strategies does *not* yield a unique solution. To do this, we simply add one or more firms to the existing duopoly. We will see that the first of the two steps discussed in the duopoly case continues to hold, but that the process ends there. Thus, when there are more than two firms, iterated elimination of strictly dominated strategies yields only the imprecise prediction that each firm's quantity will not exceed the monopoly quantity (much as in Figure 1.1.4, where no strategies were eliminated by this process).

For concreteness, we consider the three-firm case. Let Q_{-i} denote the sum of the quantities chosen by the firms other than i, and let $\pi_i(q_i, Q_{-i}) = q_i(a - q_i - Q_{-i} - c)$ provided $q_i + Q_{-i} < a$ (whereas $\pi_i(q_i, Q_{-i}) = -cq_i$ if $q_i + Q_{-i} \geq a$). It is again true that the monopoly quantity $q_m = (a - c)/2$ strictly dominates any higher quantity. That is, for any $x > 0$, $\pi_i(q_m, Q_{-i}) > \pi_i(q_m + x, Q_{-i})$ for all $Q_{-i} \geq 0$, just as in the first step in the duopoly case. Since

---

firm i's best response when firm i is uncertain about q_j. Suppose firm i is uncertain about q_j but believes that the expected value of q_j is $E(q_j)$. Because $\pi_i(q_i, q_j)$ is linear in q_j, firm i's best response when it is uncertain in this way simply equals its best response when it is certain that firm j will choose $E(q_j)$—a case covered in the text.

there are two firms other than firm i, however, all we can say about Q_{-i} is that it is between zero and $a - c$, because q_j and q_k are between zero and $(a - c)/2$. But this implies that no quantity $q_i \geq 0$ is strictly dominated for firm i, because for each q_i between zero and $(a - c)/2$ there exists a value of Q_{-i} between zero and $a - c$ (namely, $Q_{-i} = a - c - 2q_i$) such that q_i is firm i's best response to Q_{-i}. Thus, no further strategies can be eliminated.

1.2.B Bertrand Model of Duopoly

We next consider a different model of how two duopolists might interact, based on Bertrand's (1883) suggestion that firms actually choose prices, rather than quantities as in Cournot's model. It is important to note that Bertrand's model is a *different game* than Cournot's model: the strategy spaces are different, the payoff functions are different, and (as will become clear) the behavior in the Nash equilibria of the two models is different. Some authors summarize these differences by referring to the Cournot and Bertrand equilibria. Such usage may be misleading: it refers to the difference between the Cournot and Bertrand games, and to the difference between the equilibrium behavior in these games, *not* to a difference in the equilibrium concept used in the games. *In both games, the equilibrium concept used is the Nash equilibrium defined in the previous section.*

We consider the case of differentiated products. (See Problem 1.7 for the case of homogeneous products.) If firms 1 and 2 choose prices p_1 and p_2, respectively, the quantity that consumers demand from firm i is

$$q_i(p_i, p_j) = a - p_i + bp_j,$$

where $b > 0$ reflects the extent to which firm i's product is a substitute for firm j's product. (This is an unrealistic demand function because demand for firm i's product is positive even when firm i charges an arbitrarily high price, provided firm j also charges a high enough price. As will become clear, the problem makes sense only if $b < 2$.) As in our discussion of the Cournot model, we assume that there are no fixed costs of production and that marginal costs are constant at c, where $c < a$, and that the firms act (i.e., choose their prices) simultaneously.

As before, the first task in the process of finding the Nash equilibrium is to translate the problem into a normal-form game. There are again two players. This time, however, the strategies available to each firm are the different prices it might charge, rather than the different quantities it might produce. We will assume that negative prices are not feasible but that any nonnegative price can be charged—there is no restriction to prices denominated in pennies, for instance. Thus, each firm's strategy space can again be represented as $S_i = [0, \infty)$, the nonnegative real numbers, and a typical strategy s_i is now a price choice, $p_i \geq 0$.

We will again assume that the payoff function for each firm is just its profit. The profit to firm i when it chooses the price p_i and its rival chooses the price p_j is

$$\pi_i(p_i, p_j) = q_i(p_i, p_j)[p_i - c] = [a - p_i + bp_j][p_i - c].$$

Thus, the price pair (p_1^*, p_2^*) is a Nash equilibrium if, for each firm i, p_i^* solves

$$\max_{0 \leq p_i < \infty} \pi_i(p_i, p_j^*) = \max_{0 \leq p_i < \infty} [a - p_i + bp_j^*][p_i - c].$$

The solution to firm i's optimization problem is

$$p_i^* = \frac{1}{2}(a + bp_j^* + c).$$

Therefore, if the price pair (p_1^*, p_2^*) is to be a Nash equilibrium, the firms' price choices must satisfy

$$p_1^* = \frac{1}{2}(a + bp_2^* + c)$$

and

$$p_2^* = \frac{1}{2}(a + bp_1^* + c).$$

Solving this pair of equations yields

$$p_1^* = p_2^* = \frac{a + c}{2 - b}.$$

1.2.C   Final-Offer Arbitration

Many public-sector workers are forbidden to strike; instead, wage disputes are settled by binding arbitration. (Major league baseball may be a higher-profile example than the public sector but is substantially less important economically.) Many other disputes, including medical malpractice cases and claims by shareholders against their stockbrokers, also involve arbitration. The two major forms of arbitration are *conventional* and *final-offer* arbitration. In final-offer arbitration, the two sides make wage offers and then the arbitrator picks one of the offers as the settlement. In conventional arbitration, in contrast, the arbitrator is free to impose any wage as the settlement. We now derive the Nash equilibrium wage offers in a model of final-offer arbitration developed by Farber (1980).[9]

Suppose the parties to the dispute are a firm and a union and the dispute concerns wages. Let the timing of the game be as follows. First, the firm and the union simultaneously make offers, denoted by w_f and w_u, respectively. Second, the arbitrator chooses one of the two offers as the settlement. (As in many so-called static games, this is really a dynamic game of the kind to be discussed in Chapter 2, but here we reduce it to a static game between the firm and the union by making assumptions about the arbitrator's behavior in the second stage.) Assume that the arbitrator has an ideal settlement she would like to impose, denoted by x. Assume further that, after observing the parties' offers, w_f and w_u, the arbitrator simply chooses the offer that is closer to x: provided that $w_f < w_u$ (as is intuitive, and will be shown to be true), the arbitrator chooses w_f if $x < (w_f + w_u)/2$ and chooses w_u if $x > (w_f + w_u)/2$; see Figure 1.2.3. (It will be immaterial what happens if $x = (w_f + w_u)/2$. Suppose the arbitrator flips a coin.)

The arbitrator knows x but the parties do not. The parties believe that x is randomly distributed according to a cumulative probability distribution denoted by $F(x)$, with associated probability density function denoted by $f(x)$.[10] Given our specification of the arbitrator's behavior, if the offers are w_f and w_u

---

[9]This application involves some basic concepts in probability: a cumulative probability distribution, a probability density function, and an expected value. Terse definitions are given as needed; for more detail, consult any introductory probability text.

[10]That is, the probability that x is less than an arbitrary value x^* is denoted $F(x^*)$, and the derivative of this probability with respect to x^* is denoted $f(x^*)$. Since $F(x^*)$ is a probability, we have $0 \leq F(x^*) \leq 1$ for any x^*. Furthermore, if $x^{**} > x^*$ then $F(x^{**}) \geq F(x^*)$, so $f(x^*) \geq 0$ for every x^*.

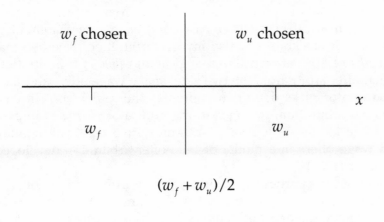

Figure 1.2.3.

then the parties believe that the probabilities Prob$\{w_f$ chosen$\}$ and Prob$\{w_u$ chosen$\}$ can be expressed as

$$\text{Prob}\{w_f \text{ chosen}\} = \text{Prob}\left\{x < \frac{w_f + w_u}{2}\right\} = F\left(\frac{w_f + w_u}{2}\right)$$

and

$$\text{Prob}\{w_u \text{ chosen}\} = 1 - F\left(\frac{w_f + w_u}{2}\right).$$

Thus, the expected wage settlement is

$$w_f \cdot \text{Prob}\{w_f \text{ chosen}\} + w_u \cdot \text{Prob}\{w_u \text{ chosen}\}$$
$$= w_f \cdot F\left(\frac{w_f + w_u}{2}\right) + w_u \cdot \left[1 - F\left(\frac{w_f + w_u}{2}\right)\right].$$

We assume that the firm wants to minimize the expected wage settlement imposed by the arbitrator and the union wants to maximize it.

If the pair of offers (w_f^*, w_u^*) is to be a Nash equilibrium of the game between the firm and the union, w_f^* must solve[11]

$$\min_{w_f} \; w_f \cdot F\left(\frac{w_f + w_u^*}{2}\right) + w_u^* \cdot \left[1 - F\left(\frac{w_f + w_u^*}{2}\right)\right]$$

and w_u^* must solve

$$\max_{w_u} \; w_f^* \cdot F\left(\frac{w_f^* + w_u}{2}\right) + w_u \cdot \left[1 - F\left(\frac{w_f^* + w_u}{2}\right)\right].$$

Thus, the wage-offer pair (w_f^*, w_u^*) must solve the first-order conditions for these optimization problems,

$$(w_u^* - w_f^*) \cdot \frac{1}{2} f\left(\frac{w_f^* + w_u^*}{2}\right) = F\left(\frac{w_f^* + w_u^*}{2}\right)$$

and

$$(w_u^* - w_f^*) \cdot \frac{1}{2} f\left(\frac{w_f^* + w_u^*}{2}\right) = \left[1 - F\left(\frac{w_f^* + w_u^*}{2}\right)\right].$$

(We defer considering whether these first-order conditions are sufficient.) Since the left-hand sides of these first-order conditions are equal, the right-hand sides must also be equal, which implies that

$$F\left(\frac{w_f^* + w_u^*}{2}\right) = \frac{1}{2}; \tag{1.2.2}$$

that is, the average of the offers must equal the median of the arbitrator's preferred settlement. Substituting (1.2.2) into either of the first-order conditions then yields

$$w_u^* - w_f^* = \frac{1}{f\left(\frac{w_f^* + w_u^*}{2}\right)}; \tag{1.2.3}$$

that is, the gap between the offers must equal the reciprocal of the value of the density function at the median of the arbitrator's preferred settlement.

---

[11]In formulating the firm's and the union's optimization problems, we have assumed that the firm's offer is less than the union's offer. It is straightforward to show that this inequality must hold in equilibrium.

In order to produce an intuitively appealing comparative-static result, we now consider an example. Suppose the arbitrator's preferred settlement is normally distributed with mean m and variance σ^2, in which case the density function is

$$f(x) = \frac{1}{\sqrt{2\pi\sigma^2}} \exp\left\{-\frac{1}{2\sigma^2}(x-m)^2\right\}.$$

(In this example, one can show that the first-order conditions given earlier are sufficient.) Because a normal distribution is symmetric around its mean, the median of the distribution equals the mean of the distribution, m. Therefore, (1.2.2) becomes

$$\frac{w_f^* + w_u^*}{2} = m$$

and (1.2.3) becomes

$$w_u^* - w_f^* = \frac{1}{f(m)} = \sqrt{2\pi\sigma^2},$$

so the Nash equilibrium offers are

$$w_u^* = m + \sqrt{\frac{\pi\sigma^2}{2}} \quad \text{and} \quad w_f^* = m - \sqrt{\frac{\pi\sigma^2}{2}}.$$

Thus, in equilibrium, the parties' offers are centered around the expectation of the arbitrator's preferred settlement (i.e., m), and the gap between the offers increases with the parties' uncertainty about the arbitrator's preferred settlement (i.e., σ^2).

The intuition behind this equilibrium is simple. Each party faces a trade-off. A more aggressive offer (i.e., a lower offer by the firm or a higher offer by the union) yields a better payoff if it is chosen as the settlement by the arbitrator but is less likely to be chosen. (We will see in Chapter 3 that a similar trade-off arises in a first-price, sealed-bid auction: a lower bid yields a better payoff if it is the winning bid but reduces the chances of winning.) When there is more uncertainty about the arbitrator's preferred settlement (i.e., σ^2 is higher), the parties can afford to be more aggressive because an aggressive offer is less likely to be wildly at odds with the arbitrator's preferred settlement. When there is hardly any uncertainty, in contrast, neither party can afford to make an offer far from the mean because the arbitrator is very likely to prefer settlements close to m.

1.2.D The Problem of the Commons

Since at least Hume (1739), political philosophers and economists have understood that if citizens respond only to private incentives, public goods will be underprovided and public resources overutilized. Today, even a casual inspection of the earth's environment reveals the force of this idea. Hardin's (1968) much cited paper brought the problem to the attention of noneconomists. Here we analyze a bucolic example.

Consider the n farmers in a village. Each summer, all the farmers graze their goats on the village green. Denote the number of goats the ith farmer owns by g_i and the total number of goats in the village by $G = g_1 + \cdots + g_n$. The cost of buying and caring for a goat is c, independent of how many goats a farmer owns. The value to a farmer of grazing a goat on the green when a total of G goats are grazing is $v(G)$ *per goat*. Since a goat needs at least a certain amount of grass in order to survive, there is a maximum number of goats that can be grazed on the green, G_{max}: $v(G) > 0$ for $G < G_{max}$ but $v(G) = 0$ for $G \geq G_{max}$. Also, since the first few goats have plenty of room to graze, adding one more does little harm to those already grazing, but when so many goats are grazing that they are all just barely surviving (i.e., G is just below G_{max}), then adding one more dramatically harms the rest. Formally: for $G < G_{max}, v'(G) < 0$ and $v''(G) < 0$, as in Figure 1.2.4.

During the spring, the farmers simultaneously choose how many goats to own. Assume goats are continuously divisible. A strategy for farmer i is the choice of a number of goats to graze on the village green, g_i. Assuming that the strategy space is $[0, \infty)$ covers all the choices that could possibly be of interest to the farmer; $[0, G_{max})$ would also suffice. The payoff to farmer i from grazing g_i goats when the numbers of goats grazed by the other farmers are $(g_1, \ldots, g_{i-1}, g_{i+1}, \ldots, g_n)$ is

$$g_i v(g_1 + \cdots + g_{i-1} + g_i + g_{i+1} + \cdots + g_n) - c g_i. \qquad (1.2.4)$$

Thus, if $(g_1^*, \ldots, g_n^*)$ is to be a Nash equilibrium then, for each i, g_i^* must maximize (1.2.4) given that the other farmers choose $(g_1^*, \ldots, g_{i-1}^*, g_{i+1}^*, \ldots, g_n^*)$. The first-order condition for this optimization problem is

$$v(g_i + g_{-i}^*) + g_i v'(g_i + g_{-i}^*) - c = 0, \qquad (1.2.5)$$

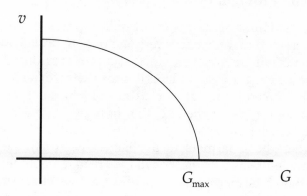

Figure 1.2.4.

where g^*_{-i} denotes $g^*_1 + \cdots + g^*_{i-1} + g^*_{i+1} + \cdots + g^*_n$. Substituting g^*_i into (1.2.5), summing over all n farmers' first-order conditions, and then dividing by n yields

$$v(G^*) + \frac{1}{n}G^*v'(G^*) - c = 0, \tag{1.2.6}$$

where G^* denotes $g^*_1 + \cdots + g^*_n$. In contrast, the social optimum, denoted by G^{**}, solves

$$\max_{0 \leq G < \infty} Gv(G) - Gc,$$

the first-order condition for which is

$$v(G^{**}) + G^{**}v'(G^{**}) - c = 0. \tag{1.2.7}$$

Comparing (1.2.6) to (1.2.7) shows[12] that $G^* > G^{**}$: too many goats are grazed in the Nash equilibrium, compared to the social optimum. The first-order condition (1.2.5) reflects the incentives faced by a farmer who is already grazing g_i goats but is consider-

---

[12]Suppose, to the contrary, that $G^* \leq G^{**}$. Then $v(G^*) \geq v(G^{**})$, since $v' < 0$. Likewise, $0 > v'(G^*) \geq v'(G^{**})$, since $v'' < 0$. Finally, $G^*/n < G^{**}$. Thus, the left-hand side of (1.2.6) strictly exceeds the left-hand side of (1.2.7), which is impossible since both equal zero.

ing adding one more (or, strictly speaking, a tiny fraction of one more). The value of the additional goat is $v(g_i + g^*_{-i})$ and its cost is c. The harm to the farmer's existing goats is $v'(g_i + g^*_{-i})$ per goat, or $g_i v'(g_i + g^*_{-i})$ in total. The common resource is overutilized because each farmer considers only his or her own incentives, not the effect of his or her actions on the other farmers, hence the presence of $G^* v'(G^*)/n$ in (1.2.6) but $G^{**} v'(G^{**})$ in (1.2.7).

1.3 Advanced Theory: Mixed Strategies and Existence of Equilibrium

1.3.A Mixed Strategies

In Section 1.1.C we defined S_i to be the set of strategies available to player i, and the combination of strategies $(s^*_1, \ldots, s^*_n)$ to be a Nash equilibrium if, for each player i, s^*_i is player i's best response to the strategies of the $n-1$ other players:

$$u_i(s^*_1, \ldots, s^*_{i-1}, s^*_i, s^*_{i+1}, \ldots, s^*_n) \geq u_i(s^*_1, \ldots, s^*_{i-1}, s_i, s^*_{i+1}, \ldots, s^*_n) \quad \text{(NE)}$$

for every strategy s_i in S_i. By this definition, there is no Nash equilibrium in the following game, known as *Matching Pennies*.

Player 2

		Heads	Tails
Player 1	Heads	$-1,\ 1$	$1, -1$
	Tails	$1, -1$	$-1,\ 1$

Matching Pennies

In this game, each player's strategy space is {Heads, Tails}. As a story to accompany the payoffs in the bi-matrix, imagine that each player has a penny and must choose whether to display it with heads or tails facing up. If the two pennies match (i.e., both are heads up or both are tails up) then player 2 wins player 1's penny; if the pennies do not match then 1 wins 2's penny. No pair of strategies can satisfy (NE), since if the players' strategies match—(Heads, Heads) or (Tails, Tails)—then player 1 prefers to switch strategies, while if the strategies do not match—(Heads, Tails) or (Tails, Heads)—then player 2 prefers to do so.

The distinguishing feature of Matching Pennies is that each player would like to outguess the other. Versions of this game also arise in poker, baseball, battle, and other settings. In poker, the analogous question is how often to bluff: if player i is known never to bluff then i's opponents will fold whenever i bids aggressively, thereby making it worthwhile for i to bluff on occasion; on the other hand, bluffing too often is also a losing strategy. In baseball, suppose that a pitcher can throw either a fastball or a curve and that a batter can hit either pitch if (but only if) it is anticipated correctly. Similarly, in battle, suppose that the attackers can choose between two locations (or two routes, such as "by land or by sea") and that the defense can parry either attack if (but only if) it is anticipated correctly.

In any game in which each player would like to outguess the other(s), there is no Nash equilibrium (at least as this equilibrium concept was defined in Section 1.1.C) because the solution to such a game necessarily involves uncertainty about what the players will do. We now introduce the notion of a *mixed strategy*, which we will interpret in terms of one player's uncertainty about what another player will do. (This interpretation was advanced by Harsanyi [1973]; we discuss it further in Section 3.2.A.) In the next section we will extend the definition of Nash equilibrium to include mixed strategies, thereby capturing the uncertainty inherent in the solution to games such as Matching Pennies, poker, baseball, and battle.

Formally, a mixed strategy for player i is a probability distribution over (some or all of) the strategies in S_i. We will hereafter refer to the strategies in S_i as player i's *pure strategies*. In the simultaneous-move games of complete information analyzed in this chapter, a player's pure strategies are the different actions the player could take. In Matching Pennies, for example, S_i consists of the two pure strategies Heads and Tails, so a mixed strategy for player i is the probability distribution $(q, 1 - q)$, where q is the probability of playing Heads, $1 - q$ is the probability of playing Tails, and $0 \leq q \leq 1$. The mixed strategy $(0, 1)$ is simply the pure strategy Tails; likewise, the mixed strategy $(1, 0)$ is the pure strategy Heads.

As a second example of a mixed strategy, recall Figure 1.1.1, where player 2 has the pure strategies Left, Middle, and Right. Here a mixed strategy for player 2 is the probability distribution $(q, r, 1 - q - r)$, where q is the probability of playing Left, r is the probability of playing Middle, and $1 - q - r$ is the probability of playing Right. As before, $0 \leq q \leq 1$, and now also $0 \leq r \leq 1$ and $0 \leq q + r \leq 1$. In this game, the mixed strategy $(1/3, 1/3, 1/3)$ puts equal probability on Left, Middle, and Right, whereas $(1/2, 1/2, 0)$ puts equal probability on Left and Middle but no probability on Right. As always, a player's pure strategies are simply the limiting cases of the player's mixed strategies—here player 2's pure strategy Left is the mixed strategy $(1, 0, 0)$, for example.

More generally, suppose that player i has K pure strategies: $S_i = \{s_{i1}, \ldots, s_{iK}\}$. Then a mixed strategy for player i is a probability distribution $(p_{i1}, \ldots, p_{iK})$, where p_{ik} is the probability that player i will play strategy s_{ik}, for $k = 1, \ldots, K$. Since p_{ik} is a probability, we require $0 \leq p_{ik} \leq 1$ for $k = 1, \ldots, K$ and $p_{i1} + \cdots + p_{iK} = 1$. We will use p_i to denote an arbitrary mixed strategy from the set of probability distributions over S_i, just as we use s_i to denote an arbitrary pure strategy from S_i.

Definition *In the normal-form game $G = \{S_1, \ldots, S_n; u_1, \ldots, u_n\}$, suppose $S_i = \{s_{i1}, \ldots, s_{iK}\}$. Then a **mixed strategy** for player i is a probability distribution $p_i = (p_{i1}, \ldots, p_{iK})$, where $0 \leq p_{ik} \leq 1$ for $k = 1, \ldots, K$ and $p_{i1} + \cdots + p_{iK} = 1$.*

We conclude this section by returning (briefly) to the notion of strictly dominated strategies introduced in Section 1.1.B, so as to illustrate the potential roles for mixed strategies in the arguments made there. Recall that if a strategy s_i is strictly dominated then there is no belief that player i could hold (about the strategies the other players will choose) such that it would be optimal to play s_i. The converse is also true, provided we allow for mixed strategies: if there is no belief that player i could hold (about the strategies the other players will choose) such that it would be optimal to play the strategy s_i, then there exists another strategy that strictly dominates s_i.[13] The games in Figures 1.3.1 and 1.3.2

---

[13]Pearce (1984) proves this result for the two-player case and notes that it holds for the n-player case provided that the players' mixed strategies are allowed to be correlated—that is, player i's belief about what player j will do must be allowed to be correlated with i's belief about what player k will do. Aumann (1987)

Player 2

		L	R
	T	3, —	0, —
Player 1	M	0, —	3, —
	B	1, —	1, —

Figure 1.3.1.

show that this converse would be false if we restricted attention to pure strategies.

Figure 1.3.1 shows that a given pure strategy may be strictly dominated by a mixed strategy, even if the pure strategy is not strictly dominated by any other pure strategy. In this game, for any belief $(q, 1-q)$ that player 1 could hold about 2's play, 1's best response is either T (if $q \geq 1/2$) or M (if $q \leq 1/2$), but never B. Yet B is not strictly dominated by either T or M. The key is that B is strictly dominated by a mixed strategy: if player 1 plays T with probability $1/2$ and M with probability $1/2$ then 1's expected payoff is $3/2$ no matter what (pure or mixed) strategy 2 plays, and $3/2$ exceeds the payoff of 1 that playing B surely produces. This example illustrates the role of mixed strategies in finding "another strategy that strictly dominates s_i."

Player 2

		L	R
	T	3, —	0, —
Player 1	M	0, —	3, —
	B	2, —	2, —

Figure 1.3.2.

suggests that such correlation in i's beliefs is entirely natural, even if j and k make their choices completely independently: for example, i may know that both j and k went to business school, or perhaps to the same business school, but may not know what is taught there.

Figure 1.3.2 shows that a given pure strategy can be a best response to a mixed strategy, even if the pure strategy is not a best response to any other pure strategy. In this game, B is not a best response for player 1 to either L or R by player 2, but B is the best response for player 1 to the mixed strategy $(q, 1 - q)$ by player 2, provided $1/3 < q < 2/3$. This example illustrates the role of mixed strategies in the "belief that player i could hold."

1.3.B Existence of Nash Equilibrium

In this section we discuss several topics related to the existence of Nash equilibrium. First, we extend the definition of Nash equilibrium given in Section 1.1.C to allow for mixed strategies. Second, we apply this extended definition to Matching Pennies and the Battle of the Sexes. Third, we use a graphical argument to show that any two-player game in which each player has two pure strategies has a Nash equilibrium (possibly involving mixed strategies). Finally, we state and discuss Nash's (1950) Theorem, which guarantees that any finite game (i.e., any game with a finite number of players, each of whom has a finite number of pure strategies) has a Nash equilibrium (again, possibly involving mixed strategies).

Recall that the definition of Nash equilibrium given in Section 1.1.C guarantees that each player's pure strategy is a best response to the other players' pure strategies. To extend the definition to include mixed strategies, we simply require that each player's mixed strategy be a best response to the other players' mixed strategies. Since any pure strategy can be represented as the mixed strategy that puts zero probability on all of the player's other pure strategies, this extended definition subsumes the earlier one.

Computing player i's best response to a mixed strategy by player j illustrates the interpretation of player j's mixed strategy as representing player i's uncertainty about what player j will do. We begin with Matching Pennies as an example. Suppose that player 1 believes that player 2 will play Heads with probability q and Tails with probability $1 - q$; that is, 1 believes that 2 will play the mixed strategy $(q, 1 - q)$. Given this belief, player 1's expected payoffs are $q \cdot (-1) + (1 - q) \cdot 1 = 1 - 2q$ from playing Heads and $q \cdot 1 + (1 - q) \cdot (-1) = 2q - 1$ from playing Tails. Since $1 - 2q > 2q - 1$ if and only if $q < 1/2$, player 1's best pure-strategy response is

Heads if $q < 1/2$ and Tails if $q > 1/2$, and player 1 is indifferent between Heads and Tails if $q = 1/2$. It remains to consider possible mixed-strategy responses by player 1.

Let $(r, 1 - r)$ denote the mixed strategy in which player 1 plays Heads with probability r. For each value of q between zero and one, we now compute the value(s) of r, denoted $r^*(q)$, such that $(r, 1 - r)$ is a best response for player 1 to $(q, 1 - q)$ by player 2. The results are summarized in Figure 1.3.3. Player 1's expected payoff from playing $(r, 1 - r)$ when 2 plays $(q, 1 - q)$ is

$$rq \cdot (-1) + r(1 - q) \cdot 1 + (1 - r)q \cdot 1 + (1 - r)(1 - q) \cdot (-1)$$
$$= (2q - 1) + r(2 - 4q), \quad (1.3.1)$$

where rq is the probability of (Heads, Heads), $r(1-q)$ the probability of (Heads, Tails), and so on.[14] Since player 1's expected payoff is increasing in r if $2 - 4q > 0$ and decreasing in r if $2 - 4q < 0$, player 1's best response is $r = 1$ (i.e., Heads) if $q < 1/2$ and $r = 0$ (i.e., Tails) if $q > 1/2$, as indicated by the two horizontal segments of $r^*(q)$ in Figure 1.3.3. This statement is stronger than the closely related statement in the previous paragraph: there we considered only pure strategies and found that if $q < 1/2$ then Heads is the best pure strategy and that if $q > 1/2$ then Tails is the best pure strategy; here we consider all pure and mixed strategies but again find that if $q < 1/2$ then Heads is the best of all (pure or mixed) strategies and that if $q > 1/2$ then Tails is the best of all strategies.

The nature of player 1's best response to $(q, 1 - q)$ changes when $q = 1/2$. As noted earlier, when $q = 1/2$ player 1 is indifferent between the pure strategies Heads and Tails. Furthermore, because player 1's expected payoff in (1.3.1) is independent of r when $q = 1/2$, player 1 is also indifferent among all mixed strategies $(r, 1 - r)$. That is, when $q = 1/2$ the mixed strategy $(r, 1 - r)$

---

[14]The events A and B are *independent* if Prob{A and B} = Prob{A}·Prob{B}. Thus, in writing rq for the probability that 1 plays Heads and 2 plays Heads, we are assuming that 1 and 2 make their choices independently, as befits the description we gave of simultaneous-move games. See Aumann (1974) for the definition of *correlated equilibrium*, which applies to games in which the players' choices can be correlated (because the players observe the outcome of a random event, such as a coin flip, before choosing their strategies).

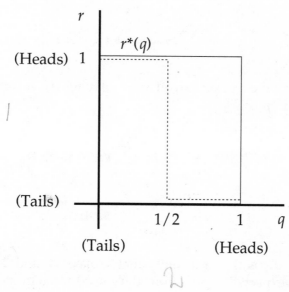

Figure 1.3.3.

is a best response to $(q, 1 - q)$ for any value of r between zero and one. Thus, $r^*(1/2)$ is the entire interval $[0, 1]$, as indicated by the vertical segment of $r^*(q)$ in Figure 1.3.3. In the analysis of the Cournot model in Section 1.2.A, we called $R_i(q_j)$ firm i's best-response *function*. Here, because there exists a value of q such that $r^*(q)$ has more than one value, we call $r^*(q)$ player 1's best-response *correspondence*.

To derive player i's best response to player j's mixed strategy more generally, and to give a formal statement of the extended definition of Nash equilibrium, we now restrict attention to the two-player case, which captures the main ideas as simply as possible. Let J denote the number of pure strategies in S_1 and K the number in S_2. We will write $S_1 = \{s_{11}, \ldots, s_{1J}\}$ and $S_2 = \{s_{21}, \ldots, s_{2K}\}$, and we will use s_{1j} and s_{2k} to denote arbitrary pure strategies from S_1 and S_2, respectively.

If player 1 believes that player 2 will play the strategies $(s_{21}, \ldots, s_{2K})$ with the probabilities $(p_{21}, \ldots, p_{2K})$ then player 1's expected payoff from playing the pure strategy s_{1j} is

$$\sum_{k=1}^{K} p_{2k} u_1(s_{1j}, s_{2k}), \tag{1.3.2}$$

and player 1's expected payoff from playing the mixed strategy $p_1 = (p_{11}, \ldots, p_{1J})$ is

$$
v_1(p_1, p_2) = \sum_{j=1}^{J} p_{1j} \left[\sum_{k=1}^{K} p_{2k} u_1(s_{1j}, s_{2k}) \right]
$$

$$
= \sum_{j=1}^{J} \sum_{k=1}^{K} p_{1j} \cdot p_{2k} u_1(s_{1j}, s_{2k}), \tag{1.3.3}
$$

where $p_{1j} \cdot p_{2k}$ is the probability that 1 plays s_{1j} and 2 plays s_{2k}. Player 1's expected payoff from the mixed strategy p_1, given in (1.3.3), is the weighted sum of the expected payoff for each of the pure strategies $\{s_{11}, \ldots, s_{1J}\}$, given in (1.3.2), where the weights are the probabilities $(p_{11}, \ldots, p_{1J})$. Thus, for the mixed strategy $(p_{11}, \ldots, p_{1J})$ to be a best response for player 1 to 2's mixed strategy p_2, it must be that $p_{1j} > 0$ only if

$$\sum_{k=1}^{K} p_{2k} u_1(s_{1j}, s_{2k}) \geq \sum_{k=1}^{K} p_{2k} u_1(s_{1j'}, s_{2k})$$

for every $s_{1j'}$ in S_1. That is, for a mixed strategy to be a best response to p_2 it must put positive probability on a given pure strategy only if the pure strategy is itself a best response to p_2. Conversely, if player 1 has several pure strategies that are best responses to p_2, then any mixed strategy that puts all its probability on some or all of these pure-strategy best responses (and zero probability on all other pure strategies) is also a best response for player 1 to p_2.

To give a formal statement of the extended definition of Nash equilibrium, we need to compute player 2's expected payoff when players 1 and 2 play the mixed strategies p_1 and p_2 respectively. If player 2 believes that player 1 will play the strategies $(s_{11}, \ldots, s_{1J})$ with the probabilities $(p_{11}, \ldots, p_{1J})$, then player 2's expected payoff from playing the strategies $(s_{21}, \ldots, s_{2K})$ with the probabilities $(p_{21}, \ldots, p_{2K})$ is

$$
\begin{aligned}
v_2(p_1, p_2) \quad &= \quad \sum_{k=1}^{K} p_{2k} \left[\sum_{j=1}^{J} p_{1j} u_2(s_{1j}, s_{2k}) \right] \\
&= \quad \sum_{j=1}^{J} \sum_{k=1}^{K} p_{1j} \cdot p_{2k} u_2(s_{1j}, s_{2k}).
\end{aligned}
$$

Given $v_1(p_1, p_2)$ and $v_2(p_1, p_2)$ we can restate the requirement of Nash equilibrium that each player's mixed strategy be a best response to the other player's mixed strategy: for the pair of mixed strategies (p_1^*, p_2^*) to be a Nash equilibrium, p_1^* must satisfy

$$
v_1(p_1^*, p_2^*) \geq v_1(p_1, p_2^*) \tag{1.3.4}
$$

for every probability distribution p_1 over S_1, and p_2^* must satisfy

$$
v_2(p_1^*, p_2^*) \geq v_2(p_1^*, p_2) \tag{1.3.5}
$$

for every probability distribution p_2 over S_2.

Definition *In the two-player normal-form game $G = \{S_1, S_2; u_1, u_2\}$, the mixed strategies (p_1^*, p_2^*) are a **Nash equilibrium** if each player's mixed strategy is a best response to the other player's mixed strategy: (1.3.4) and (1.3.5) must hold.*

We next apply this definition to Matching Pennies and the Battle of the Sexes. To do so, we use the graphical representation of player i's best response to player j's mixed strategy introduced in Figure 1.3.3. To complement Figure 1.3.3, we now compute the value(s) of q, denoted $q^*(r)$, such that $(q, 1 - q)$ is a best response for player 2 to $(r, 1 - r)$ by player 1. The results are summarized in Figure 1.3.4. If $r < 1/2$ then 2's best response is Tails, so $q^*(r) = 0$; likewise, if $r > 1/2$ then 2's best response is Heads, so $q^*(r) = 1$. If $r = 1/2$ then player 2 is indifferent not only between Heads and Tails but also among all the mixed strategies $(q, 1 - q)$, so $q^*(1/2)$ is the entire interval $[0, 1]$.

After flipping and rotating Figure 1.3.4, we have Figure 1.3.5. Figure 1.3.5 is less convenient than Figure 1.3.4 as a representation

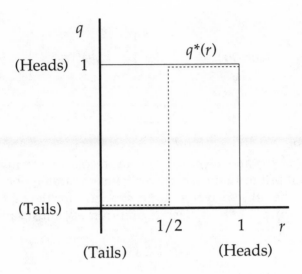

Figure 1.3.4.

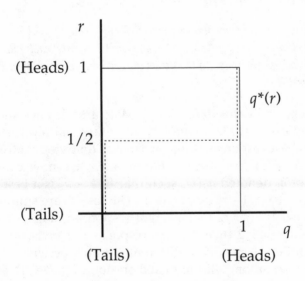

Figure 1.3.5.

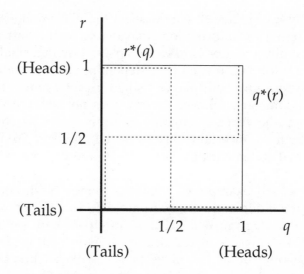

Figure 1.3.6.

of player 2's best response to player 1's mixed strategy, but it can be combined with Figure 1.3.3 to produce Figure 1.3.6.

Figure 1.3.6 is analogous to Figure 1.2.1 from the Cournot analysis in Section 1.2.A. Just as the intersection of the best-response functions $R_2(q_1)$ and $R_1(q_2)$ gave the Nash equilibrium of the Cournot game, the intersection of the best-response correspondences $r^*(q)$ and $q^*(r)$ yields the (mixed-strategy) Nash equilibrium in Matching Pennies: if player i plays $(1/2, 1/2)$ then $(1/2, 1/2)$ is a best response for player j, as required for Nash equilibrium.

It is worth emphasizing that such a mixed-strategy Nash equilibrium does *not* rely on any player flipping coins, rolling dice, or otherwise choosing a strategy at random. Rather, we interpret player j's mixed strategy as a statement of player i's uncertainty about player j's choice of a (pure) strategy. In baseball, for example, the pitcher might decide whether to throw a fastball or a curve based on how well each pitch was thrown during pregame practice. If the batter understands how the pitcher will make a choice but did not observe the pitcher's practice, then the batter may believe that the pitcher is equally likely to throw a fastball or a curve. We would then represent the batter's belief by the pitcher's mixed strategy $(1/2, 1/2)$, when in fact the pitcher chooses a pure strategy based on information unavailable to the batter. Stated more generally, the idea is to endow player j with a small amount of private information such that, depending on the realization of the private information, player j slightly prefers one of the relevant pure strategies. Since player i does not observe j's private information, however, i remains uncertain about j's choice, and we represent i's uncertainty by j's mixed strategy. We provide a more formal statement of this interpretation of a mixed strategy in Section 3.2.A.

As a second example of a mixed-strategy Nash equilibrium, consider the Battle of the Sexes from Section 1.1.C. Let $(q, 1-q)$ be the mixed strategy in which Pat plays Opera with probability q, and let $(r, 1-r)$ be the mixed strategy in which Chris plays Opera with probability r. If Pat plays $(q, 1-q)$ then Chris's expected payoffs are $q \cdot 2 + (1-q) \cdot 0 = 2q$ from playing Opera and $q \cdot 0 + (1-q) \cdot 1 = 1-q$ from playing Fight. Thus, if $q > 1/3$ then Chris's best response is Opera (i.e., $r = 1$), if $q < 1/3$ then Chris's best response is Fight (i.e., $r = 0$), and if $q = 1/3$ then any value of r is a best response. Similarly, if Chris plays $(r, 1-r)$ then Pat's expected payoffs are $r \cdot 1 + (1-r) \cdot 0 = r$ from playing Opera and $r \cdot 0 + (1-r) \cdot 2 = 2(1-r)$ from playing Fight. Thus, if $r > 2/3$ then Pat's best response is Opera (i.e., $q = 1$), if $r < 2/3$ then Pat's best response is Fight (i.e., $q = 0$), and if $r = 2/3$ then any value of q is a best response. As shown in Figure 1.3.7, the mixed strategies $(q, 1-q) = (1/3, 2/3)$ for Pat and $(r, 1-r) = (2/3, 1/3)$ for Chris are therefore a Nash equilibrium.

Unlike in Figure 1.3.6, where there was only one intersection of the players' best-response correspondences, there are three intersections of $r^*(q)$ and $q^*(r)$ in Figure 1.3.7: $(q = 0, r = 0)$ and $(q = 1, r = 1)$, as well as $(q = 1/3, r = 2/3)$. The other two intersections represent the pure-strategy Nash equilibria (Fight, Fight) and (Opera, Opera) described in Section 1.1.C.

In any game, a Nash equilibrium (involving pure or mixed strategies) appears as an intersection of the players' best-response correspondences, even when there are more than two players, and even when some or all of the players have more than two pure strategies. Unfortunately, the only games in which the players' best-response correspondences have simple graphical representations are two-player games in which each player has only two

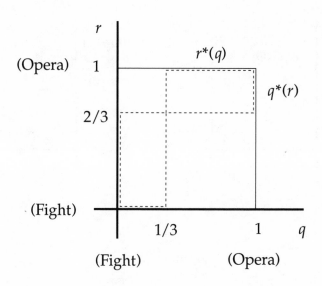

Figure 1.3.7.

Player 2

		Left	Right
Player 1	Up	$x, —$	$y, —$
	Down	$z, —$	$w, —$

Figure 1.3.8.

strategies. We turn next to a graphical argument that any such game has a Nash equilibrium (possibly involving mixed strategies).

Consider the payoffs for player 1 given in Figure 1.3.8. There are two important comparisons: x versus z, and y versus w. Based on these comparisons, we can define four main cases: (i) $x > z$ and $y > w$, (ii) $x < z$ and $y < w$, (iii) $x > z$ and $y < w$, and (iv) $x < z$ and $y > w$. We first discuss these four main cases, and then turn to the remaining cases involving $x = z$ or $y = w$.

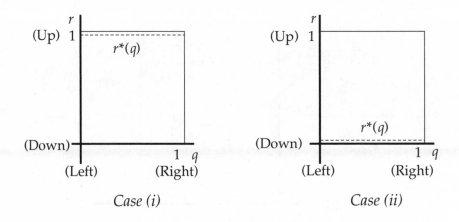

Figure 1.3.9.

In case (i) Up strictly dominates Down for player 1, and in case (ii) Down strictly dominates Up. Recall from the previous section that a strategy s_i is strictly dominated if and only if there is no belief that player i could hold (about the strategies the other players will choose) such that it would be optimal to play s_i. Thus, if $(q, 1-q)$ is a mixed strategy for player 2, where q is the probability that 2 will play Left, then in case (i) there is no value of q such that Down is optimal for player 1, and in case (ii) there is no value of q such that Up is optimal. Letting $(r, 1-r)$ denote a mixed strategy for player 1, where r is the probability that 1 will play Up, we can represent the best-response correspondences for cases (i) and (ii) as in Figure 1.3.9. (In these two cases the best-response correspondences are in fact best-response functions, since there is no value of q such that player 1 has multiple best responses.)

In cases (iii) and (iv), neither Up nor Down is strictly dominated. Thus, Up must be optimal for some values of q and Down optimal for others. Let $q' = (w - y)/(x - z + w - y)$. Then in case (iii) Up is optimal for $q > q'$ and Down for $q < q'$, whereas in case (iv) the reverse is true. In both cases, any value of r is optimal when $q = q'$. These best-response correspondences are given in Figure 1.3.10.

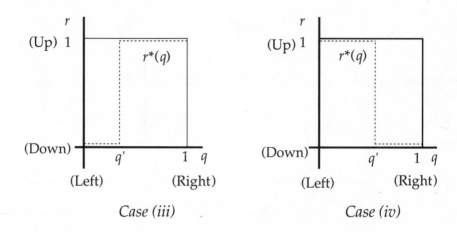

Figure 1.3.10.

Since $q' = 1$ if $x = z$ and $q' = 0$ if $y = w$, the best-response correspondences for cases involving either $x = z$ or $y = w$ are L-shaped (i.e., two adjacent sides of the unit square), as would occur in Figure 1.3.10 if $q' = 0$ or 1 in cases (iii) or (iv).

Adding arbitrary payoffs for player 2 to Figure 1.3.8 and performing the analogous computations yields the same four best-response correspondences, except that the horizontal axis measures r and the vertical q, as in Figure 1.3.4. Flipping and rotating these four figures, as was done to produce Figure 1.3.5, yields Figures 1.3.11 and 1.3.12. (In the latter figures, r' is defined analogously to q' in Figure 1.3.10.)

The crucial point is that given any of the four best-response correspondences for player 1, $r^*(q)$ from Figures 1.3.9 or 1.3.10, and any of the four for player 2, $q^*(r)$ from Figures 1.3.11 or 1.3.12, the pair of best-response correspondences has at least one intersection, so the game has at least one Nash equilibrium. Checking all sixteen possible pairs of best-response correspondences is left as an exercise. Instead, we describe the qualitative features that can result. There can be: (1) a single pure-strategy Nash equilibrium; (2) a single mixed-strategy equilibrium; or (3) two pure-strategy equilibria and a single mixed-strategy equilibrium. Recall from Figure 1.3.6 that Matching Pennies is an example of case (2), and from Figure 1.3.7 that the Battle of the Sexes is an example of

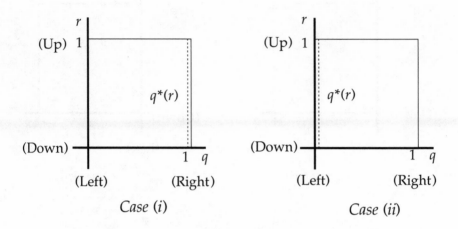

Figure 1.3.11.

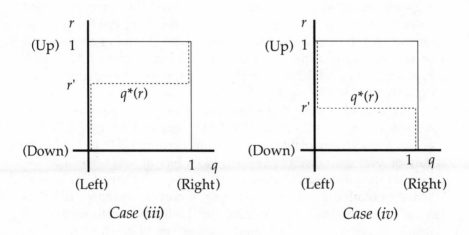

Figure 1.3.12.

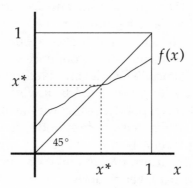

Figure 1.3.13.

case (3). The Prisoners' Dilemma is an example of case (1); it results from combining case (i) or (ii) of $r^*(q)$ with case (i) or (ii) or $q^*(r)$.[15]

We conclude this section with a discussion of the existence of a Nash equilibrium in more general games. If the above arguments for two-by-two games are stated mathematically rather than graphically, then they can be generalized to apply to n-player games with arbitrary finite strategy spaces.

Theorem (Nash 1950): *In the n-player normal-form game $G = \{S_1, \ldots, S_n; u_1, \ldots, u_n\}$, if n is finite and S_i is finite for every i then there exists at least one Nash equilibrium, possibly involving mixed strategies.*

The proof of Nash's Theorem involves a *fixed-point theorem*. As a simple example of a fixed-point theorem, suppose $f(x)$ is a continuous function with domain $[0, 1]$ and range $[0, 1]$. Then Brouwer's Fixed-Point Theorem guarantees that there exists at least one fixed point — that is, there exists at least one value x^* in $[0, 1]$ such that $f(x^*) = x^*$. Figure 1.3.13 provides an example.

---

[15]The cases involving $x = z$ or $y = w$ do not violate the claim that the pair of best-response correspondences has at least one intersection. On the contrary, in addition to the qualitative features described in the text, there can now be two pure-strategy Nash equilibria without a mixed-strategy Nash equilibrium, and a continuum of mixed-strategy Nash equilibria.

Applying a fixed-point theorem to prove Nash's Theorem involves two steps: (1) showing that any fixed point of a certain correspondence is a Nash equilibrium; (2) using an appropriate fixed-point theorem to show that this correspondence must have a fixed point. The relevant correspondence is the n-player best-response correspondence. The relevant fixed-point theorem is due to Kakutani (1941), who generalized Brouwer's theorem to allow for (well-behaved) correspondences as well as functions.

The n-player best-response correspondence is computed from the n individual players' best-response correspondences as follows. Consider an arbitrary combination of mixed strategies $(p_1, \ldots, p_n)$. For each player i, derive i's best response(s) to the other players' mixed strategies $(p_1, \ldots, p_{i-1}, p_{i+1}, \ldots, p_n)$. Then construct the set of all possible combinations of one such best response for each player. (Formally, derive each player's best-response correspondence and then construct the cross-product of these n individual correspondences.) A combination of mixed strategies $(p_1^*, \ldots, p_n^*)$ is a fixed point of this correspondence if $(p_1^*, \ldots, p_n^*)$ belongs to the set of all possible combinations of the players' best responses to $(p_1^*, \ldots, p_n^*)$. That is, for each i, p_i^* must be (one of) player i's best response(s) to $(p_1^*, \ldots, p_{i-1}^*, p_{i+1}^*, \ldots, p_n^*)$, but this is precisely the statement that $(p_1^*, \ldots, p_n^*)$ is a Nash equilibrium. This completes step (1).

Step (2) involves the fact that each player's best-response correspondence is continuous, in an appropriate sense. The role of continuity in Brouwer's fixed-point theorem can be seen by modifying $f(x)$ in Figure 1.3.13: if $f(x)$ is discontinuous then it need not have a fixed point. In Figure 1.3.14, for example, $f(x) > x$ for all $x < x'$, but $f(x') < x'$ for $x \geq x'$.[16]

To illustrate the differences between $f(x)$ in Figure 1.3.14 and a player's best-response correspondence, consider Case (iii) in Figure 1.3.10: at $q = q'$, $r^*(q')$ includes zero, one, and the entire interval in between. (A bit more formally, $r^*(q')$ includes the limit of $r^*(q)$ as q approaches q' from the left, the limit of $r^*(q)$ as q approaches q' from the right, and all the values of r in between these two limits.) If $f(x')$ in Figure 1.3.14 behaved analogously to

---

[16]The value of $f(x')$ is indicated by the solid circle. The open circle indicates that $f(x')$ does not include this value. The dotted line is included only to indicate that both circles occur at $x = x'$; it does not indicate further values of $f(x')$.

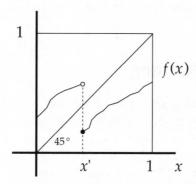

Figure 1.3.14.

player 1's best-response correspondence $r^*(q')$, then $f(x')$ would include not only the solid circle (as in the figure) but also the open circle and the entire interval in between, in which case $f(x)$ would have a fixed point at x'.

Each player's best-response correspondence always behaves the way $r^*(q')$ does in Figure 1.3.14: it always includes (the appropriate generalizations of) the limit from the left, the limit from the right, and all the values in between. The reason for this is that, as shown earlier for the two-player case, if player i has several pure strategies that are best responses to the other players' mixed strategies, then any mixed strategy p_i that puts all its probability on some or all of player i's pure-strategy best responses (and zero probability on all of player i's other pure strategies) is also a best response for player i. Because each player's best-response correspondence always behaves in this way, the n-player best-response correspondence does too; these properties satisfy the hypotheses of Kakutani's Theorem, so the latter correspondence has a fixed point.

Nash's Theorem guarantees that an equilibrium exists in a broad class of games, but none of the applications analyzed in Section 1.2 are members of this class (because each application has infinite strategy spaces). This shows that the hypotheses of Nash's Theorem are sufficient but not necessary conditions for an equilibrium to exist—there are many games that do not satisfy the hypotheses of the Theorem but nonetheless have one or more Nash equilibria.

1.4   Further Reading

On the assumptions underlying iterated elimination of strictly dominated strategies and Nash equilibrium, and on the interpretation of mixed strategies in terms of the players' beliefs, see Brandenburger (1992). On the relation between (Cournot-type) models where firms choose quantities and (Bertrand-type) models where firms choose prices, see Kreps and Scheinkman (1983), who show that in some circumstances the Cournot outcome occurs in a Bertrand-type model in which firms face capacity constraints (which they choose, at a cost, prior to choosing prices). On arbitration, see Gibbons (1988), who shows how the arbitrator's preferred settlement can depend on the information content of the parties' offers, in both final-offer and conventional arbitration. Finally, on the existence of Nash equilibrium, including pure-strategy equilibria in games with continuous strategy spaces, see Dasgupta and Maskin (1986).

1.5   Problems

Section 1.1

1.1.   What is a game in normal form? What is a strictly dominated strategy in a normal-form game? What is a pure-strategy Nash equilibrium in a normal-form game?

1.2.   In the following normal-form game, what strategies survive iterated elimination of strictly dominated strategies? What are the pure-strategy Nash equilibria?

	L	C	R
T	2,0	1,1	4,2
M	3,4	1,2	2,3
B	1,3	0,2	3,0

1.3. Players 1 and 2 are bargaining over how to split one dollar. Both players simultaneously name shares they would like to have, s_1 and s_2, where $0 \leq s_1, s_2 \leq 1$. If $s_1 + s_2 \leq 1$, then the players receive the shares they named; if $s_1 + s_2 > 1$, then both players receive zero. What are the pure-strategy Nash equilibria of this game?

Section 1.2

1.4. Suppose there are n firms in the Cournot oligopoly model. Let q_i denote the quantity produced by firm i, and let $Q = q_1 + \cdots + q_n$ denote the aggregate quantity on the market. Let P denote the market-clearing price and assume that inverse demand is given by $P(Q) = a - Q$ (assuming $Q < a$, else $P = 0$). Assume that the total cost of firm i from producing quantity q_i is $C_i(q_i) = cq_i$. That is, there are no fixed costs and the marginal cost is constant at c, where we assume $c < a$. Following Cournot, suppose that the firms choose their quantities simultaneously. What is the Nash equilibrium? What happens as n approaches infinity?

1.5. Consider the following two finite versions of the Cournot duopoly model. First, suppose each firm must choose either half the monopoly quantity, $q_m/2 = (a - c)/4$, or the Cournot equilibrium quantity, $q_c = (a - c)/3$. No other quantities are feasible. Show that this two-action game is equivalent to the Prisoners' Dilemma: each firm has a strictly dominated strategy, and both are worse off in equilibrium than they would be if they cooperated. Second, suppose each firm can choose either $q_m/2$, or q_c, or a third quantity, q'. Find a value for q' such that the game is equivalent to the Cournot model in Section 1.2.A, in the sense that (q_c, q_c) is a unique Nash equilibrium and both firms are worse off in equilibrium than they could be if they cooperated, but neither firm has a strictly dominated strategy.

1.6. Consider the Cournot duopoly model where inverse demand is $P(Q) = a - Q$ but firms have asymmetric marginal costs: c_1 for firm 1 and c_2 for firm 2. What is the Nash equilibrium if $0 < c_i < a/2$ for each firm? What if $c_1 < c_2 < a$ but $2c_2 > a + c_1$?

1.7. In Section 1.2.B, we analyzed the Bertrand duopoly model with differentiated products. The case of homogeneous products yields a stark conclusion. Suppose that the quantity that consumers demand from firm i is $a - p_i$ when $p_i < p_j$, 0 when $p_i > p_j$, and $(a - p_i)/2$ when $p_i = p_j$. Suppose also that there are no fixed costs and that marginal costs are constant at c, where $c < a$. Show that if the firms choose prices simultaneously, then the unique Nash equilibrium is that both firms charge the price c.

Similar to MWG icecream vendor problem

1.8.   Consider a population of voters uniformly distributed along the ideological spectrum from left ($x = 0$) to right ($x = 1$). Each of the candidates for a single office simultaneously chooses a campaign platform (i.e., a point on the line between $x = 0$ and $x = 1$). The voters observe the candidates' choices, and then each voter votes for the candidate whose platform is closest to the voter's position on the spectrum. If there are two candidates and they choose platforms $x_1 = .3$ and $x_2 = .6$, for example, then all voters to the left of $x = .45$ vote for candidate 1, all those to the right vote for candidate 2, and candidate 2 wins the election with 55 percent of the vote. Suppose that the candidates care only about being elected—they do not really care about their platforms at all! If there are two candidates, what is the pure-strategy Nash equilibrium? If there are three candidates, exhibit a pure-strategy Nash equilibrium. (Assume that any candidates who choose the same platform equally split the votes cast for that platform, and that ties among the leading vote-getters are resolved by coin flips.) See Hotelling (1929) for an early model along these lines.

Section 1.3

1.9.   What is a mixed strategy in a normal-form game? What is a mixed-strategy Nash equilibrium in a normal-form game?

1.10.   Show that there are no mixed-strategy Nash equilibria in the three normal-form games analyzed in Section 1.1—the Prisoners' Dilemma, Figure 1.1.1, and Figure 1.1.4.

1.11.   Solve for the mixed-strategy Nash equilibria in the game in Problem 1.2.

1.12. Find the mixed-strategy Nash equilibrium of the following normal-form game.

	L	R
T	2,1	0,2
B	1,2	3,0

1.13. Each of two firms has one job opening. Suppose that (for reasons not discussed here but relating to the value of filling each opening) the firms offer different wages: firm i offers the wage w_i, where $(1/2)w_1 < w_2 < 2w_1$. Imagine that there are two workers, each of whom can apply to only one firm. The workers simultaneously decide whether to apply to firm 1 or to firm 2. If only one worker applies to a given firm, that worker gets the job; if both workers apply to one firm, the firm hires one worker at random and the other worker is unemployed (which has a payoff of zero). Solve for the Nash equilibria of the workers' normal-form game. (For more on the wages the firms will choose, see Montgomery [1991].)

		Worker 2	
		Apply to Firm 1	Apply to Firm 2
Worker 1	Apply to Firm 1	$\frac{1}{2}w_1, \frac{1}{2}w_1$	w_1, w_2
	Apply to Firm 2	w_2, w_1	$\frac{1}{2}w_2, \frac{1}{2}w_2$

1.14. Show that Proposition B in Appendix 1.1.C holds for mixed- as well as pure-strategy Nash equilibria: the strategies played with positive probability in a mixed-strategy Nash equilibrium survive the process of iterated elimination of strictly dominated strategies.

1.6 References

Aumann, R. 1974. "Subjectivity and Correlation in Randomized Strategies." *Journal of Mathematical Economics* 1:67–96.

————. 1976. "Agreeing to Disagree." *Annals of Statistics* 4:1236–39.

————. 1987. "Correlated Equilibrium as an Expression of Bayesian Rationality." *Econometrica* 55:1–18.

Bertrand, J. 1883. "Théorie Mathématique de la Richesse Sociale." *Journal des Savants* 499–508.

Brandenburger, A. 1992. "Knowledge and Equilibrium in Games." Forthcoming in *Journal of Economic Perspectives*.

Cournot, A. 1838. *Recherches sur les Principes Mathématiques de la Théorie des Richesses.* English edition: *Researches into the Mathematical Principles of the Theory of Wealth.* Edited by N. Bacon. New York: Macmillan, 1897.

Dasgupta, P., and E. Maskin. 1986. "The Existence of Equilibrium in Discontinuous Economic Games, I: Theory." *Review of Economic Studies* 53:1–26.

Farber, H. 1980. "An Analysis of Final-Offer Arbitration." *Journal of Conflict Resolution* 35:683–705.

Friedman, J. 1971. "A Noncooperative Equilibrium for Supergames." *Review of Economic Studies* 28:1–12.

Gibbons, R. 1988. "Learning in Equilibrium Models of Arbitration." *American Economic Review* 78:896–912.

Hardin, G. 1968. "The Tragedy of the Commons." *Science* 162:1243–48.

Harsanyi, J. 1973. "Games with Randomly Disturbed Payoffs: A New Rationale for Mixed Strategy Equilibrium Points." *International Journal of Game Theory* 2:1–23.

Hotelling, H. 1929. "Stability in Competition." *Economic Journal* 39:41–57.

Hume, D. 1739. *A Treatise of Human Nature.* Reprint. London: J. M. Dent. 1952.

Kakutani, S. 1941. "A Generalization of Brouwer's Fixed Point Theorem." *Duke Mathematical Journal* 8:457–59.

Kreps, D., and J. Scheinkman. 1983. "Quantity Precommitment and Bertrand Competition Yield Cournot Outcomes." *Bell Journal of Economics* 14:326–37.

Montgomery, J. 1991. "Equilibrium Wage Dispersion and Interindustry Wage Differentials." *Quarterly Journal of Economics* 106:163–79.

Nash, J. 1950. "Equilibrium Points in n-Person Games." *Proceedings of the National Academy of Sciences* 36:48–49.

Pearce, D. 1984. "Rationalizable Strategic Behavior and the Problem of Perfection." *Econometrica* 52:1029–50.

Stackelberg, H. von. 1934. *Marktform und Gleichgewicht*. Vienna: Julius Springer.

Chapter 2

Dynamic Games of Complete Information

In this chapter we introduce dynamic games. We again restrict attention to games with complete information (i.e., games in which the players' payoff functions are common knowledge); see Chapter 3 for the introduction to games of incomplete information. In Section 2.1 we analyze dynamic games that have not only complete but also *perfect information*, by which we mean that at each move in the game the player with the move knows the full history of the play of the game thus far. In Sections 2.2 through 2.4 we consider games of complete but imperfect information: at some move the player with the move does not know the history of the game.

The central issue in all dynamic games is credibility. As an example of a noncredible threat, consider the following two-move game. First, player 1 chooses between giving player 2 $1,000 and giving player 2 nothing. Second, player 2 observes player 1's move and then chooses whether or not to explode a grenade that will kill both players. Suppose player 2 threatens to explode the grenade unless player 1 pays the $1,000. If player 1 believes the threat, then player 1's best response is to pay the $1,000. But player 1 should not believe the threat, because it is noncredible: if player 2 were given the opportunity to carry out the threat, player 2 would choose not to carry it out. Thus, player 1 should pay player 2 nothing.[1]

In Section 2.1 we analyze the following class of dynamic games of complete and perfect information: first player 1 moves, then player 2 observes player 1's move, then player 2 moves and the game ends. The grenade game belongs to this class, as do Stackelberg's (1934) model of duopoly and Leontief's (1946) model of wage and employment determination in a unionized firm. We define the *backwards-induction outcome* of such games and briefly discuss its relation to Nash equilibrium (deferring the main discussion of this relation until Section 2.4). We solve for this outcome in the Stackelberg and Leontief models. We also derive the analogous outcome in Rubinstein's (1982) bargaining model, although this game has a potentially infinite sequence of moves and so does not belong to the above class of games.

In Section 2.2 we enrich the class of games analyzed in the previous section: first players 1 and 2 move simultaneously, then players 3 and 4 observe the moves chosen by 1 and 2, then players 3 and 4 move simultaneously and the game ends. As will be explained in Section 2.4, the simultaneity of moves here means that these games have imperfect information. We define the *subgame-perfect outcome* of such games, which is the natural extension of backwards induction to these games. We solve for this outcome in Diamond and Dybvig's (1983) model of bank runs, in a model of tariffs and imperfect international competition, and in Lazear and Rosen's (1981) model of tournaments.

In Section 2.3 we study *repeated games*, in which a fixed group of players plays a given game repeatedly, with the outcomes of all previous plays observed before the next play begins. The theme of the analysis is that (credible) threats and promises about future behavior can influence current behavior. We define *subgame-perfect Nash equilibrium* for repeated games and relate it to the backwards-induction and subgame-perfect outcomes defined in Sections 2.1 and 2.2. We state and prove the Folk Theorem for infinitely re-

---

[1]Player 1 might wonder whether an opponent who threatens to explode a grenade is crazy. We model such doubts as incomplete information—player 1 is unsure about player 2's payoff function. See Chapter 3.

peated games, and we analyze Friedman's (1971) model of collusion between Cournot duopolists, Shapiro and Stiglitz's (1984) model of efficiency wages, and Barro and Gordon's (1983) model of monetary policy.

In Section 2.4 we introduce the tools necessary to analyze a general dynamic game of complete information, whether with perfect or imperfect information. We define the *extensive-form* representation of a game and relate it to the normal-form representation introduced in Chapter 1. We also define subgame-perfect Nash equilibrium for general games. The main point (of both this section and the chapter as a whole) is that a dynamic game of complete information may have many Nash equilibria, but some of these may involve noncredible threats or promises. The subgame-perfect Nash equilibria are those that pass a credibility test.

2.1   Dynamic Games of Complete and Perfect Information

2.1.A   Theory: Backwards Induction

The grenade game is a member of the following class of simple games of complete and perfect information:

1. Player 1 chooses an action a_1 from the feasible set A_1.

2. Player 2 observes a_1 and then chooses an action a_2 from the feasible set A_2.

3. Payoffs are $u_1(a_1, a_2)$ and $u_2(a_1, a_2)$.

Many economic problems fit this description.[2]   Two examples

---

[2]Player 2's feasible set of actions, A_2, could be allowed to depend on player 1's action, a_1. Such dependence could be denoted by $A_2(a_1)$ or could be incorporated into player 2's payoff function, by setting $u_2(a_1, a_2) = -\infty$ for values of a_2 that are not feasible for a given a_1. Some moves by player 1 could even end the game, without player 2 getting a move; for such values of a_1, the set of feasible actions $A_2(a_1)$ contains only one element, so player 2 has no choice to make.

(discussed later in detail) are Stackelberg's model of duopoly and Leontief's model of wages and employment in a unionized firm. Other economic problems can be modeled by allowing for a longer sequence of actions, either by adding more players or by allowing players to move more than once. (Rubinstein's bargaining game, discussed in Section 2.1.D, is an example of the latter.) The key features of a dynamic game of complete and perfect information are that (i) the moves occur in sequence, (ii) all previous moves are observed before the next move is chosen, and (iii) the players' payoffs from each feasible combination of moves are common knowledge.

We solve a game from this class by backwards induction, as follows. When player 2 gets the move at the second stage of the game, he or she will face the following problem, given the action a_1 previously chosen by player 1:

$$\max_{a_2 \in A_2} u_2(a_1, a_2).$$

Assume that for each a_1 in A_1, player 2's optimization problem has a unique solution, denoted by $R_2(a_1)$. This is player 2's *reaction* (or best response) to player 1's action. Since player 1 can solve 2's problem as well as 2 can, player 1 should anticipate player 2's reaction to each action a_1 that 1 might take, so 1's problem at the first stage amounts to

$$\max_{a_1 \in A_1} u_1(a_1, R_2(a_1)).$$

Assume that this optimization problem for player 1 also has a unique solution, denoted by a_1^*. We will call $(a_1^*, R_2(a_1^*))$ the *backwards-induction outcome* of this game. The backwards-induction outcome does not involve noncredible threats: player 1 anticipates that player 2 will respond optimally to *any* action a_1 that 1 might choose, by playing $R_2(a_1)$; player 1 gives no credence to threats by player 2 to respond in ways that will not be in 2's self-interest when the second stage arrives.

Recall that in Chapter 1 we used the normal-form representation to study static games of complete information, and we focused on the notion of Nash equilibrium as a solution concept for such games. In this section's discussion of dynamic games, however, we have made no mention of either the normal-form representation or Nash equilibrium. Instead, we have given a verbal description of a game in (1)–(3), and we have defined the backwards-induction outcome as the solution to that game. In Section 2.4.A we will see that the verbal description in (1)–(3) is the extensive-form representation of the game. We will relate the extensive- and normal-form representations, but we will find that for dynamic games the extensive-form representation is often more convenient. In Section 2.4.B we will define subgame-perfect Nash equilibrium: a Nash equilibrium is subgame-perfect if it does not involve a noncredible threat, in a sense to be made precise. We will find that there may be multiple Nash equilibria in a game from the class defined by (1)–(3), but that the only subgame-perfect Nash equilibrium is the equilibrium associated with the backwards-induction outcome. This is an example of the observation in Section 1.1.C that some games have multiple Nash equilibria but have one equilibrium that stands out as the compelling solution to the game.

We conclude this section by exploring the rationality assumptions inherent in backwards-induction arguments. Consider the following three-move game, in which player 1 moves twice:

1. Player 1 chooses L or R, where L ends the game with payoffs of 2 to player 1 and 0 to player 2.

2. Player 2 observes 1's choice. If 1 chose R then 2 chooses L' or R', where L' ends the game with payoffs of 1 to both players.

3. Player 1 observes 2's choice (and recalls his or her own choice in the first stage). If the earlier choices were R and R' then 1 chooses L'' or R'', both of which end the game, L'' with payoffs of 3 to player 1 and 0 to player 2 and R'' with analogous payoffs of 0 and 2.

All these words can be translated into the following succinct game tree. (This is the extensive-form representation of the game, to be defined more generally in Section 2.4.) The top payoff in the pair of payoffs at the end of each branch of the game tree is player 1's, the bottom player 2's.

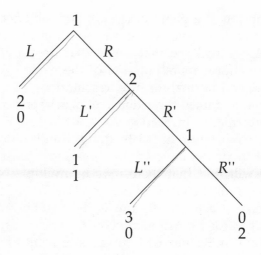

To compute the backwards-induction outcome of this game, we begin at the third stage (i.e., player 1's second move). Here player 1 faces a choice between a payoff of 3 from L'' and a payoff of 0 from R'', so L'' is optimal. Thus, at the second stage, player 2 anticipates that if the game reaches the third stage then 1 will play L'', which would yield a payoff of 0 for player 2. The second-stage choice for player 2 therefore is between a payoff of 1 from L' and a payoff of 0 from R', so L' is optimal. Thus, at the first stage, player 1 anticipates that if the game reaches the second stage then 2 will play L', which would yield a payoff of 1 for player 1. The first-stage choice for player 1 therefore is between a payoff of 2 from L and a payoff of 1 from R, so L is optimal.

This argument establishes that the backwards-induction outcome of this game is for player 1 to choose L in the first stage, thereby ending the game. Even though backwards induction predicts that the game will end in the first stage, an important part of the argument concerns what would happen if the game did not end in the first stage. In the second stage, for example, when player 2 anticipates that if the game reaches the third stage then 1 will play L'', 2 is assuming that 1 is rational. This assumption may seem inconsistent with the fact that 2 gets to move in the second stage only if 1 deviates from the backwards-induction outcome of the game. That is, it may seem that if 1 plays R in the first stage then 2 cannot assume in the second stage that 1 is rational, but this is not the case: if 1 plays R in the first stage then it cannot be common knowledge that both players are rational, but there remain reasons for 1 to have chosen R that do not contradict 2's assumption that 1 is rational.[3] One possibility is that it is common knowledge that player 1 is rational but not that player 2 is rational: if 1 thinks that 2 might not be rational, then 1 might choose R in the first stage, hoping that 2 will play R' in the second stage, thereby giving 1 the chance to play L'' in the third stage. Another possibility is that it is common knowledge that player 2 is rational but not that player 1 is rational: if 1 is rational but thinks that 2 thinks that 1 might not be rational, then 1 might choose R in the first stage, hoping that 2 will think that 1 is not rational and so play R' in the hope that 1 will play R'' in the third stage. Backwards induction assumes that 1's choice of R could be explained along these lines. For some games, however, it may be more reasonable to assume that 1 played R because 1 is indeed irrational. In such games, backwards induction loses much of its appeal as a prediction of play, just as Nash equilibrium does in games where game theory does not provide a unique solution and no convention will develop.

2.1.B   Stackelberg Model of Duopoly

Stackelberg (1934) proposed a dynamic model of duopoly in which a dominant (or leader) firm moves first and a subordinate (or follower) firm moves second. At some points in the history of the U.S. automobile industry, for example, General Motors has seemed to play such a leadership role. (It is straightforward to extend what follows to allow for more than one following firm, such as Ford, Chrysler, and so on.) Following Stackelberg, we will develop the model under the assumption that the firms choose quantities, as in the Cournot model (where the firms' choices are simultaneous, rather than sequential as here). We leave it as an exercise to develop the analogous sequential-move model in which firms choose prices, as they do (simultaneously) in the Bertrand model.

The timing of the game is as follows: (1) firm 1 chooses a quantity $q_1 \geq 0$; (2) firm 2 observes q_1 and then chooses a quantity

---

[3]Recall from the discussion of iterated elimination of strictly dominated strategies (in Section 1.1.B) that it is common knowledge that the players are rational if all the players are rational, and all the players know that all the players are rational, and all the players know that all the players know that all the players are rational, and so on, ad infinitum.

$q_2 \geq 0$; (3) the payoff to firm i is given by the profit function

$$\pi_i(q_i, q_j) = q_i[P(Q) - c],$$

where $P(Q) = a - Q$ is the market-clearing price when the aggregate quantity on the market is $Q = q_1 + q_2$, and c is the constant marginal cost of production (fixed costs being zero).

To solve for the backwards-induction outcome of this game, we first compute firm 2's reaction to an arbitrary quantity by firm 1. $R_2(q_1)$ solves

$$\max_{q_2 \geq 0} \pi_2(q_1, q_2) = \max_{q_2 \geq 0} q_2[a - q_1 - q_2 - c],$$

which yields

$$R_2(q_1) = \frac{a - q_1 - c}{2},$$

provided $q_1 < a - c$. The same equation for $R_2(q_1)$ appeared in our analysis of the simultaneous-move Cournot game in Section 1.2.A. The difference is that here $R_2(q_1)$ is truly firm 2's reaction to firm 1's observed quantity, whereas in the Cournot analysis $R_2(q_1)$ is firm 2's best response to a hypothesized quantity to be simultaneously chosen by firm 1.

Since firm 1 can solve firm 2's problem as well as firm 2 can solve it, firm 1 should anticipate that the quantity choice q_1 will be met with the reaction $R_2(q_1)$. Thus, firm 1's problem in the first stage of the game amounts to

$$\max_{q_1 \geq 0} \pi_1(q_1, R_2(q_1)) = \max_{q_1 \geq 0} q_1[a - q_1 - R_2(q_1) - c]$$

$$= \max_{q_1 \geq 0} q_1 \frac{a - q_1 - c}{2},$$

which yields

$$q_1^* = \frac{a - c}{2} \quad \text{and} \quad R_2(q_1^*) = \frac{a - c}{4}$$

as the backwards-induction outcome of the Stackelberg duopoly game.[4]

---

[4]Just as "Cournot equilibrium" and "Bertrand equilibrium" typically refer to the Nash equilibria of the Cournot and Bertrand games, references to

Recall from Chapter 1 that in the Nash equilibrium of the Cournot game each firm produces $(a-c)/3$. Thus, aggregate quantity in the backwards-induction outcome of the Stackelberg game, $3(a-c)/4$, is greater than aggregate quantity in the Nash equilibrium of the Cournot game, $2(a-c)/3$, so the market-clearing price is lower in the Stackelberg game. In the Stackelberg game, however, firm 1 could have chosen its Cournot quantity, $(a-c)/3$, in which case firm 2 would have responded with its Cournot quantity. Thus, in the Stackelberg game, firm 1 could have achieved its Cournot profit level but chose to do otherwise, so firm 1's profit in the Stackelberg game must exceed its profit in the Cournot game. But the market-clearing price is lower in the Stackelberg game, so aggregate profits are lower, so the fact that firm 1 is better off implies that firm 2 is worse off in the Stackelberg than in the Cournot game.

The observation that firm 2 does worse in the Stackelberg than in the Cournot game illustrates an important difference between single- and multi-person decision problems. In single-person decision theory, having more information can never make the decision maker worse off. In game theory, however, having more information (or, more precisely, having it known to the other players that one has more information) *can* make a player worse off.

In the Stackelberg game, the information in question is firm 1's quantity: firm 2 knows q_1, and (as importantly) firm 1 knows that firm 2 knows q_1. To see the effect this information has, consider the modified sequential-move game in which firm 1 chooses q_1, after which firm 2 chooses q_2 but does so without observing q_1. If firm 2 believes that firm 1 has chosen its Stackelberg quantity $q_1^* = (a-c)/2$, then firm 2's best response is again $R_2(q_1^*) = (a-c)/4$. But if firm 1 anticipates that firm 2 will hold this belief and so choose this quantity, then firm 1 prefers to choose its best response to $(a-c)/4$—namely, $3(a-c)/8$—rather than its Stackelberg quantity $(a-c)/2$. Thus, firm 2 should not believe that firm 1 has chosen its Stackelberg quantity. Rather, the unique Nash equilibrium of this

---

"Stackelberg equilibrium" often mean that the game is sequential- rather than simultaneous-move. As noted in the previous section, however, sequential-move games sometimes have multiple Nash equilibria, only one of which is associated with the backwards-induction outcome of the game. Thus, "Stackelberg equilibrium" can refer both to the sequential-move nature of the game and to the use of a stronger solution concept than simply Nash equilibrium.

modified sequential-move game is for both firms to choose the quantity $(a-c)/3$—precisely the Nash equilibrium of the Cournot game, where the firms move simultaneously.[5] Thus, having firm 1 know that firm 2 knows q_1 hurts firm 2.

2.1.C   Wages and Employment in a Unionized Firm

In Leontief's (1946) model of the relationship between a firm and a monopoly union (i.e., a union that is the monopoly seller of labor to the firm), the union has exclusive control over wages, but the firm has exclusive control over employment. (Similar qualitative conclusions emerge in a more realistic model in which the firm and the union bargain over wages but the firm retains exclusive control over employment.) The union's utility function is $U(w, L)$, where w is the wage the union demands from the firm and L is employment. Assume that $U(w, L)$ increases in both w and L. The firm's profit function is $\pi(w, L) = R(L) - wL$, where $R(L)$ is the revenue the firm can earn if it employs L workers (and makes the associated production and product-market decisions optimally). Assume that $R(L)$ is increasing and concave.

Suppose the timing of the game is: (1) the union makes a wage demand, w; (2) the firm observes (and accepts) w and then chooses employment, L; (3) payoffs are $U(w, L)$ and $\pi(w, L)$. We can say a great deal about the backwards-induction outcome of this game even though we have not assumed specific functional forms for $U(w, L)$ and $R(L)$ and so are not able to solve for this outcome explicitly.

First, we can characterize the firm's best response in stage (2), $L^*(w)$, to an arbitrary wage demand by the union in stage (1), w. Given w, the firm chooses $L^*(w)$ to solve

$$\max_{L \geq 0} \pi(w, L) = \max_{L \geq 0} R(L) - wL,$$

the first-order condition for which is

$$R'(L) - w = 0.$$

---

[5]This is an example of a claim we made in Section 1.1.A: in a normal-form game the players choose their strategies simultaneously, but this does not imply that the parties necessarily *act* simultaneously; it suffices that each choose his or her action without knowledge of the others' choices. For further discussion of this point, see Section 2.4.A.

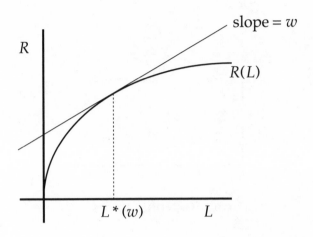

Figure 2.1.1.

To guarantee that the first-order condition $R'(L) - w = 0$ has a solution, assume that $R'(0) = \infty$ and that $R'(\infty) = 0$, as suggested in Figure 2.1.1.

Figure 2.1.2 plots $L^*(w)$ as a function of w (but uses axes that ease comparison with later figures) and illustrates that $L^*(w)$ cuts each of the firm's isoprofit curves at its maximum.[6] Holding L fixed, the firm does better when w is lower, so lower isoprofit curves represent higher profit levels. Figure 2.1.3 depicts the union's indifference curves. Holding L fixed, the union does better when w is higher, so higher indifference curves represent higher utility levels for the union.

We turn next to the union's problem at stage (1). Since the union can solve the firm's second-stage problem as well as the firm can solve it, the union should anticipate that the firm's reaction to the wage demand w will be to choose the employment level

---

[6]The latter property is merely a restatement of the fact that $L^*(w)$ maximizes $\pi(L, w)$ given w. If the union demands w', for example, then the firm's choice of L amounts to the choice of a point on the horizontal line $w = w'$. The highest feasible profit level is attained by choosing L such that the isoprofit curve through (L, w') is tangent to the constraint $w = w'$.

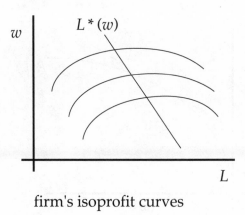

firm's isoprofit curves

Figure 2.1.2.

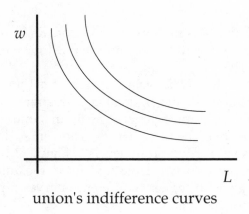

union's indifference curves

Figure 2.1.3.

$L^*(w)$. Thus, the union's problem at the first stage amounts to

$$\max_{w \geq 0} \ U(w, L^*(w)).$$

In terms of the indifference curves plotted in Figure 2.1.3, the

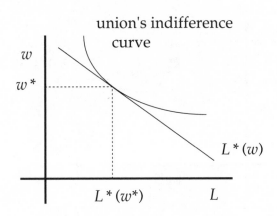

Figure 2.1.4.

union would like to choose the wage demand w that yields the outcome $(w, L^*(w))$ that is on the highest possible indifference curve. The solution to the union's problem is w^*, the wage demand such that the union's indifference curve through the point $(w^*, L^*(w^*))$ is tangent to $L^*(w)$ at that point; see Figure 2.1.4. Thus, $(w^*, L^*(w^*))$ is the backwards-induction outcome of this wage-and-employment game.

It is straightforward to see that $(w^*, L^*(w^*))$ is inefficient: both the union's utility and the firm's profit would be increased if w and L were in the shaded region in Figure 2.1.5. This inefficiency makes it puzzling that in practice firms seem to retain exclusive control over employment. (Allowing the firm and the union to bargain over the wage but leaving the firm with exclusive control over employment yields a similar inefficiency.) Espinosa and Rhee (1989) propose one answer to this puzzle, based on the fact that the union and the firm negotiate repeatedly over time (often every three years, in the United States). There may exist an equilibrium of such a repeated game in which the union's choice of w and the firm's choice of L lie in the shaded region of Figure 2.1.5, even though such values of w and L cannot arise as the backwards-induction outcome of a single negotiation. See Section 2.3 on repeated games and Problem 2.16 on the Espinosa-Rhee model.

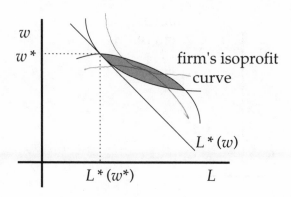

Figure 2.1.5.

2.1.D   Sequential Bargaining

We begin with a three-period bargaining model from the class of games analyzed in Section 2.1.A. We then discuss Rubinstein's (1982) model, in which the number of periods is (potentially) infinite. In both models, settlement occurs immediately—protracted negotiations (such as strikes) do not occur. In Sobel and Takahashi's (1983) model of sequential bargaining under asymmetric information, in contrast, strikes occur with positive probability in the unique (perfect Bayesian) equilibrium; see Section 4.3.B.

Players 1 and 2 are bargaining over one dollar. They alternate in making offers: first player 1 makes a proposal that player 2 can accept or reject; if 2 rejects then 2 makes a proposal that 1 can accept or reject; and so on. Once an offer has been rejected, it ceases to be binding and is irrelevant to the subsequent play of the game. Each offer takes one period, and the players are impatient: they discount payoffs received in later periods by the factor δ per period, where $0 < \delta < 1$.[7]

---

[7]The *discount factor* δ reflects the time-value of money. A dollar received at the beginning of one period can be put in the bank to earn interest, say at rate r per period, and so will be worth $1 + r$ dollars at the beginning of the next period. Equivalently, a dollar to be received at the beginning of the next period is worth only $1/(1 + r)$ of a dollar now. Let $\delta = 1/(1 + r)$. Then a payoff π to be received in the next period is worth only $\delta\pi$ now, a payoff π to be received two periods

A more detailed description of the timing of the three-period bargaining game is as follows.

(1a) At the beginning of the first period, player 1 proposes to take a share s_1 of the dollar, leaving $1 - s_1$ for player 2.

(1b) Player 2 either accepts the offer (in which case the game ends and the payoffs s_1 to player 1 and $1 - s_1$ to player 2 are immediately received) or rejects the offer (in which case play continues to the second period).

(2a) At the beginning of the second period, player 2 proposes that player 1 take a share s_2 of the dollar, leaving $1 - s_2$ for player 2. (Note the convention that s_t always goes to player 1, regardless of who made the offer.)

(2b) Player 1 either accepts the offer (in which case the game ends and the payoffs s_2 to player 1 and $1 - s_2$ to player 2 are immediately received) or rejects the offer (in which case play continues to the third period).

(3) At the beginning of the third period, player 1 receives a share s of the dollar, leaving $1 - s$ for player 2, where $0 < s < 1$.

In this three-period model, the third-period settlement $(s, 1 - s)$ is given exogenously. In the infinite-horizon model we later consider, the payoff s in the third period will represent player 1's payoff in the game that remains if the third period is reached (i.e., if the first two offers are rejected).

To solve for the backwards-induction outcome of this three-period game, we first compute player 2's optimal offer if the second period is reached. Player 1 can receive s in the third period by rejecting player 2's offer of s_2 this period, but the value this period of receiving s next period is only δs. Thus, player 1 will accept s_2 if and only if $s_2 \geq \delta s$. (We assume that each player will accept an offer if indifferent between accepting and rejecting.) Player 2's second-period decision problem therefore amounts to choosing

---

from now is worth only $\delta^2 \pi$ now, and so on. The value today of a future payoff is called the *present value* of that payoff.

between receiving $1 - \delta s$ this period (by offering $s_2 = \delta s$ to player 1) and receiving $1 - s$ next period (by offering player 1 any $s_2 < \delta s$). The discounted value of the latter option is $\delta(1 - s)$, which is less than the $1 - \delta s$ available from the former option, so player 2's optimal second-period offer is $s_2^* = \delta s$. Thus, if play reaches the second period, player 2 will offer s_2^* and player 1 will accept.

Since player 1 can solve player 2's second-period problem as well as player 2 can, player 1 knows that player 2 can receive $1 - s_2^*$ in the second period by rejecting player 1's offer of s_1 this period, but the value this period of receiving $1 - s_2^*$ next period is only $\delta(1 - s_2^*)$. Thus, player 2 will accept $1 - s_1$ if and only if $1 - s_1 \geq \delta(1 - s_2^*)$, or $s_1 \leq 1 - \delta(1 - s_2^*)$. Player 1's first-period decision problem therefore amounts to choosing between receiving $1 - \delta(1 - s_2^*)$ this period (by offering $1 - s_1 = \delta(1 - s_2^*)$ to player 2) and receiving s_2^* next period (by offering any $1 - s_1 < \delta(1 - s_2^*)$ to player 2). The discounted value of the latter option is $\delta s_2^* = \delta^2 s$, which is less than the $1 - \delta(1 - s_2^*) = 1 - \delta(1 - \delta s)$ available from the former option, so player 1's optimal first-period offer is $s_1^* = 1 - \delta(1 - s_2^*) = 1 - \delta(1 - \delta s)$. Thus, in the backwards-induction outcome of this three-period game, player 1 offers the settlement $(s_1^*, 1 - s_1^*)$ to player 2, who accepts.

Now consider the infinite-horizon case. The timing is as described previously, except that the exogenous settlement in step (3) is replaced by an infinite sequence of steps (3a), (3b), (4a), (4b), and so on. Player 1 makes the offer in odd-numbered periods, player 2 in even-numbered; bargaining continues until one player accepts an offer. We would like to solve for the backwards-induction outcome of the infinite-horizon game by working backwards, as in all the applications analyzed so far. Because the game could go on infinitely, however, there is no last move at which to begin such an analysis. Fortunately, the following insight (first applied by Shaked and Sutton 1984) allows us to truncate the infinite-horizon game and apply the logic from the finite-horizon case: the game beginning in the third period (should it be reached) is identical to the game as a whole (beginning in the first period)—in both cases, player 1 makes the first offer, the players alternate in making subsequent offers, and the bargaining continues until one player accepts an offer.

Since we have not formally defined a backwards-induction outcome for this infinite-horizon bargaining game, our arguments will be informal (but can be made formal). Suppose that there is a backwards-induction outcome of the game as a whole in which players 1 and 2 receive the payoffs s and $1 - s$, respectively. We can use these payoffs in the game beginning in the third period, should it be reached, and then work backwards to the first period (as in the three-period model) to compute a new backwards-induction outcome for the game as a whole. In this new backwards-induction outcome, player 1 will offer the settlement $(f(s), 1 - f(s))$ in the first period and player 2 will accept, where $f(s) = 1 - \delta(1 - \delta s)$ is the share taken by player 1 in the first period of the three-period model above when the settlement $(s, 1 - s)$ is exogenously imposed in the third period.

Let s_H be the highest payoff player 1 can achieve in any backwards-induction outcome of the game as a whole. Imagine using s_H as the third-period payoff to player 1, as previously described: this will produce a new backwards-induction outcome in which player 1's first-period payoff is $f(s_H)$. Since $f(s) = 1 - \delta + \delta^2 s$ is increasing in s, $f(s_H)$ is the highest possible first-period payoff because s_H is the highest possible third-period payoff. But s_H is also the highest possible first-period payoff, so $f(s_H) = s_H$. Parallel arguments show that $f(s_L) = s_L$, where s_L is the lowest payoff player 1 can achieve in any backwards-induction outcome of the game as a whole. The only value of s that satisfies $f(s) = s$ is $1/(1 + \delta)$, which we will denote by s^*. Thus, $s_H = s_L = s^*$, so there is a unique backwards-induction outcome in the game as a whole: in the first period, player 1 offers the settlement $(s^* = 1/(1 + \delta)$, $1 - s^* = \delta/(1 + \delta))$ to player 2, who accepts.

2.2   Two-Stage Games of Complete but Imperfect Information

2.2.A   Theory: Subgame Perfection

We now enrich the class of games analyzed in the previous section. As in dynamic games of complete and perfect information, we continue to assume that play proceeds in a sequence of stages, with the moves in all previous stages observed before the next stage begins. Unlike in the games analyzed in the previous section, however, we now allow there to be simultaneous moves within each stage. As will be explained in Section 2.4, this simultaneity of moves within stages means that the games analyzed in this section have imperfect information. Nonetheless, these games share important features with the perfect-information games considered in the previous section.

We will analyze the following simple game, which we (uninspiredly!) call a two-stage game of complete but imperfect information:

1. Players 1 and 2 simultaneously choose actions a_1 and a_2 from feasible sets A_1 and A_2, respectively.

2. Players 3 and 4 observe the outcome of the first stage, (a_1, a_2), and then simultaneously choose actions a_3 and a_4 from feasible sets A_3 and A_4, respectively.

3. Payoffs are $u_i(a_1, a_2, a_3, a_4)$ for $i = 1, 2, 3, 4$.

Many economic problems fit this description.[8] Three examples (later discussed in detail) are bank runs, tariffs and imperfect international competition, and tournaments (e.g., competition among several vice presidents in a firm to be the next president). Other economic problems can be modeled by allowing for a longer sequence of stages, either by adding players or by allowing players to move in more than one stage. There could also be fewer players: in some applications, players 3 and 4 are players 1 and 2; in others, either player 2 or player 4 is missing.

We solve a game from this class by using an approach in the spirit of backwards induction, but this time the first step in working backwards from the end of the game involves solving a real game (the simultaneous-move game between players 3 and 4 in stage two, given the outcome from stage one) rather than solving a single-person optimization problem as in the previous section. To keep things simple, in this section we will assume that for each feasible outcome of the first-stage game, (a_1, a_2), the second-stage game that remains between players 3 and 4 has a unique Nash equilibrium, denoted by $(a_3^*(a_1, a_2), a_4^*(a_1, a_2))$. In Section 2.3.A (on

---

[8]As in the previous section, the feasible action sets of players 3 and 4 in the second stage, A_3 and A_4, could be allowed to depend on the outcome of the first stage, (a_1, a_2). In particular, there may be values of (a_1, a_2) that end the game.

repeated games) we consider the implications of relaxing this assumption.

If players 1 and 2 anticipate that the second-stage behavior of players 3 and 4 will be given by $(a_3^*(a_1, a_2), a_4^*(a_1, a_2))$, then the first-stage interaction between players 1 and 2 amounts to the following simultaneous-move game:

1. Players 1 and 2 simultaneously choose actions a_1 and a_2 from feasible sets A_1 and A_2, respectively.

2. Payoffs are $u_i(a_1, a_2, a_3^*(a_1, a_2), a_4^*(a_1, a_2))$ for $i = 1, 2$.

Suppose (a_1^*, a_2^*) is the unique Nash equilibrium of this simultaneous-move game. We will call $(a_1^*, a_2^*, a_3^*(a_1^*, a_2^*), a_4^*(a_1^*, a_2^*))$ the *subgame-perfect outcome* of this two-stage game. This outcome is the natural analog of the backwards-induction outcome in games of complete and perfect information, and the analogy applies to both the attractive and the unattractive features of the latter. Players 1 and 2 should not believe a threat by players 3 and 4 that the latter will respond with actions that are not a Nash equilibrium in the remaining second-stage game, because when play actually reaches the second stage at least one of players 3 and 4 will not want to carry out such a threat (exactly because it is not a Nash equilibrium of the game that remains at that stage). On the other hand, suppose that player 1 is also player 3, and that player 1 does not play a_1^* in the first stage: player 4 may then want to reconsider the assumption that player 3 (i.e., player 1) will play $a_3^*(a_1, a_2)$ in the second stage.

2.2.B   Bank Runs

Two investors have each deposited D with a bank. The bank has invested these deposits in a long-term project. If the bank is forced to liquidate its investment before the project matures, a total of $2r$ can be recovered, where $D > r > D/2$. If the bank allows the investment to reach maturity, however, the project will pay out a total of $2R$, where $R > D$.

There are two dates at which the investors can make withdrawals from the bank: date 1 is before the bank's investment matures; date 2 is after. For simplicity, assume that there is no discounting. If both investors make withdrawals at date 1 then each receives r and the game ends. If only one investor makes a withdrawal at date 1 then that investor receives D, the other receives $2r - D$, and the game ends. Finally, if neither investor makes a withdrawal at date 1 then the project matures and the investors make withdrawal decisions at date 2. If both investors make withdrawals at date 2 then each receives R and the game ends. If only one investor makes a withdrawal at date 2 then that investor receives $2R - D$, the other receives D, and the game ends. Finally, if neither investor makes a withdrawal at date 2 then the bank returns R to each investor and the game ends.

In Section 2.4 we will discuss how to represent this game formally. For now, however, we will proceed informally. Let the payoffs to the two investors at dates 1 and 2 (as a function of their withdrawal decisions at these dates) be represented by the following pair of normal-form games. Note well that the normal-form game for date 1 is nonstandard: if both investors choose not to withdraw at date 1 then no payoff is specified; rather, the investors proceed to the normal-form game at date 2.

	withdraw	don't
withdraw	r, r	$D, 2r - D$
don't	$2r - D, D$	next stage

Date 1

	withdraw	don't
withdraw	R, R	$2R - D, D$
don't	$D, 2R - D$	R, R

Date 2

To analyze this game, we work backwards. Consider the normal-form game at date 2. Since $R > D$ (and so $2R - D > R$), "withdraw" strictly dominates "don't withdraw," so there is a unique Nash equilibrium in this game: both investors withdraw, leading to a payoff of (R, R). Since there is no discounting, we can simply substitute this payoff into the normal-form game at date 1, as in Figure 2.2.1. Since $r < D$ (and so $2r - D < r$), this one-period version of the two-period game has two pure-strategy Nash

	withdraw	don't
withdraw	r, r	$D, 2r - D$
don't	$2r - D, D$	R, R

Figure 2.2.1.

equilibria: (1) both investors withdraw, leading to a payoff of (r, r); (2) both investors do not withdraw, leading to a payoff of (R, R). Thus, the original two-period bank-runs game has two subgame-perfect outcomes (and so does not quite fit within the class of games defined in Section 2.2.A): (1) both investors withdraw at date 1, yielding payoffs of (r, r); (2) both investors do not withdraw at date 1 but do withdraw at date 2, yielding payoffs of (R, R) at date 2.

The first of these outcomes can be interpreted as a run on the bank. If investor 1 believes that investor 2 will withdraw at date 1 then investor 1's best response is to withdraw as well, even though both investors would be better off if they waited until date 2 to withdraw. This bank-run game differs from the Prisoners' Dilemma discussed in Chapter 1 in an important respect: both games have a Nash equilibrium that leads to a socially inefficient payoff; in the Prisoners' Dilemma this equilibrium is unique (and in dominant strategies), whereas here there also exists a second equilibrium that is efficient. Thus, this model does not predict when bank runs will occur, but does show that they can occur as an equilibrium phenomenon. See Diamond and Dybvig (1983) for a richer model.

2.2.C Tariffs and Imperfect International Competition

We turn next to an application from international economics. Consider two identical countries, denoted by $i = 1, 2$. Each country has a government that chooses a tariff rate, a firm that produces output for both home consumption and export, and consumers who buy on the home market from either the home firm or the foreign firm. If the total quantity on the market in country i is Q_i, then the market-clearing price is $P_i(Q_i) = a - Q_i$. The firm in country i (hereafter called firm i) produces h_i for home consumption and e_i for export. Thus, $Q_i = h_i + e_j$. The firms have a constant marginal cost, c, and no fixed costs. Thus, the total cost of production for firm i is $C_i(h_i, e_i) = c(h_i + e_i)$. The firms also incur tariff costs on exports: if firm i exports e_i to country j when government j has set the tariff rate t_j, then firm i must pay $t_j e_i$ to government j.

The timing of the game is as follows. First, the governments simultaneously choose tariff rates, t_1 and t_2. Second, the firms observe the tariff rates and simultaneously choose quantities for home consumption and for export, (h_1, e_1) and (h_2, e_2). Third, payoffs are profit to firm i and total welfare to government i, where total welfare to country i is the sum of the consumers' surplus[9] enjoyed by the consumers in country i, the profit earned by firm i, and the tariff revenue collected by government i from firm j:

$$\pi_i(t_i, t_j, h_i, e_i, h_j, e_j) = [a - (h_i + e_j)]h_i + [a - (e_i + h_j)]e_i$$
$$- c(h_i + e_i) - t_j e_i,$$
$$W_i(t_i, t_j, h_i, e_i, h_j, e_j) = \frac{1}{2}Q_i^2 + \pi_i(t_i, t_j, h_i, e_i, h_j, e_j) + t_i e_j.$$

Suppose the governments have chosen the tariffs t_1 and t_2. If $(h_1^*, e_1^*, h_2^*, e_2^*)$ is a Nash equilibrium in the remaining (two-market) game between firms 1 and 2 then, for each i, (h_i^*, e_i^*) must solve

$$\max_{h_i, e_i \geq 0} \pi_i(t_i, t_j, h_i, e_i, h_j^*, e_j^*).$$

Since $\pi_i(t_i, t_j, h_i, e_i, h_j^*, e_j^*)$ can be written as the sum of firm i's profits on market i (which is a function of h_i and e_j^* alone) and firm i's profits on market j (which is a function of e_i, h_j^*, and t_j alone), firm i's two-market optimization problem simplifies into a pair of problems, one for each market: h_i^* must solve

$$\max_{h_i \geq 0} h_i[a - (h_i + e_j^*) - c],$$

and e_i^* must solve

$$\max_{e_i \geq 0} e_i[a - (e_i + h_j^*) - c] - t_j e_i.$$

[9]If a consumer buys a good for price p when she would have been willing to pay the value v, then she enjoys a surplus of $v - p$. Given the inverse demand curve $P_i(Q_i) = a - Q_i$, if the quantity sold on market i is Q_i, the aggregate consumer surplus can be shown to be $(1/2)Q_i^2$.

Assuming $e_j^* \leq a - c$, we have

$$h_i^* = \frac{1}{2}(a - e_j^* - c), \tag{2.2.1}$$

and assuming $h_j^* \leq a - c - t_j$, we have

$$e_i^* = \frac{1}{2}(a - h_j^* - c - t_j). \tag{2.2.2}$$

(The results we derive are consistent with both of these assumptions.) Both of the best-response functions (2.2.1) and (2.2.2) must hold for each $i = 1, 2$. Thus, we have four equations in the four unknowns $(h_1^*, e_1^*, h_2^*, e_2^*)$. Fortunately, these equations simplify into two sets of two equations in two unknowns. The solutions are

$$h_i^* = \frac{a - c + t_i}{3} \quad \text{and} \quad e_i^* = \frac{a - c - 2t_j}{3}. \tag{2.2.3}$$

Recall (from Section 1.2.A) that the equilibrium quantity chosen by both firms in the Cournot game is $(a - c)/3$, but that this result was derived under the assumption of symmetric marginal costs. In the equilibrium described by (2.2.3), in contrast, the governments' tariff choices make marginal costs asymmetric (as in Problem 1.6). On market i, for instance, firm i's marginal cost is c but firm j's is $c + t_i$. Since firm j's cost is higher it wants to produce less. But if firm j is going to produce less, then the market-clearing price will be higher, so firm i wants to produce more, in which case firm j wants to produce even less. Thus, in equilibrium, h_i^* increases in t_i and e_j^* decreases (at a faster rate) in t_i, as in (2.2.3).

Having solved the second-stage game that remains between the two firms after the governments choose tariff rates, we can now represent the first-stage interaction between the two governments as the following simultaneous-move game. First, the governments simultaneously choose tariff rates t_1 and t_2. Second, payoffs are $W_i(t_i, t_j, h_1^*, e_1^*, h_2^*, e_2^*)$ for government $i = 1, 2$, where h_i^* and e_i^* are functions of t_i and t_j as described in (2.2.3). We now solve for the Nash equilibrium of this game between the governments.

To simplify the notation, we will suppress the dependence of h_i^* on t_i and e_i^* on t_j: let $W_i^*(t_i, t_j)$ denote $W_i(t_i, t_j, h_1^*, e_1^*, h_2^*, e_2^*)$, the payoff to government i when it chooses the tariff rate t_i, government j chooses t_j, and firms i and j then play the Nash equilibrium given in (2.2.3). If (t_1^*, t_2^*) is a Nash equilibrium of this game between the governments then, for each i, t_i^* must solve

$$\max_{t_i \geq 0} \; W_i^*(t_i, t_j^*).$$

But $W_i^*(t_i, t_j^*)$ equals

$$\frac{(2(a-c) - t_i)^2}{18} + \frac{(a-c+t_i)^2}{9} + \frac{(a-c-2t_j^*)^2}{9} + \frac{t_i(a-c-2t_i)}{3},$$

so

[handwritten: consumer surplus] *[handwritten: profit of i]* *[handwritten: profit of j]* *[handwritten: tariff paid]*

$$t_i^* = \frac{a-c}{3}$$

for each i, independent of t_j^*. Thus, in this model, choosing a tariff rate of $(a-c)/3$ is a dominant strategy for each government. (In other models, such as when marginal costs are increasing, the governments' equilibrium strategies are not dominant strategies.) Substituting $t_i^* = t_j^* = (a-c)/3$ into (2.2.3) yields

$$h_i^* = \frac{4(a-c)}{9} \quad \text{and} \quad e_i^* = \frac{a-c}{9}$$

as the firms' quantity choices in the second stage. Thus, the subgame-perfect outcome of this tariff game is ($t_1^* = t_2^* = (a-c)/3$, $h_1^* = h_2^* = 4(a-c)/9$, $e_1^* = e_2^* = (a-c)/9$).

In the subgame-perfect outcome the aggregate quantity on each market is $5(a-c)/9$. If the governments had chosen tariff rates equal to zero, however, then the aggregate quantity on each market would have been $2(a-c)/3$, just as in the Cournot model. Thus, the consumers' surplus on market i (which, as noted earlier, is simply one-half the square of the aggregate quantity on market i) is lower when the governments choose their dominant-strategy tariffs than it would be if they chose zero tariffs. In fact, zero tariffs are socially optimal, in the sense that $t_1 = t_2 = 0$ is the solution to

$$\max_{t_1, t_2 \geq 0} \; W_1^*(t_1, t_2) + W_2^*(t_2, t_1),$$

so there is an incentive for the governments to sign a treaty in which they commit to zero tariffs (i.e., free trade). (If negative tariffs—that is, subsidies—are feasible, the social optimum is for the governments to choose $t_1 = t_2 = -(a-c)$, which causes the home firm to produce zero for home consumption and to export the perfect-competition quantity to the other country.) Thus, given that firms i and j play the Nash equilibrium given in (2.2.3) in the second stage, the first-stage interaction between the governments is a Prisoners' Dilemma: the unique Nash equilibrium is in dominant strategies and is socially inefficient.

2.2.D   Tournaments

Consider two workers and their boss. Worker i (where $i = 1$ or 2) produces output $y_i = e_i + \varepsilon_i$, where e_i is effort and ε_i is noise. Production proceeds as follows. First, the workers simultaneously choose nonnegative effort levels: $e_i \geq 0$. Second, the noise terms ε_1 and ε_2 are independently drawn from a density $f(\varepsilon)$ with zero mean. Third, the workers' outputs are observed but their effort choices are not. The workers' wages therefore can depend on their outputs but not (directly) on their efforts.

Suppose the workers' boss decides to induce effort from the workers by having them compete in a tournament, as first analyzed by Lazear and Rosen (1981).[10] The wage earned by the winner of the tournament (i.e., the worker with the higher output) is w_H; the wage earned by the loser is w_L. The payoff to a worker from earning wage w and expending effort e is $u(w,e) = w - g(e)$, where the disutility of effort, $g(e)$, is increasing and convex (i.e., $g'(e) > 0$ and $g''(e) > 0$). The payoff to the boss is $y_1 + y_2 - w_H - w_L$.

We now translate this application into the terms of the class of games discussed in Section 2.2.A. The boss is player 1, whose action a_1 is choosing the wages to be paid in the tournament, w_H and w_L. There is no player 2. The workers are players 3 and 4, who observe the wages chosen in the first stage and then simultaneously choose actions a_3 and a_4, namely the effort choices e_1 and e_2. (We later consider the possibility that, given the wages chosen by the boss, the workers prefer not to participate in the tournament and accept alternative employment instead.) Finally, the players' payoffs are as given earlier. Since outputs (and so also wages) are functions not only of the players actions but also

---

[10]To keep the exposition of this application simple, we ignore several technical details, such as conditions under which the worker's first-order condition is sufficient. Nonetheless, the analysis involves more probability than others thus far. The application can be skipped without loss of continuity.

of the noise terms ε_1 and ε_2, we work with the players' expected payoffs.

Suppose the boss has chosen the wages w_H and w_L. If the effort pair (e_1^*, e_2^*) is to be a Nash equilibrium of the remaining game between the workers then, for each i, e_i^* must maximize worker i's expected wage, net of the disutility of effort: e_i^* must solve[11]

$$\max_{e_i \geq 0} \; w_H \, \text{Prob}\{y_i(e_i) > y_j(e_j^*)\} + w_L \, \text{Prob}\{y_i(e_i) \leq y_j(e_j^*)\} - g(e_i)$$

$$= (w_H - w_L) \, \text{Prob} \, \{y_i(e_i) > y_j(e_j^*)\} + w_L - g(e_i), \qquad (2.2.4)$$

where $y_i(e_i) = e_i + \varepsilon_i$. The first-order condition for (2.2.4) is

$$(w_H - w_L) \frac{\partial \text{Prob}\{y_i(e_i) > y_j(e_j^*)\}}{\partial e_i} = g'(e_i). \qquad (2.2.5)$$

That is, worker i chooses e_i such that the marginal disutility of extra effort, $g'(e_i)$, equals the marginal gain from extra effort, which is the product of the wage gain from winning the tournament, $w_H - w_L$, and the marginal increase in the probability of winning.

By Bayes' rule,[12]

$$
\begin{aligned}
\text{Prob}\{y_i(e_i) > y_j(e_j^*)\} &= \text{Prob}\{\varepsilon_i > e_j^* + \varepsilon_j - e_i\} \\
&= \int_{\varepsilon_j} \text{Prob}\{\varepsilon_i > e_j^* + \varepsilon_j - e_i \mid \varepsilon_j\} f(\varepsilon_j) \, d\varepsilon_j \\
&= \int_{\varepsilon_j} [1 - F(e_j^* - e_i + \varepsilon_j)] f(\varepsilon_j) \, d\varepsilon_j,
\end{aligned}
$$

---

[11]In writing (2.2.4), we assume that the noise density $f(\varepsilon)$ is such that the event that the workers' outputs are exactly equal happens with zero probability and so need not be considered in worker i's expected utility. (More formally, we assume that the density $f(\varepsilon)$ is atomless.) In a complete description of the tournament, it would be natural (but immaterial) to specify that the winner is determined by a coin flip or (equivalently, in this model) that both workers receive $(w_H + w_L)/2$.

[12]Bayes' rule provides a formula for $P(A \mid B)$, the (conditional) probability that an event A will occur given that an event B has already occurred. Let $P(A)$, $P(B)$, and $P(A, B)$ be the (prior) probabilities (i.e., the probabilities before either A or B has had a chance to take place) that A will occur, that B will occur, and that both A and B will occur, respectively. Bayes' rule states that $P(A \mid B) = P(A, B)/P(B)$. That is, the conditional probability of A given B equals the probability that both A and B will occur, divided by the prior probability that B will occur.

so the first-order condition (2.2.5) becomes

$$(w_H - w_L) \int_{\varepsilon_j} f(e_j^* - e_i + \varepsilon_j) f(\varepsilon_j) \, d\varepsilon_j = g'(e_i).$$

In a symmetric Nash equilibrium (i.e., $e_1^* = e_2^* = e^*$), we have

$$(w_H - w_L) \int_{\varepsilon_j} f(\varepsilon_j)^2 \, d\varepsilon_j = g'(e^*). \tag{2.2.6}$$

Since $g(e)$ is convex, a bigger prize for winning (i.e., a larger value of $w_H - w_L$) induces more effort, as is intuitive. On the other hand, holding the prize constant, it is not worthwhile to work hard when output is very noisy, because the outcome of the tournament is likely to be determined by luck rather than effort. If ε is normally distributed with variance σ^2, for example, then

$$\int_{\varepsilon_j} f(\varepsilon_j)^2 \, d\varepsilon_j = \frac{1}{2\sigma\sqrt{\pi}},$$

which decreases in σ, so e^* indeed decreases in σ.

We now work backwards to the first stage of the game. Suppose that if the workers agree to participate in the tournament (rather than accept alternative employment) then they will respond to the wages w_H and w_L by playing the symmetric Nash equilibrium characterized by (2.2.6). (We thus ignore the possibilities of asymmetric equilibria and of an equilibrium in which the workers' effort choices are given by the corner solution $e_1 = e_2 = 0$, rather than by the first-order condition (2.2.5).) Suppose also that the workers' alternative employment opportunity would provide utility U_a. Since in the symmetric Nash equilibrium each worker wins the tournament with probability one-half (i.e., Prob$\{y_i(e^*) > y_j(e^*)\} = 1/2$), if the boss intends to induce the workers to participate in the tournament then she must choose wages that satisfy

$$\frac{1}{2}w_H + \frac{1}{2}w_L - g(e^*) \geq U_a. \tag{2.2.7}$$

Assuming that U_a is low enough that the boss wants to induce the workers to participate in the tournament, she therefore chooses wages to maximize expected profit, $2e^* - w_H - w_L$, subject to (2.2.7). At the optimum, (2.2.7) holds with equality:

$$w_L = 2U_a + 2g(e^*) - w_H. \tag{2.2.8}$$

Expected profit then becomes $2e^* - 2U_a - 2g(e^*)$, so the boss wishes to choose wages such that the induced effort, e^*, maximizes $e^* - g(e^*)$. The optimal induced effort therefore satisfies the first-order condition $g'(e^*) = 1$. Substituting this into (2.2.6) implies that the optimal prize, $w_H - w_L$, solves

$$(w_H - w_L) \int_{\varepsilon_j} f(\varepsilon_j)^2 \, d\varepsilon_j = 1,$$

and (2.2.8) then determines w_H and w_L themselves.

2.3 Repeated Games

In this section we analyze whether threats and promises about future behavior can influence current behavior in repeated relationships. Much of the intuition is given in the two-period case; a few ideas require an infinite horizon. We also define subgame-perfect Nash equilibrium for repeated games. This definition is simpler to express for the special case of repeated games than for the general dynamic games of complete information we consider in Section 2.4.B. We introduce it here so as to ease the exposition later.

2.3.A   Theory: Two-Stage Repeated Games

Consider the Prisoners' Dilemma given in normal form in Figure 2.3.1. Suppose two players play this simultaneous-move game twice, observing the outcome of the first play before the second play begins, and suppose the payoff for the entire game is simply the sum of the payoffs from the two stages (i.e., there is no

Player 2

		L_2	R_2
	L_1	1, 1	5, 0
Player 1	R_1	0, 5	4, 4

Figure 2.3.1.

Player 2

	L_2	R_2
L_1	2, 2	6, 1
R_1	1, 6	5, 5

Player 1

Figure 2.3.2.

discounting). We will call this repeated game the two-stage Prisoners' Dilemma. It belongs to the class of games analyzed in Section 2.2.A. Here players 3 and 4 are identical to players 1 and 2, the action spaces A_3 and A_4 are identical to A_1 and A_2, and the payoffs $u_i(a_1, a_2, a_3, a_4)$ are simply the sum of the payoff from the first-stage outcome (a_1, a_2) and the payoff from the second-stage outcome (a_3, a_4). Furthermore, the two-stage Prisoners' Dilemma satisfies the assumption we made in Section 2.2.A: for each feasible outcome of the first-stage game, (a_1, a_2), the second-stage game that remains between players 3 and 4 has a unique Nash equilibrium, denoted by $(a_3^*(a_1, a_2), a_4^*(a_1, a_2))$. In fact, the two-stage Prisoners' Dilemma satisfies this assumption in the following stark way. In Section 2.2.A we allowed for the possibility that the Nash equilibrium of the remaining second-stage game depends on the first-stage outcome—hence the notation $(a_3^*(a_1, a_2), a_4^*(a_1, a_2))$ rather than simply (a_3^*, a_4^*). (In the tariff game, for example, the firms' equilibrium quantity choices in the second stage depend on the governments' tariff choices in the first stage.) In the two-stage Prisoners' Dilemma, however, the unique equilibrium of the second-stage game is (L_1, L_2), regardless of the first-stage outcome.

Following the procedure described in Section 2.2.A for computing the subgame-perfect outcome of such a game, we analyze the first stage of the two-stage Prisoners' Dilemma by taking into account that the outcome of the game remaining in the second stage will be the Nash equilibrium of that remaining game—namely, (L_1, L_2) with payoff $(1, 1)$. Thus, the players' first-stage interaction in the two-stage Prisoners' Dilemma amounts to the one-shot game in Figure 2.3.2, in which the payoff pair $(1, 1)$ for the second stage has been added to each first-stage payoff pair. The game in Figure 2.3.2 also has a unique Nash equilibrium: (L_1, L_2). Thus, the unique subgame-perfect outcome of the two-stage Prisoners'

Dilemma is (L_1, L_2) in the first stage, followed by (L_1, L_2) in the second stage. Cooperation—that is, (R_1, R_2)—cannot be achieved in either stage of the subgame-perfect outcome.

This argument holds more generally. (Here we temporarily depart from the two-period case to allow for any finite number of repetitions, T.) Let $G = \{A_1, \ldots, A_n; u_1, \ldots, u_n\}$ denote a static game of complete information in which players 1 through n simultaneously choose actions a_1 through a_n from the action spaces A_1 through A_n, respectively, and payoffs are $u_1(a_1, \ldots, a_n)$ through $u_n(a_1, \ldots, a_n)$. The game G will be called the *stage game* of the repeated game.

Definition *Given a stage game G, let $G(T)$ denote the **finitely repeated game** in which G is played T times, with the outcomes of all preceding plays observed before the next play begins. The payoffs for $G(T)$ are simply the sum of the payoffs from the T stage games.*

Proposition *If the stage game G has a unique Nash equilibrium then, for any finite T, the repeated game $G(T)$ has a unique subgame-perfect outcome: the Nash equilibrium of G is played in every stage.*[13]

We now return to the two-period case, but consider the possibility that the stage game G has multiple Nash equilibria, as in Figure 2.3.3. The strategies labeled L_i and M_i mimic the Prisoners' Dilemma from Figure 2.3.1, but the strategies labeled R_i have been added to the game so that there are now two pure-strategy Nash equilibria: (L_1, L_2), as in the Prisoners' Dilemma, and now also (R_1, R_2). It is of course artificial to add an equilibrium to the Prisoners' Dilemma in this way, but our interest in this game is expositional rather than economic. In the next section we will see that infinitely repeated games share this multiple-equilibria spirit even if the stage game being repeated infinitely has a unique Nash equilibrium, as does the Prisoners' Dilemma. Thus, in this section we

---

[13]Analogous results hold if the stage game G is a dynamic game of complete information. Suppose G is a dynamic game of complete and perfect information from the class defined in Section 2.1.A. If G has a unique backwards-induction outcome, then $G(T)$ has a unique subgame-perfect outcome: the backwards-induction outcome of G is played in every stage. Similarly, suppose G is a two-stage game from the class defined in Section 2.2.A. If G has a unique subgame-perfect outcome, then $G(T)$ has a unique subgame-perfect outcome: the subgame-perfect outcome of G is played in every stage.

finite Repeated game is interesting w/ multiple NE

	L_2	M_2	R_2
L_1	1,1	5,0	0,0
M_1	0,5	4,4	0,0
R_1	0,0	0,0	3,3

Figure 2.3.3.

analyze an artificial stage game in the simple two-period frame-work, and thereby prepare for our later analysis of an economi-cally interesting stage game in the infinite-horizon framework.

Suppose the stage game in Figure 2.3.3 is played twice, with the first-stage outcome observed before the second stage begins. We will show that there is a subgame-perfect outcome of this re-peated game in which the strategy pair (M_1, M_2) is played in the first stage.[14] As in Section 2.2.A, assume that in the first stage the players anticipate that the second-stage outcome will be a Nash equilibrium of the stage game. Since this stage game has more than one Nash equilibrium, it is now possible for the players to anticipate that different first-stage outcomes will be followed by different stage-game equilibria in the second stage. Suppose, for example, that the players anticipate that (R_1, R_2) will be the second-stage outcome if the first-stage outcome is (M_1, M_2), but that (L_1, L_2) will be the second-stage outcome if any of the eight other first-stage outcomes occurs. The players' first-stage inter-action then amounts to the one-shot game in Figure 2.3.4, where $(3,3)$ has been added to the (M_1, M_2)-cell and $(1,1)$ has been added to the eight other cells.

There are three pure-strategy Nash equilibria in the game in Figure 2.3.4: (L_1, L_2), (M_1, M_2), and (R_1, R_2). As in Figure 2.3.2,

---

[14]Strictly speaking, we have defined the notion of a subgame-perfect outcome only for the class of games defined in Section 2.2.A. The two-stage Prisoner's Dilemma belongs to this class because for each feasible outcome of the first-stage game there is a unique Nash equilibrium of the remaining second-stage game. The two-stage repeated game based on the stage game in Figure 2.3.3 does not belong to this class, however, because the stage game has multiple Nash equilibria. We will not formally extend the definition of a subgame-perfect outcome so that it applies to all two-stage repeated games, both because the change in the definition is minuscule and because even more general definitions appear in Sections 2.3.B and 2.4.B.

	L_2	M_2	R_2
L_1	2, 2	6, 1	1, 1
M_1	1, 6	7, 7	1, 1
R_1	1, 1	1, 1	4, 4

Figure 2.3.4.

Nash equilibria of this one-shot game correspond to subgame-perfect outcomes of the original repeated game. Let $((w, x), (y, z))$ denote an outcome of the repeated game—(w, x) in the first stage and (y, z) in the second. The Nash equilibrium (L_1, L_2) in Figure 2.3.4 corresponds to the subgame-perfect outcome $((L_1, L_2), (L_1, L_2))$ in the repeated game, because the anticipated second-stage outcome is (L_1, L_2) following anything but (M_1, M_2) in the first stage. Likewise, the Nash equilibrium (R_1, R_2) in Figure 2.3.4 corresponds to the subgame-perfect outcome $((R_1, R_2), (L_1, L_2))$ in the repeated game. These two subgame-perfect outcomes of the repeated game simply concatenate Nash equilibrium outcomes from the stage game, but the third Nash equilibrium in Figure 2.3.4 yields a qualitatively different result: (M_1, M_2) in Figure 2.3.4 corresponds to the subgame-perfect outcome $((M_1, M_2), (R_1, R_2))$ in the repeated game, because the anticipated second-stage outcome is (R_1, R_2) following (M_1, M_2). Thus, as claimed earlier, cooperation can be achieved in the first stage of a subgame-perfect outcome of the repeated game. This is an example of a more general point: if $G = \{A_1, \ldots, A_n; u_1, \ldots, u_n\}$ is a static game of complete information with multiple Nash equilibria then there may be subgame-perfect outcomes of the repeated game $G(T)$ in which, for any $t < T$, the outcome in stage t is not a Nash equilibrium of G. We return to this idea in the infinite-horizon analysis in the next section.

The main point to extract from this example is that credible threats or promises about future behavior can influence current behavior. A second point, however, is that subgame-perfection may not embody a strong enough definition of credibility. In deriving the subgame-perfect outcome $((M_1, M_2), (R_1, R_2))$, for example, we assumed that the players anticipate that (R_1, R_2) will be the second-stage outcome if the first-stage outcome is (M_1, M_2)

	L_2	M_2	R_2	P_2	Q_2
L_1	1,1	5,0	0,0	0,0	0,0
M_1	0,5	4,4	0,0	0,0	0,0
R_1	0,0	0,0	3,3	0,0	0,0
P_1	0,0	0,0	0,0	$4,\frac{1}{2}$	0,0
Q_1	0,0	0,0	0,0	0,0	$\frac{1}{2},4$

Figure 2.3.5.

and that (L_1, L_2) will be the second-stage outcome if any of the eight other first-stage outcomes occurs. But playing (L_1, L_2) in the second stage, with its payoff of $(1, 1)$, may seem silly when (R_1, R_2), with its payoff of $(3, 3)$, is also available as a Nash equilibrium of the remaining stage game. Loosely put, it would seem natural for the players to renegotiate.[15] If (M_1, M_2) does not occur as the first-stage outcome, so that (L_1, L_2) is supposed to be played in the second stage, then each player might reason that bygones are bygones and that the unanimously preferred stage-game equilibrium (R_1, R_2) should be played instead. But if (R_1, R_2) is to be the second-stage outcome after every first-stage outcome, then the incentive to play (M_1, M_2) in the first stage is destroyed: the first-stage interaction between the two players simply amounts to the one-shot game in which the payoff $(3, 3)$ has been added to each cell of the stage game in Figure 2.3.3, so L_i is player i's best response to M_j.

To suggest a solution to this renegotiation problem, we consider the game in Figure 2.3.5, which is even more artificial than the game in Figure 2.3.3. Once again, our interest in this game is expositional rather than economic. The ideas we develop here to address renegotiation in this artificial game can also be applied to renegotiation in infinitely repeated games; see Farrell and Maskin (1989), for example.

---

[15]This is loose usage because "renegotiate" suggests that communication (or even bargaining) occurs between the first and second stages. If such actions are possible, then they should be included in the description and analysis of the game. Here we assume that no such actions are possible, so by "renegotiate" we have in mind an analysis based on introspection.

This stage game adds the strategies P_i and Q_i to the stage game in Figure 2.3.3. There are four pure-strategy Nash equilibria of the stage game: (L_1, L_2) and (R_1, R_2), and now also (P_1, P_2) and (Q_1, Q_2). As before, the players unanimously prefer (R_1, R_2) to (L_1, L_2). More importantly, there is no Nash equilibrium (x, y) in Figure 2.3.5 such that the players unanimously prefer (x, y) to (P_1, P_2), or (Q_1, Q_2), or (R_1, R_2). We say that (R_1, R_2) *Pareto-dominates* (L_1, L_2), and that (P_1, P_2), (Q_1, Q_2), and (R_1, R_2) are on the *Pareto frontier* of the payoffs to Nash equilibria of the stage game in Figure 2.3.5.

Suppose the stage game in Figure 2.3.5 is played twice, with the first-stage outcome observed before the second stage begins. Suppose further that the players anticipate that the second-stage outcome will be as follows: (R_1, R_2) if the first-stage outcome is (M_1, M_2); (P_1, P_2) if the first-stage outcome is (M_1, w), where w is anything but M_2; (Q_1, Q_2) if the first-stage outcome is (x, M_2), where x is anything but M_1; and (R_1, R_2) if the first-stage outcome is (y, z), where y is anything but M_1 and z is anything but M_2. Then $((M_1, M_2), (R_1, R_2))$ is a subgame-perfect outcome of the repeated game, because each player gets $4 + 3$ from playing M_i and then R_i but only $5 + 1/2$ from deviating to L_i in the first stage (and even less from other deviations). More importantly, the difficulty in the previous example does not arise here. In the two-stage repeated game based on Figure 2.3.3, the only way to punish a player for deviating in the first stage was to play a Pareto-dominated equilibrium in the second stage, thereby also punishing the punisher. Here, in contrast, there are three equilibria on the Pareto frontier—one to reward good behavior by both players in the first stage, and two others to be used not only to punish a player who deviates in the first stage but also to reward the punisher. Thus, if punishment is called for in the second stage, there is no other stage-game equilibrium the punisher would prefer, so the punisher cannot be persuaded to renegotiate the punishment.

2.3.B   Theory: Infinitely Repeated Games

We now turn to infinitely repeated games. As in the finite-horizon case, the main theme is that credible threats or promises about future behavior can influence current behavior. In the finite-horizon case we saw that if there are multiple Nash equilibria of the stage

Finite game ·unique NE ⇒ NE of stage game will be SPNE of repeated G
· multiple NE ⇒ NE's will be SPNE of repeated G, but you
and you play NE in previous stages, t ≤ T
don't play NE in previous stages, t ≤ T
∪ only play NE in last stage T.

Repeated Games 89

Infinite game ·unique NE ⇒ for t ≤ T, you don't play NE of G.

game G then there may be subgame-perfect outcomes of the repeated game $G(T)$ in which, for any $t < T$, the outcome of stage t is
not a Nash equilibrium of G. A stronger result is true in infinitely
repeated games: even if the stage game has a unique Nash equilibrium, there may be subgame-perfect outcomes of the infinitely
repeated game in which no stage's outcome is a Nash equilibrium
of G.

We begin by studying the infinitely repeated Prisoners' Dilemma. We then consider the class of infinitely repeated games analogous to the class of finitely repeated games defined in the previous
section: a static game of complete information, G, is repeated infinitely, with the outcomes of all previous stages observed before
the current stage begins. For these classes of finitely and infinitely
repeated games, we define a player's strategy, a subgame, and
a subgame-perfect Nash equilibrium. (In Section 2.4.B we define
these concepts for general dynamic games of complete information, not just for these classes of repeated games.) We then use
these definitions to state and prove Friedman's (1971) Theorem
(also called the Folk Theorem).[16]

Suppose the Prisoners' Dilemma in Figure 2.3.6 is to be repeated infinitely and that, for each t, the outcomes of the $t - 1$
preceding plays of the stage game are observed before the tth stage
begins. Simply summing the payoffs from this infinite sequence
of stage games does not provide a useful measure of a player's
payoff in the infinitely repeated game. Receiving a payoff of 4 in
every period is better than receiving a payoff of 1 in every period,
for example, but the sum of the payoffs is infinity in both cases.
Recall (from Rubinstein's bargaining model in Section 2.1.D) that
the discount factor $\delta = 1/(1 + r)$ is the value today of a dollar to
be received one stage later, where r is the interest rate per stage.
Given a discount factor and a player's payoffs from an infinite

---

[16]The original Folk Theorem concerned the payoffs of all the Nash equilibria
of an infinitely repeated game. This result was called the Folk Theorem because it was widely known among game theorists in the 1950s, even though
no one had published it. Friedman's (1971) Theorem concerns the payoffs of
certain subgame-perfect Nash equilibria of an infinitely repeated game, and so
strengthens the original Folk Theorem by using a stronger equilibrium concept—
subgame-perfect Nash equilibrium rather than Nash equilibrium. The earlier
name has stuck, however: Friedman's Theorem (and later results) are sometimes
called Folk Theorems, even though they were not widely known among game
theorists before they were published.

Player 2

		L_2	R_2
Player 1	L_1	1,1	5,0
	R_1	0,5	4,4

Figure 2.3.6.

sequence of stage games, we can compute the *present value* of the payoffs—the lump-sum payoff that could be put in the bank now so as to yield the same bank balance at the end of the sequence.

Definition   *Given the discount factor δ, the **present value** of the infinite sequence of payoffs $\pi_1, \pi_2, \pi_3, \ldots$ is*

$$\pi_1 + \delta\pi_2 + \delta^2\pi_3 + \cdots = \sum_{t=1}^{\infty} \delta^{t-1}\pi_t.$$

We can also use δ to reinterpret what we call an infinitely repeated game as a repeated game that ends after a random number of repetitions. Suppose that after each stage is played a (weighted) coin is flipped to determine whether the game will end. If the probability is p that the game ends immediately, and therefore $1 - p$ that the game continues for at least one more stage, then a payoff π to be received in the next stage (if it is played) is worth only $(1 - p)\pi/(1 + r)$ before this stage's coin flip occurs. Likewise, a payoff π to be received two stages from now (if both it and the intervening stage are played) is worth only $(1 - p)^2\pi/(1 + r)^2$ before this stage's coin flip occurs. Let $\delta = (1 - p)/(1 + r)$. Then the present value $\pi_1 + \delta\pi_2 + \delta^2\pi_3 + \cdots$ reflects both the time-value of money and the possibility that the game will end.

Consider the infinitely repeated Prisoners' Dilemma in which each player's discount factor is δ and each player's payoff in the repeated game is the present value of the player's payoffs from the stage games. We will show that cooperation—that is, (R_1, R_2)—can occur in every stage of a subgame-perfect outcome of the infinitely repeated game, even though the only Nash equilibrium in the stage game is noncooperation—that is, (L_1, L_2). The argument is in the spirit of our analysis of the two-stage repeated game based on Figure 2.3.3 (the stage game in which we added a second Nash equilibrium to the Prisoners' Dilemma): if the players cooperate today then they play a high-payoff equilibrium tomorrow; otherwise they play a low-payoff equilibrium tomorrow. The difference between the two-stage repeated game and the infinitely repeated game is that here the high-payoff equilibrium that might be played tomorrow is not artificially added to the stage game but rather represents continuing to cooperate tomorrow and thereafter.

Suppose player i begins the infinitely repeated game by cooperating and then cooperates in each subsequent stage game if and only if both players have cooperated in every previous stage. Formally, player i's strategy is:

> Play R_i in the first stage. In the tth stage, if the outcome of all $t-1$ preceding stages has been (R_1, R_2) then play R_i; otherwise, play L_i.

This strategy is an example of a *trigger strategy*, so called because player i cooperates until someone fails to cooperate, which triggers a switch to noncooperation forever after. If both players adopt this trigger strategy then the outcome of the infinitely repeated game will be (R_1, R_2) in every stage. We first argue that if δ is close enough to one then it is a Nash equilibrium of the infinitely repeated game for both players to adopt this strategy. We then argue that such a Nash equilibrium is subgame-perfect, in a sense to be made precise.

To show that it is a Nash equilibrium of the infinitely repeated game for both players to adopt the trigger strategy, we will assume that player i has adopted the trigger strategy and then show that, provided δ is close enough to one, it is a best response for player j to adopt the strategy also. Since player i will play L_i forever once one stage's outcome differs from (R_1, R_2), player j's best response is indeed to play L_j forever once one stage's outcome differs from (R_1, R_2). It remains to determine player j's best response in the first stage, and in any stage such that all the preceding outcomes have been (R_1, R_2). Playing L_j will yield a payoff of 5 this stage but will trigger noncooperation by player i (and therefore also by player j) forever after, so the payoff in every future stage will be 1. Since $1 + \delta + \delta^2 + \cdots = 1/(1-\delta)$, the present value of this sequence of payoffs is

$$5 + \delta \cdot 1 + \delta^2 \cdot 1 + \cdots = 5 + \frac{\delta}{1-\delta}.$$

Alternatively, playing R_j will yield a payoff of 4 in this stage and will lead to exactly the same choice between L_j and R_j in the next stage. Let V denote the present value of the infinite sequence of payoffs player j receives from making this choice optimally (now and every time it arises subsequently). If playing R_j is optimal then

$$V = 4 + \delta V,$$

or $V = 4/(1 - \delta)$, because playing R_j leads to the same choice next stage. If playing L_j is optimal then

$$V = 5 + \frac{\delta}{1 - \delta} \, ,$$

as derived earlier. So playing R_j is optimal if and only if

$$\frac{4}{1 - \delta} \geq 5 + \frac{\delta}{1 - \delta} \, , \tag{2.3.1}$$

or $\delta \geq 1/4$. Thus, in the first stage, and in any stage such that all the preceding outcomes have been (R_1, R_2), player j's optimal action (given that player i has adopted the trigger strategy) is R_j if and only if $\delta \geq 1/4$. Combining this observation with the fact that j's best response is to play L_j forever once one stage's outcome differs from (R_1, R_2), we have that it is a Nash equilibrium for both players to play the trigger strategy if and only if $\delta \geq 1/4$.

    We now want to argue that such a Nash equilibrium is sub-game-perfect. To do so, we define a strategy in a repeated game, a subgame in a repeated game, and a subgame-perfect Nash equilibrium in a repeated game. In order to illustrate these concepts with simple examples from the previous section, we will define them for both finitely and infinitely repeated games. In the previous section we defined the finitely repeated game $G(T)$ based on a stage game $G = \{A_1, \ldots, A_n; u_1, \ldots, u_n\}$—a static game of complete information in which players 1 through n simultaneously choose actions a_1 through a_n from the action spaces A_1 through A_n, respectively, and payoffs are $u_1(a_1, \ldots, a_n)$ through $u_n(a_1, \ldots, a_n)$. We now define the analogous infinitely repeated game.[17]

---

[17]One can of course also define a repeated game based on a dynamic stage game. In this section we restrict attention to static stage games so as to present the main ideas in a simple way. The applications in Sections 2.3.D and 2.3.E are repeated games based on dynamic stage games.

Definition *Given a stage game G, let $G(\infty, \delta)$ denote the **infinitely repeated game** in which G is repeated forever and the players share the discount factor δ. For each t, the outcomes of the $t - 1$ preceding plays of the stage game are observed before the tth stage begins. Each player's payoff in $G(\infty, \delta)$ is the present value of the player's payoffs from the infinite sequence of stage games.*

In any game (repeated or otherwise), a player's strategy is a complete plan of action—it specifies a feasible action for the player in every contingency in which the player might be called upon to act. Put slightly more colorfully, if a player left a strategy with his or her lawyer before the game began, the lawyer could play the game for the player without ever needing further instructions as to how to play. In a static game of complete information, for example, a strategy is simply an action. (This is why we described such a game as $G = \{S_1, \ldots, S_n; u_1, \ldots, u_n\}$ in Chapter 1 but can also describe it as $G = \{A_1, \ldots, A_n; u_1, \ldots, u_n\}$ here: in a static game of complete information, player i's strategy space S_i is simply the action space A_i.) In a dynamic game, however, a strategy is more complicated.

Consider the two-stage Prisoners' Dilemma analyzed in the previous section. Each player acts twice, so one might think that a strategy is simply a pair of instructions (b, c), where b is the first-stage action and c is the second-stage action. But there are four possible first-stage outcomes—(L_1, L_2), (L_1, R_2), (R_1, L_2), and (R_1, R_2)—and these represent four separate contingencies in which each player might be called upon to act. Thus, each player's strategy consists of five instructions, denoted (v, w, x, y, z), where v is the first-stage action and w, x, y, and z are the second-stage actions to be taken following the first-stage outcomes (L_1, L_2), (L_1, R_2), (R_1, L_2), and (R_1, R_2), respectively. Using this notation, the instructions "play b in the first stage, and play c in the second stage no matter what happens in the first" are written (b, c, c, c, c), but this notation also can express strategies in which the second-stage action is contingent on the first-stage outcome, such as (b, c, c, c, b), which means "play b in the first stage, and play c in the second stage unless the first-stage outcome was (R_1, R_2), in which case play b." Likewise, in the two-stage repeated game based on Figure 2.3.3, each player's strategy consists of ten instructions—a first-stage action and nine contingent second-stage actions, one to be played following each possible first-stage outcome. Recall that in analyzing this two-stage repeated game we considered a strategy in which the player's second-stage action was contingent on the first-stage outcome: play M_i in the first stage, and play L_i in the second stage unless the first-stage outcome was (M_1, M_2), in which case play R_i in the second stage.

In the finitely repeated game $G(T)$ or the infinitely repeated game $G(\infty, \delta)$, the *history of play through stage t* is the record of the players' choices in stages 1 through t. The players might have chosen $(a_{11}, \ldots, a_{n1})$ in stage 1, $(a_{12}, \ldots, a_{n2})$ in stage 2, ..., and $(a_{1t}, \ldots, a_{nt})$ in stage t, for example, where for each player i and stage s the action a_{is} belongs to the action space A_i.

Definition *In the finitely repeated game $G(T)$ or the infinitely repeated game $G(\infty, \delta)$, a player's **strategy** specifies the action the player will take in each stage, for each possible history of play through the previous stage.*

We turn next to subgames. A subgame is a piece of a game— the piece that remains to be played beginning at any point at which the complete history of the game thus far is common knowledge among the players. (Later in this section we give a precise definition for the repeated games $G(T)$ and $G(\infty, \delta)$; in Section 2.4.B, we give a precise definition for general dynamic games of complete information.) In the two-stage Prisoners' Dilemma, for example, there are four subgames, corresponding to the second-stage games that follow the four possible first-stage outcomes. Likewise, in the two-stage repeated game based on Figure 2.3.3, there are nine subgames, corresponding to the nine possible first-stage outcomes of that stage game. In the finitely repeated game $G(T)$ and the infinitely repeated game $G(\infty, \delta)$, the definition of a strategy is closely related to the definition of a subgame: a player's strategy specifies the actions the player will take in the first stage of the repeated game and in the first stage of each of its subgames.

Definition *In the finitely repeated game $G(T)$, a **subgame** beginning at stage $t + 1$ is the repeated game in which G is played $T - t$ times, denoted $G(T - t)$. There are many subgames that begin at stage $t + 1$, one for each of the possible histories of play through stage t. In the infinitely repeated game $G(\infty, \delta)$, each **subgame** beginning at stage $t + 1$ is identical to the original game $G(\infty, \delta)$. As in the finite-horizon case, there are as many subgames beginning at stage $t + 1$ of $G(\infty, \delta)$ as there are possible histories of play through stage t.*

Note well that the tth stage of a repeated game taken on its own is *not* a subgame of the repeated game (assuming $t < T$ in the finite case). A subgame is a piece of the original game that not only starts at a point where the history of play thus far is common knowledge among the players, but also includes all the moves that follow this point in the original game. Analyzing the tth stage in isolation would be equivalent to treating the tth stage as the final stage of the repeated game. Such an analysis could be conducted but would not be relevant to the original repeated game.

We are now ready for the definition of subgame-perfect Nash equilibrium, which in turn depends on the definition of Nash equilibrium. The latter is unchanged from Chapter 1, but we now appreciate the potential complexity of a player's strategy in a dynamic game: in any game, a Nash equilibrium is a collection of strategies, one for each player, such that each player's strategy is a best response to the other players' strategies.

Definition (Selten 1965): *A Nash equilibrium is **subgame-perfect** if the players' strategies constitute a Nash equilibrium in every subgame.*

Subgame-perfect Nash equilibrium is a *refinement* of Nash equilibrium. That is, to be subgame-perfect, the players' strategies must first be a Nash equilibrium and must then pass an additional test.

To show that the trigger-strategy Nash equilibrium in the infinitely repeated Prisoners' Dilemma is subgame-perfect, we must show that the trigger strategies constitute a Nash equilibrium on every subgame of that infinitely repeated game. Recall that every subgame of an infinitely repeated game is identical to the game as a whole. In the trigger-strategy Nash equilibrium of the infinitely repeated Prisoners' Dilemma, these subgames can be grouped into two classes: (i) subgames in which all the outcomes of earlier stages have been (R_1, R_2), and (ii) subgames in which the outcome of at least one earlier stage differs from (R_1, R_2). If the players adopt the trigger strategy for the game as a whole, then (i) the players' strategies in a subgame in the first class are again the trigger strategy, which we have shown to be a Nash equilibrium of the game as a whole, and (ii) the players' strategies in a subgame in the second class are simply to repeat the stage-game equilibrium (L_1, L_2) forever, which is also a Nash equilibrium of

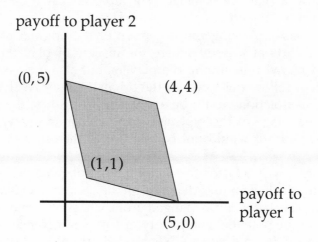

Figure 2.3.7.

the game as a whole. Thus, the trigger-strategy Nash equilibrium of the infinitely repeated Prisoners' Dilemma is subgame-perfect.

We next apply analogous arguments in the infinitely repeated game $G(\infty, \delta)$. These arguments lead to Friedman's (1971) Theorem for infinitely repeated games. To state the theorem, we need two final definitions. First, we call the payoffs $(x_1, \ldots, x_n)$ *feasible* in the stage game G if they are a convex combination (i.e., a weighted average, where the weights are all nonnegative and sum to one) of the pure-strategy payoffs of G. The set of feasible payoffs for the Prisoners' Dilemma in Figure 2.3.6 is the shaded region in Figure 2.3.7. The pure-strategy payoffs $(1,1)$, $(0,5)$, $(4,4)$, and $(5,0)$ are feasible. Other feasible payoffs include the pairs (x, x) for $1 < x < 4$, which result from weighted averages of $(1,1)$ and $(4,4)$, and the pairs (y, z) for $y + z = 5$ and $0 < y < 5$, which result from weighted averages of $(0,5)$ and $(5,0)$. The other pairs in (the interior of) the shaded region in Figure 2.3.7 are weighted averages of more than two pure-strategy payoffs. To achieve a weighted average of pure-strategy payoffs, the players could use a public randomizing device: by playing (L_1, R_2) or (R_1, L_2) depending on a flip of a (fair) coin, for example, they achieve the expected payoffs $(2.5, 2.5)$.

The second definition we need in order to state Friedman's Theorem is a rescaling of the players' payoffs. We continue to define each player's payoff in the infinitely repeated game $G(\infty, \delta)$ to be the present value of the player's infinite sequence of stage-game payoffs, but it is more convenient to express this present value in terms of the *average payoff* from the same infinite sequence of stage-game payoffs—the payoff that would have to be received in every stage so as to yield the same present value. Let the discount factor be δ. Suppose the infinite sequence of payoffs $\pi_1, \pi_2, \pi_3, \ldots$ has a present value of V. If the payoff π were received in every stage, the present value would be $\pi/(1 - \delta)$. For π to be the average payoff from the infinite sequence $\pi_1, \pi_2, \pi_3, \ldots$ with discount factor δ, these two present values must be equal, so $\pi = V(1 - \delta)$. That is, the average payoff is $(1 - \delta)$ times the present value.

Definition *Given the discount factor δ, the **average payoff** of the infinite sequence of payoffs $\pi_1, \pi_2, \pi_3, \ldots$ is*

$$(1 - \delta) \sum_{t=1}^{\infty} \delta^{t-1} \pi_t.$$

The advantage of the average payoff over the present value is that the former is directly comparable to the payoffs from the stage game. In the Prisoners' Dilemma in Figure 2.3.6, for example, both players might receive a payoff of 4 in every period. Such an infinite sequence of payoffs has an average payoff of 4 but a present value of $4/(1 - \delta)$. Since the average payoff is just a rescaling of the present value, however, maximizing the average payoff is equivalent to maximizing the present value.

We are at last ready to state the main result in our discussion of infinitely repeated games:

Theorem (Friedman 1971): *Let G be a finite, static game of complete information. Let $(e_1, \ldots, e_n)$ denote the payoffs from a Nash equilibrium of G, and let $(x_1, \ldots, x_n)$ denote any other feasible payoffs from G. If $x_i > e_i$ for every player i and if δ is sufficiently close to one, then there exists a subgame-perfect Nash equilibrium of the infinitely repeated game $G(\infty, \delta)$ that achieves $(x_1, \ldots, x_n)$ as the average payoff.*

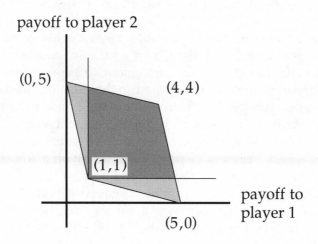

Figure 2.3.8.

The proof of this theorem parallels the arguments already given for the infinitely repeated Prisoners' Dilemma, so we relegate it to Appendix 2.3.B. It is conceptually straightforward but slightly messier notationally to extend the Theorem to well-behaved stage games that are neither finite nor static; see the applications in the next three sections for examples. In the context of the Prisoners' Dilemma in Figure 2.3.6, Friedman's Theorem guarantees that any point in the cross-hatched region in Figure 2.3.8 can be achieved as the average payoff in a subgame-perfect Nash equilibrium of the repeated game, provided the discount factor is sufficiently close to one.

We conclude this section by sketching two further developments in the theory of infinitely repeated games, both of which are obscured by the following special feature of the Prisoners' Dilemma. In the (one-shot) Prisoners' Dilemma in Figure 2.3.6, player i can guarantee receiving at least the Nash equilibrium payoff of 1 by playing L_i. In a one-shot Cournot duopoly game (such as described in Section 1.2.A), in contrast, a firm cannot guarantee receiving the Nash-equilibrium profit by producing the Nash-equilibrium quantity; rather, the only profit a firm can guarantee receiving is zero, by producing zero. Given an arbitrary stage game G, let r_i denote player i's *reservation payoff*—the largest payoff player i can guarantee receiving, no matter what the other players do. It must be that $r_i \le e_i$ (where e_i is player i's Nash-equilibrium payoff used in Friedman's Theorem), since if r_i were greater than e_i, it would not be a best response for player i to play his or her Nash-equilibrium strategy. In the Prisoners' Dilemma, $r_i = e_i$, but in the Cournot duopoly game (and typically), $r_i < e_i$.

Fudenberg and Maskin (1986) show that for two-player games, the reservation payoffs (r_1, r_2) can replace the equilibrium payoffs (e_1, e_2) in the statement of Friedman's Theorem. That is, if (x_1, x_2) is a feasible payoff from G, with $x_i > r_i$ for each i, then for δ sufficiently close to one there exists a subgame-perfect Nash equilibrium of $G(\infty, \delta)$ that achieves (x_1, x_2) as the average payoff, even if $x_i < e_i$ for one or both of the players. For games with more than two players, Fudenberg and Maskin provide a mild condition under which the reservation payoffs $(r_1, \dots, r_n)$ can replace the equilibrium payoffs $(e_1, \dots, e_n)$ in the statement of the Theorem.

A complementary question is also of interest: what average payoffs can be achieved by subgame-perfect Nash equilibria when the discount factor is not "sufficiently close to one"? One way to approach this question is to consider a fixed value of δ and determine the average payoffs that can be achieved if the players use trigger strategies that switch forever to the stage-game Nash equilibrium after any deviation. Smaller values of δ make a punishment that will begin next period less effective in deterring a deviation this period. Nonetheless, the players typically can do better than simply repeating a stage-game Nash equilibrium. A second approach, pioneered by Abreu (1988), is based on the idea that the most effective way to deter a player from deviating from a proposed strategy is to threaten to administer the strongest credible punishment should the player deviate (i.e., threaten to respond to a deviation by playing the subgame-perfect Nash equilibrium of the infinitely repeated game that yields the lowest payoff of all such equilibria for the player who deviated). In most games, switching forever to the stage-game Nash equilibrium is not the strongest credible punishment, so some average payoffs can be achieved using Abreu's approach that cannot be achieved using the trigger-strategy approach. In the Prisoners' Dilemma, however, the stage-game Nash equilibrium yields the reservation payoffs (that is, $e_i = r_i$), so the two approaches are equivalent. We give examples of both of these approaches in the next section.

Appendix 2.3.B

In this appendix we prove Friedman's Theorem. Let $(a_{e1}, \ldots, a_{en})$ be the Nash equilibrium of G that yields the equilibrium payoffs $(e_1, \ldots, e_n)$. Likewise, let $(a_{x1}, \ldots, a_{xn})$ be the collection of actions that yields the feasible payoffs $(x_1, \ldots, x_n)$. (The latter notation is only suggestive because it ignores the public randomizing device typically necessary to achieve arbitrary feasible payoffs.) Consider the following trigger strategy for player i:

> Play a_{xi} in the first stage. In the tth stage, if the outcome of all $t-1$ preceding stages has been $(a_{x1}, \ldots, a_{xn})$ then play a_{xi}; otherwise, play a_{ei}.

If both players adopt this trigger strategy then the outcome of every stage of the infinitely repeated game will be $(a_{x1}, \ldots, a_{xn})$, with (expected) payoffs $(x_1, \ldots, x_n)$. We first argue that if δ is close enough to one, then it is a Nash equilibrium of the repeated game for the players to adopt this strategy. We then argue that such a Nash equilibrium is subgame-perfect.

Suppose that all the players other than player i have adopted this trigger strategy. Since the others will play $(a_{e1}, \ldots, a_{e,i-1}, a_{e,i+1}, \ldots, a_{en})$ forever once one stage's outcome differs from $(a_{x1}, \ldots, a_{xn})$, player i's best response is to play a_{ei} forever once one stage's outcome differs from $(a_{x1}, \ldots, a_{xn})$. It remains to determine player i's best response in the first stage, and in any stage such that all the preceding outcomes have been $(a_{x1}, \ldots, a_{xn})$. Let a_{di} be player i's best deviation from $(a_{x1}, \ldots, a_{xn})$. That is, a_{di} solves

$$\max_{a_i \in A_i} u_i(a_{x1}, \ldots, a_{x,i-1}, a_i, a_{x,i+1}, \ldots, a_{xn}).$$

Let d_i be i's payoff from this deviation: $d_i = u_i(a_{x1}, \ldots, a_{x,i-1}, a_{di}, a_{x,i+1}, \ldots, a_{xn})$. (Again, we ignore the role of the randomizing device: the best deviation and its payoff may depend on which pure strategies the randomizing device has prescribed.) We have $d_i \geq x_i = u_i(a_{x1}, \ldots, a_{x,i-1}, a_{xi}, a_{x,i+1}, \ldots, a_{xn}) > e_i = u_i(a_{e1}, \ldots, a_{en})$.

Playing a_{di} will yield a payoff of d_i at this stage but will trigger $(a_{e1}, \ldots, a_{e,i-1}, a_{e,i+1}, \ldots, a_{en})$ by the other players forever after, to which the best response is a_{ei} by player i, so the payoff in every future stage will be e_i. The present value of this sequence of payoffs is

$$d_i + \delta \cdot e_i + \delta^2 \cdot e_i + \cdots = d_i + \frac{\delta}{1-\delta} e_i.$$

(Since any deviation triggers the same response by the other players, the only deviation we need to consider is the most profitable one.) Alternatively, playing a_{xi} will yield a payoff of x_i this stage and will lead to exactly the same choice between a_{di} and a_{xi} in the next stage. Let V_i denote the present value of the stage-game payoffs player i receives from making this choice optimally (now and every time it arises subsequently). If playing a_{xi} is optimal, then

$$V_i = x_i + \delta V_i,$$

or $V_i = x_i/(1 - \delta)$. If playing a_{di} is optimal, then

$$V_i = d_i + \frac{\delta}{1-\delta} e_i,$$

as derived previously. (Assume that the randomizing device is serially uncorrelated. It then suffices to let d_i be the highest of the payoffs to player i's best deviations from the various pure-strategy combinations prescribed by the randomizing device.) So playing a_{xi} is optimal if and only if

$$\frac{x_i}{1-\delta} \geq d_i + \frac{\delta}{1-\delta} e_i,$$

or

$$\delta \geq \frac{d_i - x_i}{d_i - e_i}.$$

Thus, in the first stage, and in any stage such that all the preceding outcomes have been $(a_{x1}, \ldots, a_{xn})$, player i's optimal action (given that the other players have adopted the trigger strategy) is a_{xi} if and only if $\delta \geq (d_i - x_i)/(d_i - e_i)$.

Combining this observation with the fact that i's best response is to play a_{ei} forever once one stage's outcome differs from $(a_{x1}, \ldots, a_{xn})$, we have that it is a Nash equilibrium for all the players to play the trigger strategy if and only if

$$\delta \geq \max_i \frac{d_i - x_i}{d_i - e_i}.$$

Since $d_i \geq x_i > e_i$, it must be that $(d_i - x_i)/(d_i - e_i) < 1$ for every i, so the maximum of this fraction across all the players is also strictly less than one.

It remains to show that this Nash equilibrium is subgame-perfect. That is, the trigger strategies must constitute a Nash equilibrium in every subgame of $G(\infty, \delta)$. Recall that every subgame of $G(\infty, \delta)$ is identical to $G(\infty, \delta)$ itself. In the trigger-strategy Nash equilibrium, these subgames can be grouped into two classes: (i) subgames in which all the outcomes of earlier stages have been $(a_{x1}, \ldots, a_{xn})$, and (ii) subgames in which the outcome of at least one earlier stage differs from $(a_{x1}, \ldots, a_{xn})$. If the players adopt the trigger strategy for the game as a whole, then (i) the players' strategies in a subgame in the first class are again the trigger strategy, which we have just shown to be a Nash equilibrium of the game as a whole, and (ii) the players' strategies in a subgame in the second class are simply to repeat the stage-game equilibrium $(a_{e1}, \ldots, a_{en})$ forever, which is also a Nash equilibrium of the game as a whole. Thus, the trigger-strategy Nash equilibrium of the infinitely repeated game is subgame-perfect.

2.3.C Collusion between Cournot Duopolists

Friedman (1971) was the first to show that cooperation could be achieved in an infinitely repeated game by using trigger strategies that switch forever to the stage-game Nash equilibrium following any deviation. The original application was to collusion in a Cournot oligopoly, as follows.

Recall the static Cournot game from Section 1.2.A: If the aggregate quantity on the market is $Q = q_1 + q_2$, then the market-clearing price is $P(Q) = a - Q$, assuming $Q < a$. Each firm has a marginal cost of c and no fixed costs. The firms choose quantities simultaneously. In the unique Nash equilibrium, each firm produces the quantity $(a - c)/3$, which we will call the Cournot quantity and denote by q_C. Since the equilibrium aggregate quantity, $2(a - c)/3$, exceeds the monopoly quantity, $q_m \equiv (a - c)/2$, both firms would be better off if each produced half the monopoly quantity, $q_i = q_m/2$.

Consider the infinitely repeated game based on this Cournot stage game when both firms have the discount factor δ. We now compute the values of δ for which it is a subgame-perfect Nash equilibrium of this infinitely repeated game for both firms to play the following trigger strategy:

> Produce half the monopoly quantity, $q_m/2$, in the first period. In the tth period, produce $q_m/2$ if both firms have produced $q_m/2$ in each of the $t-1$ previous periods; otherwise, produce the Cournot quantity, q_C.

Since the argument parallels that given for the Prisoners' Dilemma in the previous section, we keep the discussion brief.

The profit to one firm when both produce $q_m/2$ is $(a-c)^2/8$, which we will denote by $\pi_m/2$. The profit to one firm when both produce q_C is $(a-c)^2/9$, which we will denote by π_C. Finally, if firm i is going to produce $q_m/2$ this period then the quantity that maximizes firm j's profit this period solves

$$\max_{q_j} \left(a - q_j - \frac{1}{2}q_m - c \right) q_j.$$

The solution is $q_j = 3(a-c)/8$, with associated profit of $9(a-c)^2/64$, which we denote by π_d ("d" for deviation). Thus, it is a Nash equilibrium for both firms to play the trigger strategy given earlier provided that

$$\frac{1}{1-\delta} \cdot \frac{1}{2}\pi_m \geq \pi_d + \frac{\delta}{1-\delta} \cdot \pi_C, \qquad (2.3.2)$$

analogous to (2.3.1) in the Prisoners' Dilemma analysis. Substituting the values of π_m, π_d, and π_C into (2.3.2) yields $\delta \geq 9/17$. For the same reasons as in the previous section, this Nash equilibrium is subgame-perfect.

We can also ask what the firms can achieve if $\delta < 9/17$. We will explore both approaches described in the previous section. We first determine, for a given value of δ, the most-profitable quantity the firms can produce if they both play trigger strategies that switch forever to the Cournot quantity after any deviation. We know that such trigger strategies cannot support a quantity as low as half the monopoly quantity, but for any value of δ it is a subgame-perfect Nash equilibrium simply to repeat the Cournot quantity forever. Therefore, the most-profitable quantity that trigger strategies can support is between $q_m/2$ and q_C. To compute this quantity, consider the following trigger strategy:

> Produce q^* in the first period. In the tth period, produce q^* if both firms have produced q^* in each of the

$t - 1$ previous periods; otherwise, produce the Cournot quantity, q_C.

The profit to one firm if both play q^* is $(a - 2q^* - c)q^*$, which we will denote by π^*. If firm i is going to produce q^* this period, then the quantity that maximizes firm j's profit this period solves

$$\max_{q_j} (a - q_j - q^* - c)q_j.$$

The solution is $q_j = (a - q^* - c)/2$, with associated profit of $(a - q^* - c)^2/4$, which we again denote by π_d. It is a Nash equilibrium for both firms to play the trigger strategy given above provided that

$$\frac{1}{1 - \delta} \cdot \pi^* \geq \pi_d + \frac{\delta}{1 - \delta} \cdot \pi_C.$$

Solving the resulting quadratic in q^* shows that the lowest value of q^* for which the trigger strategies given above are a subgame-perfect Nash equilibrium is

$$q^* = \frac{9 - 5\delta}{3(9 - \delta)}(a - c),$$

which is monotonically decreasing in δ, approaching $q_m/2$ as δ approaches 9/17 and approaching q_C as δ approaches zero.

We now explore the second approach, which involves threatening to administer the strongest credible punishment. Abreu (1986) applies this idea to Cournot models more general than ours using an arbitrary discount factor; we simply show that Abreu's approach can achieve the monopoly outcome in our model when $\delta = 1/2$ (which is less than 9/17). Consider the following "two-phase" (or "carrot-and-stick") strategy:

Produce half the monopoly quantity, $q_m/2$, in the first period. In the tth period, produce $q_m/2$ if both firms produced $q_m/2$ in period $t - 1$, produce $q_m/2$ if both firms produced x in period $t - 1$, and otherwise produce x.

This strategy involves a (one-period) punishment phase in which the firm produces x and a (potentially infinite) collusive phase in which the firm produces $q_m/2$. If either firm deviates from the collusive phase, then the punishment phase begins. If either firm deviates from the punishment phase, then the punishment phase begins again. If neither firm deviates from the punishment phase, then the collusive phase begins again.

The profit to one firm if both produce x is $(a-2x-c)x$, which we will denote by $\pi(x)$. Let $V(x)$ denote the present value of receiving $\pi(x)$ this period and half the monopoly profit forever after:

$$V(x) = \pi(x) + \frac{\delta}{1-\delta} \cdot \frac{1}{2}\pi_m.$$

If firm i is going to produce x this period, then the quantity that maximizes firm j's profit this period solves

$$\max_{q_j} (a - q_j - x - c)q_j.$$

The solution is $q_j = (a - x - c)/2$, with associated profit of $(a - x - c)^2/4$, which we denote by $\pi_{dp}(x)$, where dp stands for deviation from the punishment.

If both firms play the two-phase strategy above, then the subgames in the infinitely repeated game can be grouped into two classes: (i) collusive subgames, in which the outcome of the previous period was either $(q_m/2, q_m/2)$ or (x, x), and (ii) punishment subgames, in which the outcome of the previous period was neither $(q_m/2, q_m/2)$, nor (x, x). For it to be a subgame-perfect Nash equilibrium for both firms to play the two-phase strategy, it must be a Nash equilibrium to obey the strategy in each class of subgames. In the collusive subgames, each firm must prefer to receive half the monopoly profit forever than to receive π_d this period and the punishment present value $V(x)$ next period:

$$\frac{1}{1-\delta} \cdot \frac{1}{2}\pi_m \geq \pi_d + \delta V(x). \tag{2.3.3}$$

In the punishment subgames, each firm must prefer to administer the punishment than to receive π_{dp} this period and begin the punishment again next period:

$$V(x) \geq \pi_{dp}(x) + \delta V(x). \tag{2.3.4}$$

Substituting for $V(x)$ in (2.3.3) yields

$$\delta \left(\frac{1}{2}\pi_m - \pi(x) \right) \geq \pi_d - \frac{1}{2}\pi_m.$$

That is, the gain this period from deviating must not exceed the discounted value of the loss next period from the punishment. (Provided neither firm deviates from the punishment phase, there is no loss after next period, since the punishment ends and the firms return to the monopoly outcome, as though there had been no deviation.) Likewise, (2.3.4) can be rewritten as

$$\delta \left(\frac{1}{2} \pi_m - \pi(x) \right) \geq \pi_{dp} - \pi(x),$$

with an analogous interpretation. For $\delta = 1/2$, (2.3.3) is satisfied provided $x/(a - c)$ is not between 1/8 and 3/8, and (2.3.4) is satisfied if $x/(a - c)$ is between 3/10 and 1/2. Thus, for $\delta = 1/2$, the two-phase strategy achieves the monopoly outcome as a subgame-perfect Nash equilibrium provided that $3/8 \leq x/(a - c) \leq 1/2$.

There are many other models of dynamic oligopoly that enrich the simple model developed here. We conclude this section by briefly discussing two classes of such models: state-variable models, and imperfect-monitoring models. Both classes of models have many applications beyond oligopoly; for example, the efficiency-wage model in the next section is an example of imperfect monitoring.

Rotemberg and Saloner (1986, and Problem 2.14) study collusion over the business cycle by allowing the intercept of the demand function to fluctuate randomly across periods. In each period, all firms observe that period's demand intercept before taking their actions for that period; in other applications, the players could observe the realization of another state variable at the beginning of each period. The incentive to deviate from a given strategy thus depends both on the value of demand this period and on the likely realizations of demand in future periods. (Rotemberg and Saloner assume that demand is independent across periods, so the latter consideration is independent of the current value of demand, but later authors have relaxed this assumption.)

Green and Porter (1984) study collusion when deviations cannot be detected perfectly: rather than observing the other firms' quantity choices, each firm observes only the market-clearing price, which is buffeted by an unobservable shock each period. In this setting, firms cannot tell whether a low market-clearing price occurred because one or more firms deviated or because there was an adverse shock. Green and Porter examine trigger-price equilibria, in which any price below a critical level triggers a punishment period during which all firms play their Cournot quantities. In equilibrium, no firm ever deviates. Nonetheless, an especially bad shock can cause the price to fall below the critical level, triggering a punishment period. Since punishments happen by accident, infinite punishments of the kind considered in the trigger-strategy analysis in this section are not optimal. Two-phase strategies of the kind analyzed by Abreu might seem promising; indeed, Abreu, Pearce, and Stacchetti (1986) show that they can be optimal.

2.3.D Efficiency Wages

In efficiency-wage models, the output of a firm's work force depends on the wage the firm pays. In the context of developing countries, higher wages could lead to better nutrition; in developed countries, higher wages could induce more able workers to apply for jobs at the firm, or could induce an existing work force to work harder.

Shapiro and Stiglitz (1984) develop a dynamic model in which firms induce workers to work hard by paying high wages and threatening to fire workers caught shirking. As a consequence of these high wages, firms reduce their demand for labor, so some workers are employed at high wages while others are (involuntarily) unemployed. The larger the pool of unemployed workers, the longer it would take a fired worker to find a new job, so the threat of firing becomes more effective. In the competitive equilibrium, the wage w and the unemployment rate u just induce workers not to shirk, and firms' labor demands at w result in an unemployment rate of exactly u. We study the repeated-game aspects of this model (but ignore the competitive-equilibrium aspects) by analyzing the case of one firm and one worker.

Consider the following stage game. First, the firm offers the worker a wage, w. Second, the worker accepts or rejects the firm's offer. If the worker rejects w, then the worker becomes self-employed at wage w_0. If the worker accepts w, then the worker chooses either to supply effort (which entails disutility e) or to shirk (which entails no disutility). The worker's effort decision is not observed by the firm, but the worker's output is observed by both the firm and the worker. Output can be either high or low;

for simplicity, we take low output to be zero and so write high output as $y > 0$. Suppose that if the worker supplies effort then output is sure to be high, but that if the worker shirks then output is high with probability p and low with probability $1 - p$. Thus, in this model, low output is an incontrovertible sign of shirking.

If the firm employs the worker at wage w, then the players' payoffs if the worker supplies effort and output is high are $y - w$ for the firm and $w - e$ for the worker. If the worker shirks, then e becomes 0; if output is low, then y becomes 0. We assume that $y - e > w_0 > py$, so that it is efficient for the worker to be employed by the firm and to supply effort, and also better that the worker be self-employed than employed by the firm and shirking.

The subgame-perfect outcome of this stage game is rather bleak: because the firm pays w in advance, the worker has no incentive to supply effort, so the firm offers $w = 0$ (or any other $w \leq w_0$) and the worker chooses self-employment. In the infinitely repeated game, however, the firm can induce effort by paying a wage w in excess of w_0 and threatening to fire the worker if output is ever low. We show that for some parameter values, the firm finds it worthwhile to induce effort by paying such a wage premium.

One might wonder why the firm and the worker cannot sign a compensation contract that is contingent on output, so as to induce effort. One reason such contracts might be infeasible is that it is too difficult for a court to enforce them, perhaps because the appropriate measure of output includes the quality of output, unexpected difficulties in the conditions of production, and so on. More generally, output-contingent contracts are likely to be imperfect (rather than completely infeasible), but there will remain a role for the repeated-game incentives studied here.

Consider the following strategies in the infinitely repeated game, which involve the wage $w^* > w_0$ to be determined later. We will say that the history of play is *high-wage, high-output* if all previous offers have been w^*, all previous offers have been accepted, and all previous outputs have been high. The firm's strategy is to offer $w = w^*$ in the first period, and in each subsequent period to offer $w = w^*$ provided that the history of play is high-wage, high-output, but to offer $w = 0$ otherwise. The worker's strategy is to accept the firm's offer if $w \geq w_0$ (choosing self-employment otherwise) and to supply effort if the history of play, including the current offer, is high-wage, high-output (shirking otherwise).

The firm's strategy is analogous to the trigger strategies analyzed in the previous two sections: play cooperatively provided that all previous play has been cooperative, but switch forever to the subgame-perfect outcome of the stage game should cooperation ever break down. The worker's strategy is also analogous to these trigger strategies, but is slightly subtler because the worker moves second in the sequential-move stage game. In a repeated game based on a simultaneous-move stage game, deviations are detected only at the end of a stage; when the stage game is sequential-move, however, a deviation by the first mover is detected (and should be responded to) during a stage. The worker's strategy is to play cooperatively provided all previous play has been cooperative, but to respond optimally to a deviation by the firm, knowing that the subgame-perfect outcome of the stage game will be played in all future stages. In particular, if $w \neq w^*$ but $w \geq w_0$, then the worker accepts the firm's offer but shirks.

We now derive conditions under which these strategies are a subgame-perfect Nash equilibrium. As in the previous two sections, the argument consists of two parts: (i) deriving conditions under which the strategies are a Nash equilibrium, and (ii) showing that they are subgame-perfect.

Suppose the firm offers w^* in the first period. Given the firm's strategy, it is optimal for the worker to accept. If the worker supplies effort, then the worker is sure to produce high output, so the firm will again offer w^* and the worker will face the same effort-supply decision next period. Thus, if it is optimal for the worker to supply effort, then the present value of the worker's payoffs is

$$V_e = (w^* - e) + \delta V_e,$$

or $V_e = (w^* - e)/(1 - \delta)$. If the worker shirks, however, then the worker will produce high output with probability p, in which case the same effort-supply decision will arise next period, but the worker will produce low output with probability $1 - p$, in which case the firm will offer $w = 0$ forever after, so the worker will be self-employed forever after. Thus, if it is optimal for the worker to shirk, then the (expected) present value of the worker's payoffs is

$$V_s = w^* + \delta \left\{ pV_s + (1 - p)\frac{w_0}{1 - \delta} \right\},$$

or $V_s = [(1 - \delta)w^* + \delta(1 - p)w_0]/(1 - \delta p)(1 - \delta)$. It is optimal for the worker to supply effort if $V_e \geq V_s$, or

$$w^* \geq w_0 + \frac{1 - p\delta}{\delta(1 - p)}e = w_0 + \left(1 + \frac{1 - \delta}{\delta(1 - p)}\right)e. \qquad (2.3.5)$$

Thus, to induce effort, the firm must pay not only $w_0 + e$ to compensate the worker for the foregone opportunity of self-employment and for the disutility of effort, but also the wage premium $(1 - \delta)e/\delta(1 - p)$. Naturally, if p is near one (i.e., if shirking is rarely detected) then the wage premium must be extremely high to induce effort. If $p = 0$, on the other hand, then it is optimal for the worker to supply effort if

$$\frac{1}{1 - \delta}(w^* - e) \geq w^* + \frac{\delta}{1 - \delta}w_0, \qquad (2.3.6)$$

analogous to (2.3.1) and (2.3.2) from the perfect-monitoring analyses in the previous two sections, (2.3.6) is equivalent to

$$w^* \geq w_0 + \left(1 + \frac{1 - \delta}{\delta}\right)e,$$

which is indeed (2.3.5) with $p = 0$.

Even if (2.3.5) holds, so that the worker's strategy is a best response to the firm's strategy, it must also be worth the firm's while to pay w^*. Given the worker's strategy, the firm's problem in the first period amounts to choosing between: (1) paying $w = w^*$, thereby inducing effort by threatening to fire the worker if low output is ever observed, and so receiving the payoff $y - w^*$ each period; and (2) paying $w = 0$, thereby inducing the worker to choose self-employment, and so receiving the payoff zero in each period. Thus, the firm's strategy is a best response to the worker's if

$$y - w^* \geq 0. \qquad (2.3.7)$$

Recall that we assumed that $y - e > w_0$ (i.e., that it is efficient for the worker to be employed by the firm and to supply effort). We require more if these strategies are to be a subgame-perfect Nash equilibrium: (2.3.5) and (2.3.7) imply

$$y - e \geq w_0 + \frac{1 - \delta}{\delta(1 - p)}e,$$

which can be interpreted as the familiar restriction that δ must be sufficiently large if cooperation is to be sustained.

We have so far shown that if (2.3.5) and (2.3.7) hold, then the specified strategies are a Nash equilibrium. To show that these strategies are subgame-perfect, we first define the subgames of the repeated game. Recall that when the stage game has simultaneous moves, the subgames of the repeated game begin between the stages of the repeated game. For the sequential-move stage game considered here, the subgames begin not only between stages but also within each stage—after the worker observes the firm's wage offer. Given the players' strategies, we can group the subgames into two classes: those beginning after a high-wage, high-output history, and those beginning after all other histories. We have already shown that the players' strategies are a Nash equilibrium given a history of the former kind. It remains to do so given a history of the latter kind: since the worker will never supply effort, it is optimal for the firm to induce the worker to choose self-employment; since the firm will offer $w = 0$ in the next stage and forever after, the worker should not supply effort in this stage and should accept the current offer only if $w \geq w_0$.

In this equilibrium, self-employment is permanent: if the worker is ever caught shirking, then the firm offers $w = 0$ forever after; if the firm ever deviates from offering $w = w^*$, then the worker will never supply effort again, so the firm cannot afford to employ the worker. There are several reasons to question whether it is reasonable for self-employment to be permanent. In our single-firm, single-worker model, both players would prefer to return to the high-wage, high-output equilibrium of the infinitely repeated game rather than play the subgame-perfect outcome of the stage game forever. This is the issue of renegotiation introduced in Section 2.3.A. Recall that if the players know that punishments will not be enforced, then cooperation induced by the threat of such punishments is no longer an equilibrium.

In the labor-market context, the firm may prefer not to renegotiate if it employs many workers, since renegotiating with one worker may upset the high-wage, high-output equilibrium still being played (or yet to begin) with other workers. If there are many firms, the question becomes whether firm j will hire workers formerly employed by firm i. It may be that firm j will not, because it fears upsetting the high-wage, high-output equilibrium with its current workers, just as in the single-firm case. Something like this may explain the lack of mobility of prime-age, white-collar male workers among large firms in Japan.

Alternatively, if fired workers can always find new jobs that they prefer to self-employment, then it is the wage in those new jobs (net of any disutility of effort) that plays the role of the self-employment wage w_0 here. In the extreme case in which a fired worker suffers no loss at all, there are no punishments for shirking available in the infinitely repeated game, and hence no subgame-perfect Nash equilibrium in which the worker supplies effort. See Bulow and Rogoff (1989) for an elegant application of similar ideas in the context of sovereign debt: if an indebted country can replicate the long-term loans it receives from creditor countries by making short-term cash-in-advance transactions in international capital markets, then there are no punishments for default available in the infinitely repeated game between debtor and creditor countries.

2.3.E   Time-Consistent Monetary Policy

Consider a sequential-move game in which employers and workers negotiate nominal wages, after which the monetary authority chooses the money supply, which in turn determines the rate of inflation. If wage contracts cannot be perfectly indexed, employers and workers will try to anticipate inflation in setting the wage. Once an imperfectly indexed nominal wage has been set, however, actual inflation above the anticipated level of inflation will erode the real wage, causing employers to expand employment and output. The monetary authority therefore faces a trade-off between the costs of inflation and the benefits of reduced unemployment and increased output that follow from surprise inflation (i.e., inflation above the anticipated level).

As in Barro and Gordon (1983), we analyze a reduced-form version of this model in the following stage game. First, employers form an expectation of inflation, π^e. Second, the monetary authority observes this expectation and chooses actual inflation, π. The payoff to employers is $-(\pi - \pi^e)^2$. That is, employers simply want to anticipate inflation correctly; they achieve their maximum payoff (namely, zero) when $\pi = \pi^e$. The monetary authority, for its part, would like inflation to be zero but output (y) to be at its efficient level (y^*). We write the payoff to the monetary authority as

$$U(\pi, y) = -c\pi^2 - (y - y^*)^2,$$

where the parameter $c > 0$ reflects the monetary authority's trade-off between its two goals. Suppose that actual output is the following function of target output and surprise inflation:

$$y = by^* + d(\pi - \pi^e),$$

where $b < 1$ reflects the presence of monopoly power in product markets (so that if there is no surprise inflation then actual output will be smaller than would be efficient) and $d > 0$ measures the effect of surprise inflation on output through real wages, as described in the previous paragraph. We can then rewrite the monetary authority's payoff as

$$W(\pi, \pi^e) = -c\pi^2 - [(b-1)y^* + d(\pi - \pi^e)]^2.$$

To solve for the subgame-perfect outcome of this stage game, we first compute the monetary authority's optimal choice of π given employers' expectation π^e. Maximizing $W(\pi, \pi^e)$ yields

$$\pi^*(\pi^e) = \frac{d}{c + d^2}[(1 - b)y^* + d\pi^e]. \qquad (2.3.8)$$

Since employers anticipate that the monetary authority will choose $\pi^*(\pi^e)$, employers choose π^e to maximize $-[\pi^*(\pi^e) - \pi^e]^2$, which yields $\pi^*(\pi^e) = \pi^e$, or

$$\pi^e = \frac{d(1 - b)}{c}y^* = \pi_s,$$

where the subscript s denotes "stage game." Equivalently, one could say that the *rational expectation* for employers to hold is the one that will subsequently be confirmed by the monetary authority, hence $\pi^*(\pi^e) = \pi^e$, and thus $\pi^e = \pi_s$. When employers hold the expectation $\pi^e = \pi_s$, the marginal cost to the monetary authority from setting π slightly above π_s exactly balances the marginal benefit from surprise inflation. In this subgame-perfect outcome, the monetary authority is expected to inflate and does so, but would be better off if it could commit to having no inflation. Indeed, if employers have rational expectations (i.e, $\pi = \pi^e$), then zero inflation maximizes the monetary authority's payoff (i.e., $W(\pi, \pi^e) = -c\pi^2 - (b-1)^2 y^{*2}$ when $\pi = \pi^e$, so $\pi = 0$ is optimal).

Now consider the infinitely repeated game in which both players share the discount factor δ. We will derive conditions under which $\pi = \pi^e = 0$ in every period in a subgame-perfect Nash equilibrium involving the following strategies. In the first period, employers hold the expectation $\pi^e = 0$. In subsequent periods they hold the expectation $\pi^e = 0$ provided that all prior expectations have been $\pi^e = 0$ and all prior actual inflations have been $\pi = 0$; otherwise, employers hold the expectation $\pi^e = \pi_s$—the rational expectation from the stage game. Similarly, the monetary authority sets $\pi = 0$ provided that the current expectation is $\pi^e = 0$, all prior expectations have been $\pi^e = 0$, and all prior actual inflations have been $\pi = 0$; otherwise, the monetary authority sets $\pi = \pi^*(\pi^e)$—its best response to the employers' expectation, as given by (2.3.8).

Suppose employers hold the expectation $\pi^e = 0$ in the first period. Given the employers' strategy (i.e., the way employers update their expectation after observing actual inflation), the monetary authority can restrict attention to two choices: (1) $\pi = 0$, which will lead to $\pi^e = 0$ next period, and hence to the same decision for the monetary authority next period; and (2) $\pi = \pi^*(0)$ from (2.3.8), which will lead to $\pi^e = \pi_s$ forever after, in which case the monetary authority will find it optimal to choose $\pi = \pi_s$ forever after. Setting $\pi = 0$ this period thus results in the payoff $W(0, 0)$ each period, while setting $\pi = \pi^*(0)$ this period results in the payoff $W(\pi^*(0), 0)$ this period, but the payoff $W(\pi_s, \pi_s)$ forever after. Thus, the monetary authority's strategy is a best response to the employers' updating rule if

$$\frac{1}{1-\delta} W(0,0) \geq W(\pi^*(0), 0) + \frac{\delta}{1-\delta} W(\pi_s, \pi_s), \qquad (2.3.9)$$

which is analogous to (2.3.6).

Simplifying (2.3.9) yields $\delta \geq c/(2c + d^2)$. Each of the parameters c and d has two effects. An increase in d, for example, makes surprise inflation more effective in increasing output, and so makes it more tempting for the monetary authority to indulge in surprise inflation, but for the same reason an increase in d also increases the stage-game outcome π_s, which makes the punishment more painful for the monetary authority. Likewise, an increase in c makes inflation more painful, which makes surprise inflation less tempting but also decreases π_s. In both cases, the latter effect outweighs the former, so the critical value of the discount factor necessary to support this equilibrium, $c/(2c + d^2)$, decreases in d and increases in c.

We have so far shown that the monetary authority's strategy is a best response to the employers' strategy if (2.3.9) holds. To show that these strategies are a Nash equilibrium, it remains to show that the latter is a best response to the former, which follows from the observation that the employers obtain their best possible pay-off (namely, zero) in every period. Showing that these strategies are subgame-perfect follows from arguments analogous to those in the previous section.

2.4   Dynamic Games of Complete but Imperfect Information

2.4.A   Extensive-Form Representation of Games

In Chapter 1 we analyzed static games by representing such games in normal form. We now analyze dynamic games by representing such games in extensive form.[18] This expositional approach may make it seem that static games must be represented in normal form and dynamic games in extensive form, but this is not the case. Any game can be represented in either normal or extensive form, although for some games one of the two forms is more convenient to analyze. We will discuss how static games can be represented using the extensive form and how dynamic games can be represented using the normal form.

Recall from Section 1.1.A that the normal-form representation of a game specifies: (1) the players in the game, (2) the strategies available to each player, and (3) the payoff received by each player for each combination of strategies that could be chosen by the players.

Definition *The **extensive-form representation** of a game specifies: (1) the players in the game, (2a) when each player has the move, (2b) what*

---

[18]We give an informal description of the extensive form. For a precise treatment, see Kreps and Wilson (1982).

*each player can do at each of his or her opportunities to move, (2c) what
each player knows at each of his or her opportunities to move, and (3) the
payoff received by each player for each combination of moves that could be
chosen by the players.*

Although we did not say so at the time, we analyzed several games
represented in extensive form in Sections 2.1 through 2.3. The
contribution of this section is to describe such games using game
trees rather than words, because the former are often simpler both
to express and to analyze.

   As an example of a game in extensive form, consider the following member of the class of two-stage games of complete and
perfect information introduced in Section 2.1.A:

1. Player 1 chooses an action a_1 from the feasible set $A_1 =
   \{L, R\}$.

2. Player 2 observes a_1 and then chooses an action a_2 from the
   set $A_2 = \{L', R'\}$.

3. Payoffs are $u_1(a_1, a_2)$ and $u_2(a_1, a_2)$, as shown in the game
   tree in Figure 2.4.1.

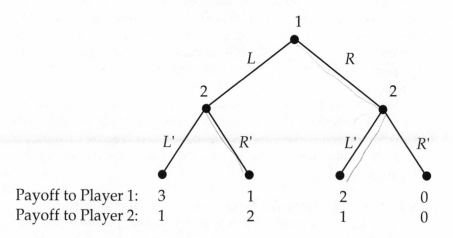

| Payoff to Player 1: | 3 | 1 | 2 | 0 |
| Payoff to Player 2: | 1 | 2 | 1 | 0 |

Figure 2.4.1.

This game tree begins with a *decision node* for player 1, where 1 chooses between *L* and *R*. If player 1 chooses *L*, then a decision node for player 2 is reached, where 2 chooses between *L'* and *R'*. Likewise, if player 1 chooses *R*, then another decision node for player 2 is reached, where 2 chooses between *L'* and *R'*. Following each of player 2's choices, a *terminal node* is reached (i.e., the game ends) and the indicated payoffs are received.

It is straightforward to extend the game tree in Figure 2.4.1 to represent any dynamic game of complete and perfect information —that is, any game in which the players move in sequence, all previous moves are common knowledge before the next move is chosen, and the players' payoffs from each feasible combination of moves are common knowledge. (Continuous action spaces, as in the Stackelberg model, or an infinite horizon, as in the Rubinstein model, present graphical but not conceptual difficulties.) We next derive the normal-form representation of the dynamic game in Figure 2.4.1. We then conclude this section by showing that static games can be given extensive-form representations, and by describing how to construct extensive-form representations of dynamic games with complete but imperfect information.

As the numbering conventions in the definitions of the normal and extensive forms suggest, there is a close connection between a player's feasible strategies (item 2) given in the normal form and the description of when a player moves, what he or she can do, and what he or she knows (items 2a, 2b, and 2c) in the extensive form. To represent a dynamic game in normal form, we need to translate the information in the extensive form into the description of each player's strategy space in the normal form. To do this, recall the definition of a strategy given (informally) in Section 2.3.B:

Definition *A **strategy** for a player is a complete plan of action—it specifies a feasible action for the player in every contingency in which the player might be called on to act.*

It may seem unnecessary to require a player's strategy to specify a feasible action for every contingency in which the player might be called upon to move. It will become clear, however, that we could not apply the notion of Nash equilibrium to dynamic games of complete information if we allowed a player's strategy to leave the actions in some contingencies unspecified. For player *j* to compute a best response to player i's strategy, j may need to consider how i would act in every contingency, not just in the contingencies i or j thinks likely to arise.

In the game in Figure 2.4.1, player 2 has two actions but four strategies, because there are two different contingencies (namely, after observing L by player 1 and after observing R by player 1) in which player 2 could be called upon to act.

> *Strategy 1*: If player 1 plays L then play L', if player 1 plays R then play L', denoted by (L', L').

> *Strategy 2*: If player 1 plays L then play L', if player 1 plays R then play R', denoted by (L', R').

> *Strategy 3*: If player 1 plays L then play R', if player 1 plays R then play L', denoted by (R', L').

> *Strategy 4*: If player 1 plays L then play R', if player 1 plays R then play R', denoted by (R', R').

Player 1, however, has two actions but only two strategies: play L and play R. The reason player 1 has only two strategies is that there is only one contingency in which player 1 might be called upon to act (namely, the first move of the game, when player 1 will certainly be called upon to act), so player 1's strategy space is equivalent to the action space $A_1 = \{L, R\}$.

Given these strategy spaces for the two players, it is straightforward to derive the normal-form representation of the game from its extensive-form representation. Label the rows of the normal form with player 1's feasible strategies, label the columns with player 2's feasible strategies, and compute the payoffs to the players for each possible combination of strategies, as shown in Figure 2.4.2.

Having now demonstrated that a dynamic game can be represented in normal form, we turn next to showing how a static (i.e., simultaneous-move) game can be represented in extensive form. To do so, we rely on the observation made in Section 1.1.A (in connection with the Prisoners' Dilemma) that the players need not act simultaneously: it suffices that each choose a strategy without knowledge of the other's choice, as would be the case in the Prisoners' Dilemma if the prisoners reached decisions at arbitrary times while in separate cells. Thus, we can represent a (so-called)

Player 2

		(L',L')	(L',R')	(R',L')	(R',R')
	L	3,1	3,1	1,2	1,2
Player 1	R	2,1	0,0	2,1	0,0

Figure 2.4.2.

simultaneous-move game between players 1 and 2 as follows.

1. Player 1 chooses an action a_1 from the feasible set A_1.

2. Player 2 does not observe player 1's move but chooses an action a_2 from the feasible set A_2.

3. Payoffs are $u_1(a_1, a_2)$ and $u_2(a_1, a_2)$.

Alternatively, player 2 could move first and player 1 could then move without observing 2's action. Recall that in Section 2.1.B we showed that a quantity-choice game with this timing and information structure differs importantly from the Stackelberg game with the same timing but an information structure in which firm 2 observes firm 1's move, and we argued that this sequential-move, unobserved-action game has the same Nash equilibrium as the simultaneous-move Cournot game.

   To represent this kind of ignorance of previous moves in an extensive-form game, we introduce the notion of a player's *information set*.

Definition *An **information set** for a player is a collection of decision nodes satisfying:*

   (i) *the player has the move at every node in the information set, and*

   (ii) *when the play of the game reaches a node in the information set, the player with the move does not know which node in the information set has (or has not) been reached.*

Part (ii) of this definition implies that the player must have the same set of feasible actions at each decision node in an information

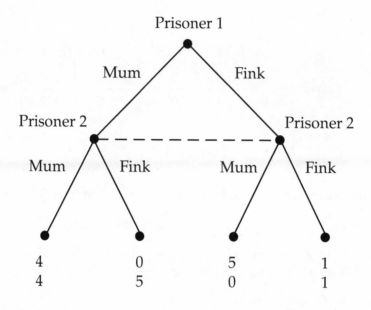

Figure 2.4.3.

set, else the player would be able to infer from the set of actions available that some node(s) had or had not been reached.

In an extensive-form game, we will indicate that a collection of decision nodes constitutes an information set by connecting the nodes by a dotted line, as in the extensive-form representation of the Prisoners' Dilemma given in Figure 2.4.3. We will sometimes indicate which player has the move at the nodes in an information set by labeling each node in the information set, as in Figure 2.4.3; alternatively, we may simply label the dotted line connecting these nodes, as in Figure 2.4.4. The interpretation of Prisoner 2's information set in Figure 2.4.3 is that when Prisoner 2 gets the move, all he knows is that the information set has been reached (i.e., that Prisoner 1 has moved), not which node has been reached (i.e., what she did). We will see in Chapter 4 that Prisoner 2 may have a conjecture or belief about what Prisoner 1 did, even if he did not observe what she did, but we will ignore this issue until then.

As a second example of the use of an information set in representing ignorance of previous play, consider the following

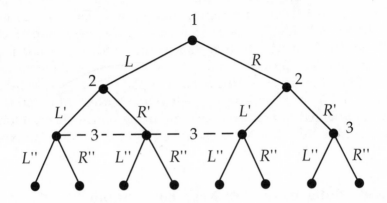

Figure 2.4.4.

dynamic game of complete but imperfect information:

1. Player 1 chooses an action a_1 from the feasible set $A_1 = \{L, R\}$.

2. Player 2 observes a_1 and then chooses an action a_2 from the feasible set $A_2 = \{L', R'\}$.

3. Player 3 observes whether or not $(a_1, a_2) = (R, R')$ and then chooses an action a_3 from the feasible set $A_3 = \{L'', R''\}$.

The extensive-form representation of this game (with payoffs ignored for simplicity) is given in Figure 2.4.4. In this extensive form, player 3 has two information sets: a singleton information set following R by player 1 and R' by player 2, and a nonsingleton information set that includes every other node at which player 3 has the move. Thus, all player 3 observes is whether or not $(a_1, a_2) = (R, R')$.

Now that we have defined the notion of an information set, we can offer an alternative definition of the distinction between perfect and imperfect information. We previously defined perfect information to mean that at each move in the game the player with the move knows the full history of the play of the game thus far. An equivalent definition of perfect information is that every information set is a singleton; imperfect information, in contrast, means that there is at least one nonsingleton information set.[19] Thus, the extensive-form representation of a simultaneous-move game (such as the Prisoners' Dilemma) is a game of imperfect information. Similarly, the two-stage games studied in Section 2.2.A have imperfect information because the actions of players 1 and 2 are simultaneous, as are the actions of players 3 and 4. More generally, a dynamic game of complete but imperfect information can be represented in extensive form by using nonsingleton information sets to indicate what each player knows (and does not know) when he or she has the move, as was done in Figure 2.4.4.

2.4.B Subgame-Perfect Nash Equilibrium

In Section 2.3.B we gave the general definition of subgame-perfect Nash equilibrium. We applied the definition only to repeated games, however, because we defined a strategy and a subgame only for repeated games. In Section 2.4.A we gave the general definition of a strategy. We now give the general definition of a subgame, after which we will be able to apply the definition of a subgame-perfect Nash equilibrium to general dynamic games of complete information.

Recall that in Section 2.3.B we informally defined a subgame as the piece of a game that remains to be played beginning at any point at which the complete history of the game thus far is common knowledge among the players, and we gave a formal definition for the repeated games we considered there. We now give a formal definition for a general dynamic game of complete information, in terms of the game's extensive-form representation.

Definition *A **subgame** in an extensive-form game*

(a) *begins at a decision node n that is a singleton information set (but is not the game's first decision node),*

(b) *includes all the decision and terminal nodes following n in the game tree (but no nodes that do not follow n), and*

---

[19]This characterization of perfect and imperfect information in terms of singleton and nonsingleton information sets is restricted to games of complete information because, as we will see in Chapter 4, the extensive-form representation of a game with perfect but incomplete information has a nonsingleton information set. In this chapter, however, we restrict attention to complete information.

(c) does not cut any information sets (i.e., if a decision node n' follows n in the game tree, then all other nodes in the information set containing n' must also follow n, and so must be included in the subgame).

Because of the parenthetical remark in part (a), we do not count the whole game as a subgame, but this is only a matter of style: dropping that parenthetical remark from the definition would have no effect in what follows.

We can use the game in Figure 2.4.1 and the Prisoners' Dilemma in Figure 2.4.3 to illustrate parts (a) and (b) of this definition. In Figure 2.4.1 there are two subgames, one beginning at each of player 2's decision nodes. In the Prisoners' Dilemma (or any other simultaneous-move game) there are no subgames. To illustrate part (c) of the definition, consider the game in Figure 2.4.4. There is only one subgame; it begins at player 3's decision node following R by player 1 and R' by player 2. Because of part (c), a subgame does not begin at either of player 2's decision nodes in this game, even though both of these nodes are singleton information sets.

One way to motivate part (c) is to say that we want to be able to analyze a subgame on its own, and we want the analysis to be relevant to the original game. In Figure 2.4.4, if we attempted to define a subgame beginning at player 2's decision node following L by player 1, then we would be creating a subgame in which player 3 is ignorant about player 2's move but knows player 1's move. Such a subgame would not be relevant to the original game because in the latter player 3 does not know player 1's move but instead observes only whether or not $(a_1, a_2) = (R, R')$. Recall the related argument for why the tth stage game in a repeated game taken on its own is not a subgame of the repeated game, assuming $t < T$ in the finite case.

Another way to motivate part (c) is to note that part (a) guarantees only that the player with the move at node n knows the complete history of the game thus far, not that the other players also know this history. Part (c) guarantees that the complete history of the game thus far is to be common knowledge among all the players, in the following sense: at any node that follows n, say n', the player with the move at n' knows that the play of the game reached node n. Thus, even if n' belongs to a nonsingleton information set, all the nodes in that information set follow n, so the player with the move at that information set knows that the game has reached a node that follows n. (If the last two statements seem awkward, it is in part because the extensive-form representation of a game specifies what player i knows at each of i's decision nodes but does not explicitly specify what i knows at j's decision nodes.) As described earlier, Figure 2.4.4 offers an example of how part (c) could be violated. We can now reinterpret this example: if we (informally) characterized what player 3 knows at player 2's decision node following L by player 1, we would say that 3 does not know the history of the game thus far, because 3 has subsequent decision nodes at which 3 does not know whether 1 played L or R.

Given the general definition of a subgame, we can now apply the definition of subgame-perfect Nash equilibrium from Section 2.3.B.

Definition (Selten 1965): *A Nash equilibrium is **subgame-perfect** if the players' strategies constitute a Nash equilibrium in every subgame.*

It is straightforward to show that any finite dynamic game of complete information (i.e., any dynamic game in which each of a finite number of players has a finite set of feasible strategies) has a subgame-perfect Nash equilibrium, perhaps in mixed strategies. The argument is by construction, involving a procedure in the spirit of backwards induction, and is based on two observations. First, although we presented Nash's Theorem in the context of static games of complete information, it applies to all finite normal-form games of complete information, and we have seen that such games can be static or dynamic. Second, a finite dynamic game of complete information has a finite number of subgames, each of which satisfies the hypotheses of Nash's Theorem.[20]

---

[20]To construct a subgame-perfect Nash equilibrium, first identify all the smallest subgames that contain terminal nodes in the original game tree (where a subgame is a smallest subgame if it does not contain any other subgames). Then replace each such subgame with the payoffs from one of its Nash equilibria. Now think of the initial nodes in these subgames as the terminal nodes in a truncated version of the original game. Identify all the smallest subgames in this truncated game that contain such terminal nodes, and replace each of these subgames with the payoffs from one of its Nash equilibria. Working backwards through the tree in this way yields a subgame-perfect Nash equilibrium because the players' strategies constitute a Nash equilibrium (in fact, a subgame-perfect Nash equilibrium) in every subgame.

We have already encountered two ideas that are intimately related to subgame-perfect Nash equilibrium: the backwards-induction outcome defined in Section 2.1.A, and the subgame-perfect outcome defined in Section 2.2.A. Put informally, the difference is that an equilibrium is a collection of strategies (and a strategy is a complete plan of action), whereas an outcome describes what will happen only in the contingencies that are expected to arise, not in every contingency that might arise. To be more precise about the difference between an equilibrium and an outcome, and to illustrate the notion of subgame-perfect Nash equilibrium, we now reconsider the games defined in Sections 2.1.A and 2.2.A.

Definition *In the two-stage game of complete and perfect information defined in Section 2.1.A, the* backwards-induction outcome *is $(a_1^*, R_2(a_1^*))$ but the* **subgame-perfect Nash equilibrium** *is $(a_1^*, R_2(a_1))$.*

In this game, the action a_1^* is a strategy for player 1 because there is only one contingency in which player 1 can be called upon to act—the beginning of the game. For player 2, however, $R_2(a_1^*)$ is an action (namely, 2's best response to a_1^*) but not a strategy, because a strategy for player 2 must specify the action 2 will take following each of 1's possible first-stage actions. The best-response function $R_2(a_1)$, on the other hand, is a strategy for player 2. In this game, the subgames begin with (and consist solely of) player 2's move in the second stage. There is one subgame for each of player 1's feasible actions, a_1 in A_1. To show that $(a_1^*, R_2(a_1))$ is a subgame-perfect Nash equilibrium, we therefore must show that $(a_1^*, R_2(a_1))$ is a Nash equilibrium and that the players' strategies constitute a Nash equilibrium in each of these subgames. Since the subgames are simply single-person decision problems, the latter reduces to requiring that player 2's action be optimal in every subgame, which is exactly the problem that the best-response function $R_2(a_1)$ solves. Finally, $(a_1^*, R_2(a_1))$ is a Nash equilibrium because the players' strategies are best responses to each other: a_1^* is a best response to $R_2(a_1)$—that is, a_1^* maximizes $u_1(a_1, R_2(a_1))$, and $R_2(a_1)$ is a best response to a_1^*—that is, $R_2(a_1^*)$ maximizes $u_2(a_1^*, a_2)$.

The arguments are analogous for the games considered in Section 2.2.A, so we do not give as much detail.

Definition *In the two-stage game of complete but imperfect information defined in Section 2.2.A, the* subgame-perfect outcome *is $(a_1^*, a_2^*,$*

$a_3^*(a_1^*, a_2^*), a_4^*(a_1^*, a_2^*))$ *but the subgame-perfect Nash equilibrium is* $(a_1^*, a_2^*, a_3^*(a_1, a_2), a_4^*(a_1, a_2))$.

In this game, the action pair $(a_3^*(a_1^*, a_2^*), a_4^*(a_1^*, a_2^*))$ is the Nash equilibrium of a single subgame between players 3 and 4 (namely, the game that remains after players 1 and 2 choose (a_1^*, a_2^*)), whereas $(a_3^*(a_1, a_2), a_4^*(a_1, a_2))$ is a strategy for player 3 and a strategy for player 4—complete plans of action describing a response to every feasible pair of moves by players 1 and 2. In this game, the subgames consist of the second-stage interaction between players 3 and 4, given the actions taken by players 1 and 2 in the first stage. As required for a subgame-perfect Nash equilibrium, the strategy pair $(a_3^*(a_1, a_2), a_4^*(a_1, a_2))$ specifies a Nash equilibrium in each of these subgames.

We conclude this section (and this chapter) with an example that illustrates the main theme of the chapter: subgame-perfection eliminates Nash equilibria that rely on noncredible threats or promises. Recall the extensive-form game in Figure 2.4.1. Had we encountered this game in Section 2.1.A, we would have solved it by backwards induction, as follows. If player 2 reaches the decision node following L by player 1, then 2's best response is to play R' (which yields a payoff of 2) rather than to play L' (which yields a payoff of 1). If 2 reaches the decision node following R by player 1, then 2's best response is to play L' (which yields a payoff of 1) rather than to play R' (which yields a payoff of 0). Since player 1 can solve player 2's problem as well as 2 can, 1's problem at the first stage amounts to choosing between L (which leads to a payoff of 1 for player 1, after player 2 plays R') and R (which leads to a payoff of 2 for player 1, after player 2 plays L'). Thus, player 1's best response to the anticipated behavior by player 2 is to play R in the first stage, so the backwards-induction outcome of the game is (R, L'), as indicated by the bold path beginning at player 1's decision node in Figure 2.4.5. There is an additional bold path emanating from player 2's decision node following L by player 1. This partial path through the game tree indicates that player 2 would have chosen R' if that decision node had been reached.

Recall that the normal-form representation of this game was given in Figure 2.4.2. If we had encountered this normal-form game in Section 1.1.C, we would have solved for its (pure-strategy) Nash equilibria. They are $(R, (R', L'))$ and $(L, (R', R'))$. We can

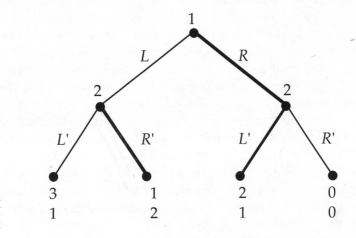

Figure 2.4.5.

now compare these Nash equilibria in the normal-form game in Figure 2.4.2 with the results of the backwards-induction procedure in the extensive-form game in Figure 2.4.5: the Nash equilibrium $(R, (R', L'))$ in the normal-form representation corresponds to *all* the bold paths in Figure 2.4.5. In Section 2.1.A we called (R, L') the backwards-induction *outcome* of the game. It would be natural to call $(R, (R', L'))$ the backwards-induction Nash *equilibrium* of the game, but we will use more general terminology and call it the subgame-perfect Nash equilibrium. The difference between the outcome and the equilibrium is that the outcome specifies only the bold path beginning at the game's first decision node and concluding at a terminal node, whereas the equilibrium also specifies the additional bold path emanating from player 2's decision node following L by player 1. That is, the equilibrium specifies a complete strategy for player 2.

But what about the other Nash equilibrium, $(L, (R', R'))$? In this equilibrium, player 2's strategy is to play R' not only if player 1 chooses L (as was also the case in the first Nash equilibrium) but also if player 1 chooses R. Because R' (following R) leads to a payoff of 0 for player 1, player 1's best response to this strategy by player 2 is to play L, thereby achieving a payoff of 1 for player 1 (after player 2 chooses R'), which is better than 0. Using loose but evocative language, one might say that player 2 is threatening to play R' if player 1 plays R. (Strictly speaking, there is no opportunity for 2 to make such a threat before 1 chooses an action. If there were, it would be included in the extensive form.) If this threat works (i.e., if 1 chooses to play L), then 2 is not given the opportunity to carry out the threat. The threat should not work, however, because it is not credible: if player 2 were given the opportunity to carry it out (i.e., if player 1 played R), then player 2 would decide to play L' rather than R'. Put more formally, the Nash equilibrium $(L, (R', R'))$ is not subgame-perfect, because the players' strategies do not constitute a Nash equilibrium in one of the subgames. In particular, player 2's choice of R' is not optimal in the subgame beginning at (and consisting solely of) player 2's decision node following R by player 1.

In a game of complete and perfect information, backwards induction eliminates noncredible threats. Because every information set is a singleton, each decision node in the tree represents a contingency that could arise in which a player would be called upon to act. The process of working backwards through the extensive form, node by node, thus amounts to forcing each player to consider carrying out each threat the player might make. In a game of imperfect information, however, things are not so simple, because such a game involves at least one nonsingleton information set. One could try the same approach: work backwards through the extensive form and eventually reach a decision node that is contained in a nonsingleton information set. But forcing the player to consider what he or she would do if that decision node were reached is *not* equivalent to forcing the player to consider a contingency that could arise in which the player would be called on to act, because if that information set is reached by the play of the game then the player does not know whether or not that decision node has been reached, precisely because the decision node is contained in a nonsingleton information set.

One way to handle the problem of nonsingleton information sets in backwards induction is to work backwards through the extensive form until one encounters a nonsingleton information set, but skip over it and proceed up the tree until a singleton information set is found. Then consider not only what the player with the move at that singleton information set would do if that decision node were reached, but also what action would be taken by the player with the move at each of the nonsingleton information sets that has been skipped. Roughly speaking, this procedure yields a subgame-perfect Nash equilibrium. A second way to handle the problem is to work backwards through the extensive form until one encounters a nonsingleton information set. Then force the player with the move at that information set to consider what he or she would do if that information set were reached. (Doing this requires that the player have a probability assessment concerning which node in the information set has been reached. Such an assessment will of course depend on the players' possible moves higher up the game tree, so one pass through the tree from the bottom up cannot yield a solution using this method.) Roughly speaking, this procedure yields a perfect Bayesian equilibrium; see Chapter 4.

2.5 Further Reading

Section 2.1: On wages and employment in unionized firms, see Espinosa and Rhee (1989; Problem 2.10) for a model of repeated negotiations, and Staiger (1991) for a model of a single negotiation in which the firm can choose whether to bargain over wages and employment or over only wages. On sequential bargaining, see Fernandez and Glazer (1991) for a Rubinstein-style model of bargaining between a firm and a union, with the new feature that the union must decide whether to go on strike after either it or the firm rejects an offer. There are multiple efficient subgame-perfect equilibria, which in turn support inefficient subgame-perfect equilibria (i.e., equilibria involving strikes), even though there is complete information. Osborne and Rubinstein's (1990) book surveys many game-theoretic bargaining models, relates them to Nash's axiomatic approach to bargaining, and uses bargaining models as a foundation for the theory of markets.

Section 2.2: On bank runs, see Jacklin and Bhattacharya (1988). McMillan's (1986) book surveys the early applications of game theory to international economics; see Bulow and Rogoff (1989) for more recent work on sovereign debt. On tournaments, see Lazear (1989; Problem 2.8) for a model in which workers can both increase their own outputs and sabotage others', and see Rosen (1986) on the prizes necessary to maintain incentives in a sequence of tournaments in which losers in one round do not proceed to the next.

Section 2.3: Benoit and Krishna (1985) analyze finitely repeated games. On renegotiation, see Benoit and Krishna (1989) for finitely repeated games and Farrell and Maskin (1989) for infinitely repeated games and a review of the literature. Tirole (1988, Chapter 6) surveys dynamic oligopoly models. Akerlof and Yellen's (1986) book collects many of the important papers on efficiency wages and provides an integrative introduction. On monetary policy, see Ball (1990) for a summary of the stylized facts, a review of existing models, and a model that explains the time-path of inflation.

Section 2.4: See Kreps and Wilson (1982) for a formal treatment of extensive-form games, and Kreps (1990, Chapter 11) for a more discursive account.

2.6   Problems

Section 2.1

2.1. Suppose a parent and child play the following game, first analyzed by Becker (1974). First, the child takes an action, A, that produces income for the child, $I_C(A)$, and income for the parent, $I_P(A)$. (Think of $I_C(A)$ as the child's income net of any costs of the action A.) Second, the parent observes the incomes I_C and I_P and then chooses a bequest, B, to leave to the child. The child's payoff is $U(I_C + B)$; the parent's is $V(I_P - B) + kU(I_C + B)$, where $k > 0$ reflects the parent's concern for the child's well-being. Assume that: the action is a nonnegative number, $A \geq 0$; the income functions $I_C(A)$ and $I_P(A)$ are strictly concave and are maximized at $A_C > 0$ and $A_P > 0$, respectively; the bequest B can be positive or negative; and the utility functions U and V are increasing and strictly concave. Prove the "Rotten Kid" Theorem: in the backwards-induction outcome, the child chooses the action that maximizes the family's aggregate income, $I_C(A) + I_P(A)$, even though only the parent's payoff exhibits altruism.

2.2. Now suppose the parent and child play a different game, first analyzed by Buchanan (1975). Let the incomes I_C and I_P be fixed exogenously. First, the child decides how much of the income I_C to save (S) for the future, consuming the rest $(I_C - S)$ today. Second, the parent observes the child's choice of S and chooses a bequest, B. The child's payoff is the sum of current and future utilities: $U_1(I_C - S) + U_2(S + B)$. The parent's payoff is $V(I_P - B) + k[U_1(I_C - S) + U_2(S + B)]$. Assume that the utility functions U_1, U_2, and V are increasing and strictly concave. Show that there is a "Samaritan's Dilemma": in the backwards-induction outcome, the child saves too little, so as to induce the parent to leave a larger bequest (i.e., both the parent's and child's payoffs could be increased if S were suitably larger and B suitably smaller).

2.3. Suppose the players in Rubinstein's infinite-horizon bargaining game have different discount factors: δ_1 for player 1 and δ_2 for player 2. Adapt the argument in the text to show that in the backwards-induction outcome, player 1 offers the settlement

Peter did in Section

$$\left(\frac{1 - \delta_2}{1 - \delta_1 \delta_2}, \frac{\delta_2(1 - \delta_1)}{1 - \delta_1 \delta_2} \right)$$

to player 2, who accepts.

2.4. Two partners would like to complete a project. Each partner receives the payoff V when the project is completed but neither receives any payoff before completion. The cost remaining before the project can be completed is R. Neither partner can commit to making a future contribution towards completing the project, so they decide to play the following two-period game: In period one partner 1 chooses to contribute c_1 towards completion. If this contribution is sufficient to complete the project then the game ends and each partner receives V. If this contribution is not sufficient to complete the project (i.e., $c_1 < R$) then in period two partner 2 chooses to contribute c_2 towards completion. If the (undiscounted) sum of the two contributions is sufficient to complete the project then the game ends and each partner receives V. If this sum is not sufficient to complete the project then the game ends and both partners receive zero.

Each partner must generate the funds for a contribution by taking money away from other profitable activities. The optimal way to do this is to take money away from the least profitable alternatives first. The resulting (opportunity) cost of a contribution is thus convex in the size of the contribution. Suppose that the

cost of a contribution c is c^2 for each partner. Assume that partner 1 discounts second-period benefits by the discount factor δ.
Compute the unique backwards-induction outcome of this two-
period contribution game for each triple of parameters $\{V, R, \delta\}$;
see Admati and Perry (1991) for the infinite-horizon case.

2.5. Suppose a firm wants a worker to invest in a firm-specific
skill, S, but the skill is too nebulous for a court to verify whether
the worker has acquired it. (For example, the firm might ask the
worker to "familiarize yourself with how we do things around
here," or "become an expert on this new market we might enter.")
The firm therefore cannot contract to repay the worker's cost of
investing: even if the worker invests, the firm can claim that the
worker did not invest, and the court cannot tell whose claim is
true. Likewise, the worker cannot contract to invest if paid in
advance.

It may be that the firm can use the (credible) promise of a
promotion as an incentive for the worker to invest, as follows.
Suppose that there are two jobs in the firm, one easy (E) and the
other difficult (D), and that the skill is valuable on both jobs but
more so on the difficult job: $y_{D0} < y_{E0} < y_{ES} < y_{DS}$, where y_{ij} is the
worker's output in job i ($= E$ or D) when the worker's skill level
is j ($= 0$ or S). Assume that the firm can commit to paying different
wages in the two jobs, w_E and w_D, but that neither wage can be less
than the worker's alternative wage, which we normalize to zero.

The timing of the game is as follows: At date 0 the firm chooses
w_E and w_D and the worker observes these wages. At date 1 the
worker joins the firm and can acquire the skill S at cost C. (We
ignore production and wages during this first period. Since the
worker has not yet acquired the skill, the efficient assignment is
to job E.) Assume that $y_{DS} - y_{E0} > C$, so that it is efficient for
the worker to invest. At date 2 the firm observes whether the
worker has acquired the skill and then decides whether to promote
the worker to job D for the worker's second (and last) period of
employment.

The firm's second-period profit is $y_{ij} - w_i$ when the worker is
in job i and has skill level j. The worker's payoff from being in
job i in the second period is w_i or $w_i - C$, depending on whether
the worker invested in the first period. Solve for the backwards-
induction outcome. See Prendergast (1992) for a richer model.

Section 2.2

2.6. Three oligopolists operate in a market with inverse demand given by $P(Q) = a - Q$, where $Q = q_1 + q_2 + q_3$ and q_i is the quantity produced by firm i. Each firm has a constant marginal cost of production, c, and no fixed cost. The firms choose their quantities as follows: (1) firm 1 chooses $q_1 \geq 0$; (2) firms 2 and 3 observe q_1 and then simultaneously choose q_2 and q_3, respectively. What is the subgame-perfect outcome?

2.7. Suppose a union is the sole supplier of labor to all the firms in an oligopoly, such as the United Auto Workers is to General Motors, Ford, Chrysler, and so on. Let the timing of moves be analogous to the model in Section 2.1.C: (1) the union makes a single wage demand, w, that applies to *all* the firms; (2) the firms observe (and accept) w and then simultaneously choose employment levels, L_i for firm i; (3) payoffs are $(w - w_a)L$ for the union, where w_a is the wage that union members can earn in alternative employment and $L = L_1 + \cdots + L_n$ is total employment in the unionized firms, and profit $\pi(w, L_i)$ for firm i, where the determinants of firm i's profit are described next.

All firms have the following production function: output equals labor; $q_i = L_i$. The market-clearing price is $P(Q) = a - Q$ when the aggregate quantity on the market is $Q = q_1 + \cdots + q_n$. To keep things simple, suppose that firms have no costs other than wages. What is the subgame-perfect outcome of this game? How (and why) does the number of firms affect the union's utility in the subgame-perfect outcome?

2.8. Modify the tournament model in Section 2.2.D so that worker i's output is $y_i = e_i - (1/2)s_j + \varepsilon_i$, where $s_j \geq 0$ represents sabotage by worker j, and worker i's disutility of (productive and destructive) effort is $g(e_i) + g(s_i)$, as in Lazear (1989). Show that the optimal prize $w_H - w_L$ is smaller than when there is no possibility of sabotage (as in the text).

2.9. Consider two countries. At date 1, the countries both have such high tariffs that there is no trade. Within each country, wages and employment are determined as in the monopoly-union model in Section 2.1.C. At date 2, all tariffs disappear. Now each union sets the wage in its country but each firm produces for both markets.

Assume that in each country inverse demand is $P(Q) = a - Q$, where Q is the aggregate quantity on the market in that country. Let the production function for each firm be $q = L$, so that wages are the firm's only cost, and let the union's utility function be $U(w, L) = (w - w_0)L$, where w_0 is the workers' alternative wage. Solve for the backwards-induction outcome at date 1.

Now consider the following game at date 2. First, the two unions simultaneously choose wages, w_1 and w_2. Then the firms observe the wages and choose production levels for the domestic and foreign markets, denoted by h_i and e_i for the firm in country i. All of firm i's production occurs at home, so the total cost is $w_i(h_i + e_i)$. Solve for the subgame-perfect outcome. Show that wages, employment, and profit (and therefore also the union's utility and consumer surplus) all increase when the tariffs disappear. See Huizinga (1989) for other examples along these lines.

Section 2.3

2.10. The accompanying simultaneous-move game is played twice, with the outcome of the first stage observed before the second stage begins. There is no discounting. The variable x is greater than 4, so that $(4, 4)$ is not an equilibrium payoff in the one-shot game. For what values of x is the following strategy (played by both players) a subgame-perfect Nash equilibrium?

> Play Q_i in the first stage. If the first-stage outcome is (Q_1, Q_2), play P_i in the second stage. If the first-stage outcome is (y, Q_2) where $y \neq Q_1$, play R_i in the second stage. If the first-stage outcome is (Q_1, z) where $z \neq Q_2$, play S_i in the second stage. If the first-stage outcome is (y, z) where $y \neq Q_1$ and $z \neq Q_2$, play P_i in the second stage.

$x > 4$

	P_2	Q_2	R_2	S_2
P_1	2, 2	x, 0	-1, 0	0, 0
Q_1	0, x	4, 4	-1, 0	0, 0
R_1	0, 0	0, 0	0, 2	0, 0
S_1	0, -1	0, -1	-1, -1	2, 0

2.11. The simultaneous-move game (below) is played twice, with the outcome of the first stage observed before the second stage begins. There is no discounting. Can the payoff $(4,4)$ be achieved in the first stage in a pure-strategy subgame-perfect Nash equilibrium? If so, give strategies that do so. If not, prove why not.

	L	C	R
T	3,1	0,0	5,0
M	2,1	1,2	3,1
B	1,2	0,1	4,4

[handwritten annotation: Although, (4,4) is not an eqlb payoff in the one-shot game, it can be achieved in the first stage of a two stage game SPNE.]

2.12. What is a strategy in a repeated game? What is a subgame in a repeated game? What is a subgame-perfect Nash equilibrium?

2.13. Recall the static Bertrand duopoly model (with homogeneous products) from Problem 1.7: the firms name prices simultaneously; demand for firm i's product is $a - p_i$ if $p_i < p_j$, is 0 if $p_i > p_j$, and is $(a - p_i)/2$ if $p_i = p_j$; marginal costs are $c < a$. Consider the infinitely repeated game based on this stage game. Show that the firms can use trigger strategies (that switch forever to the stage-game Nash equilibrium after any deviation) to sustain the monopoly price level in a subgame-perfect Nash equilibrium if and only if $\delta \geq 1/2$.

2.14. Suppose that demand fluctuates randomly in the infinitely repeated Bertrand game described in Problem 2.13: in each period, the demand intercept is a_H with probability π and a_L $(< a_H)$ with probability $1 - \pi$; demands in different periods are independent. Suppose that each period the level of demand is revealed to both firms before they choose their prices for that period. What are the monopoly price levels (p_H and p_L) for the two levels of demand? Solve for δ^*, the lowest value of δ such that the firms can use trigger strategies to sustain these monopoly price levels (i.e., to play p_i when demand is a_i, for $i = H, L$) in a subgame-perfect Nash equilibrium. For each value of δ between $1/2$ and δ^*, find the highest price $p(\delta)$ such that the firms can use trigger strategies to sustain the price $p(\delta)$ when demand is high and the price p_L

when demand is low in a subgame-perfect Nash equilibrium. (See Rotemburg and Saloner 1986.)

2.15.   Suppose there are n firms in a Cournot oligopoly. Inverse demand is given by $P(Q) = a - Q$, where $Q = q_1 + \cdots + q_n$. Consider the infinitely repeated game based on this stage game. What is the lowest value of δ such that the firms can use trigger strategies to sustain the monopoly output level in a subgame-perfect Nash equilibrium? How does the answer vary with n, and why? If δ is too small for the firms to use trigger strategies to sustain the monopoly output, what is the most-profitable symmetric subgame-perfect Nash equilibrium that can be sustained using trigger strategies?

2.16.   In the model of wages and employment analyzed in Section 2.1.C, the backwards-induction outcome is not socially efficient. In practice, however, a firm and a union negotiate today over the terms of a three-year contract, then negotiate three years from today over the terms of a second contract, and so on. Thus, the relationship may be more accurately characterized as a repeated game, as in Espinosa and Rhee (1989).

This problem derives conditions under which a subgame-perfect Nash equilibrium in the infinitely repeated game is Pareto-superior to the backwards-induction outcome of the one-shot game. Denote the union's utility and the firm's profit in the backwards-induction outcome of the one-shot game by U^* and π^*, respectively. Consider an alternative utility-profit pair (U, π) associated with an alternative wage-employment pair (w, L). Suppose that the parties share the discount factor δ (per three-year period). Derive conditions on (w, L) such that (1) (U, π) Pareto-dominates (U^*, π^*) and (2) (U, π) is the outcome of a subgame-perfect Nash equilibrium of the infinitely repeated game, where (U^*, π^*) is played forever following a deviation.

2.17.   Consider the following infinite-horizon game between a single firm and a sequence of workers, each of whom lives for one period. In each period the worker chooses either to expend effort and so produce output y at effort cost c or to expend no effort, produce no output, and incur no cost. If output is produced, the firm owns it but can share it with the worker by paying a wage, as described next. Assume that at the beginning of the period the worker has an alternative opportunity worth zero (net of effort cost) and that the worker cannot be forced to accept a wage less than zero. Assume also that $y > c$ so that expending effort is efficient.

Within each period, the timing of events is as follows: first the worker chooses an effort level, then output is observed by both the firm and the worker, and finally the firm chooses a wage to pay the worker. Assume that no wage contracts can be enforced: the firm's choice of a wage is completely unconstrained. In a one-period game, therefore, subgame-perfection implies that the firm will offer a wage of zero independent of the worker's output, so the worker will not expend any effort.

Now consider the infinite-horizon problem. Recall that each worker lives for only one period. Assume, however, that at the beginning of period t, the history of the game through period $t-1$ is observed by the worker who will work in period t. (Think of this knowledge as being passed down through the generations of workers.) Suppose the firm discounts the future according to the discount factor δ per period. Describe strategies for the firm and each worker in a subgame-perfect equilibrium in the infinite-horizon game in which in equilibrium each worker expends effort and so produces output y, provided the discount factor is high enough. Give a necessary and sufficient condition for your equilibrium to exist.

Section 2.4

2.18. What is a strategy (in an arbitrary game)? What is an information set? What is a subgame (in an arbitrary game)?

2.19. In the three-period version of Rubinstein's bargaining model analyzed in Section 2.1.D, we solved for the backwards-induction outcome. What is the subgame-perfect Nash equilibrium?

2.20. Consider the following strategies in the infinite-horizon version of Rubinstein's bargaining model. (Recall the notational convention that the offer $(s, 1 - s)$ means that Player 1 will get s and Player 2 will get $1 - s$, independent of who made the offer.) Let $s^* = 1/(1 + \delta)$. Player 1 always offers $(s^*, 1 - s^*)$ and accepts an offer $(s, 1 - s)$ only if $s \geq \delta s^*$. Player 2 always offers $(1 - s^*, s^*)$ and accepts an offer $(s, 1 - s)$ only if $1 - s \geq \delta s^*$. Show that these strategies are a Nash equilibrium. Show that this equilibrium is subgame-perfect.

2.21.   Give the extensive-form and normal-form representations of the grenade game described in Section 2.1. What are the pure-strategy Nash equilibria? What is the backwards-induction outcome? What is the subgame-perfect Nash equilibrium?

2.22.   Give the extensive- and normal-form representations of the bank-runs game discussed in Section 2.2.B. What are the pure-strategy subgame-perfect Nash equilibria?

2.23.   A buyer and seller would like to trade. Before they do, the buyer can make an investment that increases the value he or she puts on the object to be traded. This investment cannot be observed by the seller, and does not affect the value the seller puts on the object, which we normalize to zero. (As an example, think of one firm buying another. Some time before the merger, the acquirer could take steps to change the products it plans to introduce, so that they mesh with the acquired firm's products after the merger. If product development takes time and product life cycles are short, there is not enough time for this investment by the acquirer to occur after the merger.) The buyer's initial value for the object is $v > 0$; an investment of I increases the buyer's value to $v + I$ but costs I^2. The timing of the game is as follows: First, the buyer chooses an investment level I and incurs the cost I^2. Second, the seller does not observe I but offers to sell the object for the price p. Third, the buyer accepts or rejects the seller's offer: if the buyer accepts, then the buyer's payoff is $v + I - p - I^2$ and the seller's is p; if the buyer rejects, then these payoffs are $-I^2$ and zero, respectively. Show that there is no pure-strategy subgame-perfect Nash equilibrium of this game. Solve for the mixed-strategy subgame-perfect Nash equilibria in which the buyer's mixed strategy puts positive probability on only two levels of investment and the seller's mixed strategy puts positive probability on only two prices.

2.7   References

Abreu, D. 1986. "Extremal Equilibria of Oligopolistic Supergames." *Journal of Economic Theory* 39:191–225.

_____. 1988. "On the Theory of Infinitely Repeated Games with Discounting." *Econometrica* 56:383–96.

Abreu, D., D. Pearce, and E. Stacchetti. 1986. "Optimal Cartel Equilibria with Imperfect Monitoring." *Journal of Economic Theory* 39:251–69.

Admati, A., and M. Perry. 1991. "Joint Projects without Commitment." *Review of Economic Studies* 58:259–76.

Akerlof, G., and J. Yellen, eds. 1986. *Efficiency Wage Models of the Labor Market*. Cambridge, England: Cambridge University Press.

Ball, L. 1990. "Time-Consistent Policy and Persistent Changes in Inflation." National Bureau of Economic Research Working Paper #3529 (December).

Barro, R., and D. Gordon. 1983. "Rules, Discretion, and Reputation in a Model of Monetary Policy." *Journal of Monetary Economics* 12:101–21.

Becker, G. 1974. "A Theory of Social Interactions." *Journal of Political Economy* 82:1063–93.

Benoit, J-P., and V. Krishna. 1985. "Finitely Repeated Games." *Econometrica* 53:905–22.

_____. 1989. "Renegotiation in Finitely Repeated Games." Harvard Business School Working Paper #89-004.

Buchanan, J. 1975. "The Samaritan's Dilemma." In *Altruism, Morality, and Economic Theory*, E. Phelps, ed. New York: Russell Sage Foundation.

Bulow, J., and K. Rogoff. 1989. "Sovereign Debt: Is to Forgive to Forget?" *American Economic Review* 79:43–50.

Diamond, D., and P. Dybvig. 1983. "Bank Runs, Deposit Insurance, and Liquidity." *Journal of Political Economy* 91:401–19.

Espinosa, M., and C. Rhee. 1989. "Efficient Wage Bargaining as a Repeated Game." *Quarterly Journal of Economics* 104:565–88.

Farrell, J., and E. Maskin. 1989. "Renegotiation in Repeated Games." *Games and Economic Behavior* 1:327–60.

Fernandez, R., and J. Glazer. 1991. "Striking for a Bargain Between Two Completely Informed Agents." *American Economic Review* 81:240–52.

Friedman, J. 1971. "A Non-cooperative Equilibrium for Supergames." *Review of Economic Studies* 38:1–12.

Fudenberg, D., and E. Maskin. 1986. "The Folk Theorem in Repeated Games with Discounting and Incomplete Information."

Econometrica 54:533–54.

Green, E., and R. Porter. 1984. "Noncooperative Collusion Under Imperfect Price Information." *Econometrica* 52:87–100.

Huizinga, H. 1989. "Union Wage Bargaining and Industry Structure." Stanford University, Mimeo.

Jacklin, C., and S. Bhattacharya. 1988. "Distinguishing Panics and Information-based Bank Runs: Welfare and Policy Implications." *Journal of Political Economy* 96:568–92.

Kreps, D. 1990. *A Course in Microeconomic Theory.* Princeton, NJ: Princeton University Press.

Kreps, D., and R. Wilson. 1982. "Sequential Equilibrium." *Econometrica* 50:863–94.

Lazear, E. 1989. "Pay Equality and Industrial Politics." *Journal of Political Economy* 97:561–80.

Lazear, E., and S. Rosen. 1981. "Rank-Order Tournaments as Optimum Labor Contracts." *Journal of Political Economy* 89:841–64.

Leontief, W. 1946. "The Pure Theory of the Guaranteed Annual Wage Contract." *Journal of Political Economy* 54:76–79.

McMillan, J. 1986. *Game Theory in International Economics.* Chur, Switzerland: Harwood Academic Publishers.

Osborne, M., and A. Rubinstein. 1990. *Bargaining and Markets.* San Diego: Academic Press.

Prendergast, C. 1992. "The Role of Promotion in Inducing Specific Human Capital Acquisition." Forthcoming in *Quarterly Journal of Economics.*

Rosen, S. 1986. "Prizes and Incentives in Elimination Tournaments." *American Economic Review* 76:701–15.

Rotemberg, J., and G. Saloner. 1986. "A Supergame-Theoretic Model of Business Cycles and Price Wars during Booms." *American Economic Review* 76:390–407.

Rubinstein, A. 1982. "Perfect Equilibrium in a Bargaining Model." *Econometrica* 50:97–109.

Selten, R. 1965. "Spieltheoretische Behandlung eines Oligopolmodells mit Nachfragetragheit." *Zeitschrift für Gesamte Staatswissenschaft* 121:301–24.

Shaked, A., and J. Sutton. 1984. "Involuntary Unemployment as a Perfect Equilibrium in a Bargaining Model." *Econometrica* 52:1351–64.

Shapiro, C., and J. Stiglitz. 1984. "Equilibrium Unemployment as a Discipline Device." *American Economic Review* 74:433–44.

Sobel, J., and I. Takahashi. 1983. "A Multistage Model of Bargaining." *Review of Economic Studies* 50:411–26.

Stackelberg, H. von 1934. *Marktform und Gleichgewicht*. Vienna: Julius Springer.

Staiger, D. 1991. "Why Do Union Contracts Exclude Employment?" Stanford University, Mimeo.

Tirole, J. 1988. *The Theory of Industrial Organization*. Cambridge: MIT Press.

Chapter 3

Static Games of Incomplete Information

This chapter begins our study of games of *incomplete information*, also called *Bayesian games*. Recall that in a game of complete information the players' payoff functions are common knowledge. In a game of incomplete information, in contrast, at least one player is uncertain about another player's payoff function. One common example of a static game of incomplete information is a sealed-bid auction: each bidder knows his or her own valuation for the good being sold but does not know any other bidder's valuation; bids are submitted in sealed envelopes, so the players' moves can be thought of as simultaneous. Most economically interesting Bayesian games, however, are dynamic. As we will see in Chapter 4, the existence of private information leads naturally to attempts by informed parties to communicate (or mislead) and to attempts by uninformed parties to learn and respond. These are inherently dynamic issues.

In Section 3.1 we define the normal-form representation of a static Bayesian game and a Bayesian Nash equilibrium in such a game. Since these definitions are abstract and a bit complex, we introduce the main ideas with a simple example—Cournot competition under asymmetric information.

In Section 3.2 we consider three applications. First, we provide a formal discussion of the interpretation of a mixed strategy given in Chapter 1: player j's mixed strategy represents player i's uncertainty about j's choice of a pure strategy, and j's choice depends on the realization of a small amount of private information. Second, we analyze a sealed-bid auction in which the bidders' valuations are private information but the seller's valuation is known. Finally, we consider the case in which a buyer and a seller each have private information about their valuations (as when a firm knows a worker's marginal product and the worker knows his or her outside opportunity). We analyze a trading game called a double auction: the seller names an asking price and the buyer simultaneously names an offer price; trade occurs at the average of the two prices if the latter exceeds the former.

In Section 3.3 we state and prove the *Revelation Principle*, and briefly suggest how it can be applied in designing games when the players have private information.

3.1　Theory: Static Bayesian Games and Bayesian Nash Equilibrium

3.1.A　An Example: Cournot Competition under Asymmetric Information

Consider a Cournot duopoly model with inverse demand given by $P(Q) = a - Q$, where $Q = q_1 + q_2$ is the aggregate quantity on the market. Firm 1's cost function is $C_1(q_1) = cq_1$. Firm 2's cost function, however, is $C_2(q_2) = c_H q_2$ with probability θ and $C_2(q_2) = c_L q_2$ with probability $1 - \theta$, where $c_L < c_H$. Furthermore, information is asymmetric: firm 2 knows its cost function and firm 1's, but firm 1 knows its cost function and only that firm 2's marginal cost is c_H with probability θ and c_L with probability $1 - \theta$. (Firm 2 could be a new entrant to the industry, or could have just invented a new technology.) All of this is common knowledge: firm 1 knows that firm 2 has superior information, firm 2 knows that firm 1 knows this, and so on.

Naturally, firm 2 may want to choose a different (and presumably lower) quantity if its marginal cost is high than if it is low. Firm 1, for its part, should anticipate that firm 2 may tailor its quantity to its cost in this way. Let $q_2^*(c_H)$ and $q_2^*(c_L)$ denote firm 2's quantity choices as a function of its cost, and let q_1^* denote firm 1's single quantity choice. If firm 2's cost is high, it will choose $q_2^*(c_H)$ to solve

$$\max_{q_2} \ [(a - q_1^* - q_2) - c_H]q_2.$$

Similarly, if firm 2's cost is low, $q_2^*(c_L)$ will solve

$$\max_{q_2} \ [(a - q_1^* - q_2) - c_L]q_2.$$

Finally, firm 1 knows that firm 2's cost is high with probability θ and should anticipate that firm 2's quantity choice will be $q_2^*(c_H)$ or $q_2^*(c_L)$, depending on firm 2's cost. Thus, firm 1 chooses q_1^* to solve

$$\max_{q_1} \ \theta[(a - q_1 - q_2^*(c_H)) - c]q_1 + (1 - \theta)[(a - q_1 - q_2^*(c_L)) - c]q_1$$

so as to maximize expected profit.

The first-order conditions for these three optimization problems are

$$q_2^*(c_H) = \frac{a - q_1^* - c_H}{2},$$

$$q_2^*(c_L) = \frac{a - q_1^* - c_L}{2},$$

and

$$q_1^* = \frac{\theta[a - q_2^*(c_H) - c] + (1 - \theta)[(a - q_2^*(c_L) - c]}{2}.$$

Assume that these first-order conditions characterize the solutions to the earlier optimization problems. (Recall from Problem 1.6 that in a complete-information Cournot duopoly, if the firms' costs are sufficiently different then in equilibrium the high-cost firm produces nothing. As an exercise, find a sufficient condition to rule out the analogous problems here.) The solutions to the three first-order conditions are

$$q_2^*(c_H) = \frac{a - 2c_H + c}{3} + \frac{1 - \theta}{6}(c_H - c_L),$$

$$q_2^*(c_L) = \frac{a - 2c_L + c}{3} - \frac{\theta}{6}(c_H - c_L),$$

and

$$q_1^* = \frac{a - 2c + \theta c_H + (1 - \theta)c_L}{3}.$$

Compare $q_2^*(c_H)$, $q_2^*(c_L)$, and q_1^* to the Cournot equilibrium under *complete* information with costs c_1 and c_2. Assuming that the values of c_1 and c_2 are such that both firms' equilibrium quantities are both positive, firm i produces $q_i^* = (a - 2c_i + c_j)/3$ in this complete-information case. In the incomplete-information case, in contrast $q_2^*(c_H)$ is greater than $(a - 2c_H + c)/3$ and $q_2^*(c_L)$ is less than $(a - 2c_L + c)/3$. This occurs because firm 2 not only tailors its quantity to its cost but also responds to the fact that firm 1 cannot do so. If firm 2's cost is high, for example, it produces less because its cost is high but also produces more because it knows that firm 1 will produce a quantity that maximizes its expected profit and thus is smaller than firm 1 would produce if it knew firm 2's cost to be high. (A potentially misleading feature of this example is that q_1^* exactly equals the expectation of the Cournot quantities firm 1 would produce in the two corresponding games of complete information. This is typically not true; consider the case in which firm i's total cost is $c_i q_i^2$, for example.)

3.1.B Normal-Form Representation of Static Bayesian Games

Recall that the normal-form representation of an n-player game of *complete* information is $G = \{S_1 \ldots S_n; u_1 \ldots u_n\}$, where S_i is player i's strategy space and $u_i(s_1, \ldots, s_n)$ is player i's payoff when the players choose the strategies $(s_1, \ldots, s_n)$. As discussed in Section 2.3.B, however, in a simultaneous-move game of complete information a strategy for a player is simply an action, so we can write $G = \{A_1 \ldots A_n; u_1 \ldots u_n\}$, where A_i is player i's action space and $u_i(a_1, \ldots, a_n)$ is player i's payoff when the players choose the actions $(a_1, \ldots, a_n)$. To prepare for our description of the timing of a static game of *incomplete* information, we describe the timing of a static game of *complete* information as follows: (1) the players simultaneously choose actions (player i chooses a_i from the feasible set A_i), and then (2) payoffs $u_i(a_1, \ldots, a_n)$ are received.

We now want to develop the normal-form representation of a simultaneous-move game of incomplete information, also called a static Bayesian game. The first step is to represent the idea that each player knows his or her own payoff function but may be uncertain about the other players' payoff functions. Let player i's possible payoff functions be represented by $u_i(a_1, \ldots, a_n; t_i)$, where

t_i is called player i's *type* and belongs to a set of possible types (or *type space*) T_i. Each type t_i corresponds to a different payoff function that player i might have.

As an abstract example suppose player i has two possible payoff functions. We would say that player i has two types, t_{i1} and t_{i2}, that player i's type space is $T_i = \{t_{i1}t_{i2}\}$, and that player i's two payoff functions are $u_i(a_1, \ldots, a_n; t_{i1})$ and $u_i(a_1, \ldots, a_n; t_{i2})$. We can use the idea that each of a player's types corresponds to a different payoff function the player might have to represent the possibility that the player might have different sets of feasible actions, as follows. Suppose, for example, that player i's set of feasible actions is $\{a, b\}$ with probability q and $\{a, b, c\}$ with probability $1 - q$. Then we can say that i has two types (t_{i1} and t_{i2}, where the probability of t_{i1} is q) and we can define i's feasible set of actions to be $\{a, b, c\}$ for both types but define the payoff from taking action c to be $-\infty$ for type t_{i1}.

As a more concrete example, consider the Cournot game in the previous section. The firms' actions are their quantity choices, q_1 and q_2. Firm 2 has two possible cost functions and thus two possible profit or payoff functions:

$$\pi_2(q_1, q_2; c_L) = [(a - q_1 - q_2) - c_L]q_2$$

and

$$\pi_2(q_1, q_2; c_H) = [(a - q_1 - q_2) - c_H]q_2.$$

Firm 1 has only one possible payoff function:

$$\pi_1(q_1, q_2; c) = [(a - q_1 - q_2) - c]q_1.$$

We say that firm 2's type space is $T_2 = \{c_L, c_H\}$ and that firm 1's type space is $T_1 = \{c\}$.

Given this definition of a player's type, saying that player i knows his or her own payoff function is equivalent to saying that player i knows his or her type. Likewise, saying that player i may be uncertain about the other players' payoff functions is equivalent to saying that player i may be uncertain about the types of the other players, denoted by $t_{-i} = (t_1, \ldots, t_{i-1}, t_{i+1}, \ldots, t_n)$. We use T_{-i} to denote the set of all possible values of t_{-i}, and we use the probability distribution $p_i(t_{-i} \mid t_i)$ to denote player i's *belief* about the other players' types, t_{-i}, given player i's knowledge of his or her own type, t_i. In every application analyzed in Section 3.2

(and in most of the literature), the players' types are independent, in which case $p_i(t_{-i} \mid t_i)$ does not depend on t_i, so we can write player i's belief as $p_i(t_{-i})$. There are contexts in which the players' types are correlated, however, so we allow for this in our definition of a static Bayesian game by writing player i's belief as $p_i(t_{-i} \mid t_i)$.[1]

Joining the new concepts of types and beliefs with the familiar elements of the normal-form representation of a static game of complete information yields the normal-form representation of a static Bayesian game.

Definition *The **normal-form representation** of an n-player static Bayesian game specifies the players' action spaces $A_1, \ldots, A_n$, their type spaces $T_1, \ldots, T_n$, their beliefs $p_1, \ldots, p_n$, and their payoff functions $u_1, \ldots, u_n$. Player i's **type**, t_i, is privately known by player i, determines player i's payoff function, $u_i(a_1, \ldots, a_n; t_i)$, and is a member of the set of possible types, T_i. Player i's **belief** $p_i(t_{-i} \mid t_i)$ describes i's uncertainty about the $n - 1$ other players' possible types, t_{-i}, given i's own type, t_i. We denote this game by $G = \{A_1, \ldots, A_n; T_1, \ldots, T_n; p_1, \ldots, p_n; u_1, \ldots, u_n\}$.*

Following Harsanyi (1967), we will assume that the timing of a static Bayesian game is as follows: (1) nature draws a type vector $t = (t_1, \ldots, t_n)$, where t_i is drawn from the set of possible types T_i; (2) nature reveals t_i to player i but not to any other player; (3) the players simultaneously choose actions, player i choosing a_i from the feasible set A_i; and then (4) payoffs $u_i(a_1, \ldots, a_n; t_i)$ are received. By introducing the fictional moves by nature in steps (1) and (2), we have described a game of *incomplete* information as a game of *imperfect* information, where by imperfect information we mean (as in Chapter 2) that at some move in the game the player with the move does not know the complete history of the game thus far. Here, because nature reveals player i's type to player i but not to player j in step (2), player j does not know the complete history of the game when actions are chosen in step (3).

Two slightly more technical points need to be covered to complete our discussion of normal-form representations of static Bayes-

---

[1] Imagine that two firms are racing to develop a new technology. Each firm's chance of success depends in part on how difficult the technology is to develop, which is not known. Each firm knows only whether it has succeeded and not whether the other has. If firm 1 has succeeded, however, then it is more likely that the technology is easy to develop and so also more likely that firm 2 has succeeded. Thus, firm 1's belief about firm 2's type depends on firm 1's knowledge of its own type.

ian games. First there are games in which player i has private information not only about his or her own payoff function but also about another player's payoff function. In Problem 3.2, for example, the asymmetric-information Cournot model from Section 3.1.A is changed so that costs are symmetric and common knowledge but one firm knows the level of demand and the other does not. Since the level of demand affects both players' payoff functions, the informed firm's type enters the uninformed firm's payoff function. In the n-player case we capture this possibility by allowing player i's payoff to depend not only on the actions $(a_1, \ldots, a_n)$ but also on all the types $(t_1, \ldots, t_n)$. We write this payoff as $u_i(a_1, \ldots, a_n; t_1, \ldots, t_n)$.

The second technical point involves the beliefs, $p_i(t_{-i} \mid t_i)$. We will assume that it is common knowledge that in step (1) of the timing of a static Bayesian game, nature draws a type vector $t = (t_1, \ldots, t_n)$ according to the prior probability distribution $p(t)$. When nature then reveals t_i to player i, he or she can compute the belief $p_i(t_{-i} \mid t_i)$ using Bayes' rule:[2]

$$p_i(t_{-i} \mid t_i) = \frac{p(t_{-i}, t_i)}{p(t_i)} = \frac{p(t_{-i}, t_i)}{\displaystyle\sum_{t_{-i} \in T_{-i}} p(t_{-i}, t_i)} \, .$$

Furthermore, the other players can compute the various beliefs that player i might hold, depending on i's type, namely $p_i(t_{-i} \mid t_i)$ for each t_i in T_i. As already noted, we will frequently assume that the players' types are independent, in which case $p_i(t_{-i})$ does not depend on t_i but is still derived from the prior distribution $p(t)$. In this case the other players know i's belief about their types.

3.1.C Definition of Bayesian Nash Equilibrium

We now want to define an equilibrium concept for static Bayesian games. To do so, we must first define the players' strategy spaces

---

[2]Bayes' rule provides a formula for $P(A \mid B)$, the (conditional) probability that an event A will occur given that an event B has already occurred. Let $P(A)$, $P(B)$, and $P(A, B)$ be the (prior) probabilities (i.e., the probabilities before either A or B has had a chance to take place) that A will occur, that B will occur, and that both A and B will occur, respectively. Bayes' rule states that $P(A \mid B) = P(A, B)/P(B)$. That is, the conditional probability of A given B equals the probability that both A and B will occur, divided by the prior probability that B will occur.

in such a game. Recall from Sections 2.3.B and 2.4.B that a player's strategy is a complete plan of action, specifying a feasible action in every contingency in which the player might be called on to act. Given the timing of a static Bayesian game, in which nature begins the game by drawing the players' types, a (pure) strategy for player i must specify a feasible action for *each* of player i's possible types.

Definition *In the static Bayesian game $G = \{A_1, \ldots, A_n; T_1, \ldots, T_n; p_1, \ldots, p_n; u_1, \ldots, u_n\}$, a **strategy** for player i is a function $s_i(t_i)$, where for each type t_i in T_i, $s_i(t_i)$ specifies the action from the feasible set A_i that type t_i would choose if drawn by nature.*

Unlike (both static and dynamic) games of complete information, in a Bayesian game the strategy spaces are not given in the normal-form representation of the game. Instead, in a static Bayesian game the strategy spaces are constructed from the type and action spaces: player i's set of possible (pure) strategies, S_i, is the set of all possible functions with domain T_i and range A_i. In a *separating* strategy, for example, each type t_i in T_i chooses a different action a_i from A_i. In a *pooling* strategy, in contrast, all types choose the same action. This distinction between separating and pooling strategies will be important in our discussion of dynamic games of incomplete information in Chapter 4. We introduce the distinction here only to help describe the wide variety of strategies that can be constructed from a given pair of type and action spaces, T_i and A_i.

It may seem unnecessary to require player i's strategy to specify a feasible action for each of player i's possible types. After all, once nature has drawn a particular type and revealed it to a player, it may seem that the player need not be concerned with the actions he or she would have taken had nature drawn some other type. On the other hand, player i needs to consider what the other players will do, and what they will do depends on what they think player i will do, for each t_i in T_i. Thus, in deciding what to do once one type has been drawn, player i will have to think about what he or she would have done if each of the other types in T_i had been drawn.

Consider the asymmetric-information Cournot game in Section 3.1.A, for example. We argued that the solution to the game consists of three quantity choices: $q_2^*(c_H)$, $q_2^*(c_L)$, and q_1^*. In terms of the definition of a strategy just given, the pair $(q_2^*(c_H), q_2^*(c_L))$ is firm 2's strategy and q_1^* is firm 1's strategy. It is easy to imagine that firm 2 will choose different quantities depending on its cost. It is equally important to note, however, that firm 1's single quantity choice should take into account that firm 2's quantity will depend on firm 2's cost in this way. Thus, if our equilibrium concept is to require that firm 1's strategy be a best response to firm 2's strategy, then firm 2's strategy must be a *pair* of quantities, one for each possible cost type, else firm 1 simply cannot compute whether its strategy is indeed a best response to firm 2's.

More generally, we would not be able to apply the notion of Nash equilibrium to Bayesian games if we allowed a player's strategy not to specify what the player would do if some types were drawn by nature. This argument is analogous to one from Chapter 2: it may have seemed unnecessary to require player i's strategy in a dynamic game of complete information to specify a feasible action for each contingency in which player i might be called on to move, but we could not have applied the notion of Nash equilibrium to dynamic games of complete information if we had allowed a player's strategy to leave the player's actions in some contingencies unspecified.

Given the definition of a strategy in a Bayesian game, we turn next to the definition of a Bayesian Nash equilibrium. In spite of the notational complexity of the definition, the central idea is both simple and familiar: each player's strategy must be a best response to the other players' strategies. That is, a Bayesian Nash equilibrium is simply a Nash equilibrium in a Bayesian game.

Definition *In the static Bayesian game* $G = \{A_1, \ldots, A_n; T_1, \ldots, T_n; p_1, \ldots, p_n; u_1, \ldots, u_n\}$, *the strategies* $s^* = (s_1^*, \ldots, s_n^*)$ *are a (pure-strategy)* **Bayesian Nash equilibrium** *if for each player i and for each of i's types t_i in T_i, $s_i^*(t_i)$ solves*

$$\max_{a_i \in A_i} \sum_{t_{-i} \in T_{-i}} u_i(s_1^*(t_1), \ldots, s_{i-1}^*(t_{i-1}), a_i, s_{i+1}^*(t_{i+1}), \ldots, s_n^*(t_n); t) p_i(t_{-i} \mid t_i).$$

That is, no player wants to change his or her strategy, even if the change involves only one action by one type.

It is straightforward to show that in a finite static Bayesian game (i.e., a game in which n is finite and $(A_1, \ldots, A_n)$ and $(T_1, \ldots, T_n)$

are all finite sets) there exists a Bayesian Nash equilibrium, perhaps in mixed strategies. The proof closely parallels the proof of the existence of a mixed-strategy Nash equilibrium in finite games of complete information, and so is omitted here.

3.2 Applications

3.2.A Mixed Strategies Revisited

As we mentioned in Section 1.3.A, Harsanyi (1973) suggested that player j's mixed strategy represents player i's uncertainty about j's choice of a pure strategy, and that j's choice in turn depends on the realization of a small amount of private information. We can now give a more precise statement of this idea: a mixed-strategy Nash equilibrium in a game of complete information can (almost always) be interpreted as a pure-strategy Bayesian Nash equilibrium in a closely related game with a little bit of incomplete information. (We will ignore the rare cases in which such an interpretation is not possible.) Put more evocatively, the crucial feature of a mixed-strategy Nash equilibrium is not that player j chooses a strategy randomly, but rather that player i is uncertain about player j's choice; this uncertainty can arise either because of randomization or (more plausibly) because of a little incomplete information, as in the following example.

Recall that in the Battle of the Sexes there are two pure-strategy Nash equilibria (Opera, Opera) and (Fight, Fight) and a mixed-strategy Nash equilibrium in which Chris plays Opera with probability 2/3 and Pat plays Fight with probability 2/3.

		Pat	
		Opera	Fight
Chris	Opera	2, 1	0, 0
	Fight	0, 0	1, 2

The Battle of the Sexes

Now suppose that, although they have known each other for quite some time, Chris and Pat are not quite sure of each other's payoffs. In particular, suppose that: Chris's payoff if both attend the Opera is $2 + t_c$, where t_c is privately known by Chris; Pat's payoff if both attend the Fight is $2 + t_p$, where t_p is privately known by Pat; and t_c and t_p are independent draws from a uniform distribution on $[0, x]$. (The choice of a uniform distribution on $[0, x]$ is not important, but we do have in mind that the values of t_c and t_p only slightly perturb the payoffs in the original game, so think of x as small.) All the other payoffs are the same. In terms of the abstract static Bayesian game in normal form $G = \{A_c, A_p; T_c, T_p; p_c, p_p; u_c, u_p\}$, the action spaces are $A_c = A_p = \{\text{Opera, Fight}\}$, the type spaces are $T_c = T_p = [0, x]$, the beliefs are $p_c(t_p) = p_p(t_c) = 1/x$ for all t_c and t_p, and the payoffs are as follows.

Pat

		Opera	Fight
Chris	Opera	$2 + t_c, 1$	$0, 0$
	Fight	$0, 0$	$1, 2 + t_p$

The Battle of the Sexes with Incomplete Information

We will construct a pure-strategy Bayesian Nash equilibrium of this incomplete-information version of the Battle of the Sexes in which Chris plays Opera if t_c exceeds a critical value, c, and plays Fight otherwise and Pat plays Fight if t_p exceeds a critical value, p, and plays Opera otherwise. In such an equilibrium, Chris plays Opera with probability $(x - c)/x$ and Pat plays Fight with probability $(x - p)/x$. We will show that as the incomplete information disappears (i.e., as x approaches zero), the players' behavior in this pure-strategy Bayesian Nash equilibrium approaches their behavior in the mixed-strategy Nash equilibrium in the original game of complete information. That is, both $(x - c)/x$ and $(x - p)/x$ approach $2/3$ as x approaches zero.

Suppose Chris and Pat play the strategies just described. For a given value of x, we will determine values of c and p such that these strategies are a Bayesian Nash equilibrium. Given Pat's strategy, Chris's expected payoffs from playing Opera and from playing Fight are

$$\frac{p}{x}(2 + t_c) + \left[1 - \frac{p}{x}\right] \cdot 0 = \frac{p}{x}(2 + t_c)$$

and

$$\frac{p}{x} \cdot 0 + \left[1 - \frac{p}{x}\right] \cdot 1 = 1 - \frac{p}{x},$$

respectively. Thus playing Opera is optimal if and only if

$$t_c \geq \frac{x}{p} - 3 = c. \tag{3.2.1}$$

Similarly, given Chris's strategy, Pat's expected payoffs from playing Fight and from playing Opera are

$$\left[1 - \frac{c}{x}\right] \cdot 0 + \frac{c}{x}(2 + t_p) = \frac{c}{x}(2 + t_p)$$

and

$$\left[1 - \frac{c}{x}\right] \cdot 1 + \frac{c}{x} \cdot 0 = 1 - \frac{c}{x},$$

respectively. Thus, playing Fight is optimal if and only if

$$t_p \geq \frac{x}{c} - 3 = p. \tag{3.2.2}$$

Solving (3.2.1) and (3.2.2) simultaneously yields $p = c$ and $p^2 + 3p - x = 0$. Solving the quadratic then shows that the probability that Chris plays Opera, namely $(x - c)/x$, and the probability that Pat plays Fight, namely $(x - p)/x$, both equal

$$1 - \frac{-3 + \sqrt{9 + 4x}}{2x},$$

which approaches 2/3 as x approaches zero. Thus, as the incomplete information disappears, the players' behavior in this pure-strategy Bayesian Nash equilibrium of the incomplete-information game approaches their behavior in the mixed-strategy Nash equilibrium in the original game of complete information.

3.2.B An Auction

Consider the following first-price, sealed-bid auction. There are two bidders, labeled $i = 1, 2$. Bidder i has a valuation v_i for the good—that is, if bidder i gets the good and pays the price p, then i's payoff is $v_i - p$. The two bidders' valuations are independently and uniformly distributed on $[0, 1]$. Bids are constrained to be nonnegative. The bidders simultaneously submit their bids. The higher bidder wins the good and pays the price she bid; the other bidder gets and pays nothing. In case of a tie, the winner is determined by a flip of a coin. The bidders are risk-neutral. All of this is common knowledge.

In order to formulate this problem as a static Bayesian game, we must identify the action spaces, the type spaces, the beliefs, and the payoff functions. Player i's action is to submit a (nonnegative) bid, b_i, and her type is her valuation, v_i. (In terms of the abstract game $G = \{A_1, A_2; T_1, T_2; p_1, p_2; u_1, u_2\}$, the action space is $A_i = [0, \infty)$ and the type space is $T_i = [0, 1]$.) Because the valuations are independent, player i believes that v_j is uniformly distributed on $[0, 1]$, no matter what the value of v_i. Finally, player i's payoff function is

$$u_i(b_1, b_2; v_1, v_2) = \begin{cases} v_i - b_i & \text{if } b_i > b_j, \\ (v_i - b_i)/2 & \text{if } b_i = b_j, \\ 0 & \text{if } b_i < b_j. \end{cases}$$

To derive a Bayesian Nash equilibrium of this game, we begin by constructing the players' strategy spaces. Recall that in a static Bayesian game, a strategy is a function from types to actions. Thus, a strategy for player i is a function $b_i(v_i)$ specifying the bid that each of i's types (i.e., valuations) would choose. In a Bayesian Nash equilibrium, player 1's strategy $b_1(v_1)$ is a best response to player 2's strategy $b_2(v_2)$, and vice versa. Formally, the pair of strategies $(b(v_1), b(v_2))$ is a Bayesian Nash equilibrium if for each v_i in $[0, 1]$, $b_i(v_i)$ solves

$$\max_{b_i} (v_i - b_i)\text{Prob}\{b_i > b_j(v_j)\} + \frac{1}{2}(v_i - b_i)\text{Prob}\{b_i = b_j(v_j)\}.$$

We simplify the exposition by looking for a linear equilibrium: $b_1(v_1) = a_1 + c_1 v_1$ and $b_2(v_2) = a_2 + c_2 v_2$. Note well that we are *not* restricting the players' strategy spaces to include only linear strategies. Rather, we allow the players to choose arbitrary strategies but ask whether there is an equilibrium that is linear. It turns out that because the players' valuations are uniformly distributed, a linear equilibrium not only exists but is unique (in a sense to be made precise). We will find that $b_i(v_i) = v_i/2$. That is, each player submits a bid equal to half her valuation. Such a bid reflects the fundamental trade-off a bidder faces in an auction: the higher the bid, the more likely the bidder is to win; the lower the bid, the larger the gain if the bidder does win.

Suppose that player j adopts the strategy $b_j(v_j) = a_j + c_j v_j$. For a given value of v_i, player i's best response solves

$$\max_{b_i} \ (v_i - b_i)\text{Prob}\{b_i > a_j + c_j v_j\},$$

where we have used the fact that $\text{Prob}\{b_i = b_j(v_j)\} = 0$ (because $b_j(v_j) = a_j + c_j v_j$ and v_j is uniformly distributed, so b_j is uniformly distributed). Since it is pointless for player i to bid below player j's minimum bid and stupid for i to bid above j's maximum bid, we have $a_j \leq b_i \leq a_j + c_j$, so

$$\text{Prob}\{b_i > a_j + c_j v_j\} = \text{Prob}\left\{v_j < \frac{b_i - a_j}{c_j}\right\} = \frac{b_i - a_j}{c_j} \ .$$

Player i's best response is therefore

$$b_i(v_i) = \begin{cases} (v_i + a_j)/2 & \text{if } v_i \geq a_j, \\ a_j & \text{if } v_i < a_j. \end{cases}$$

If $0 < a_j < 1$ then there are some values of v_i such that $v_i < a_j$, in which case $b_i(v_i)$ is not linear; rather, it is flat at first and positively sloped later. Since we are looking for a linear equilibrium, we therefore rule out $0 < a_j < 1$, focusing instead on $a_j \geq 1$ and $a_j \leq 0$. But the former cannot occur in equilibrium: since it is optimal for a higher type to bid at least as much as a lower type's optimal bid, we have $c_j \geq 0$, but then $a_j \geq 1$ would imply that $b_j(v_j) \geq v_j$, which cannot be optimal. Thus, if $b_i(v_i)$ is to be linear, then we must have $a_j \leq 0$, in which case $b_i(v_i) = (v_i + a_j)/2$, so $a_i = a_j/2$ and $c_i = 1/2$.

We can repeat the same analysis for player j under the assumption that player i adopts the strategy $b_i(v_i) = a_i + c_i v_i$. This yields

$a_i \leq 0$, $a_j = a_i/2$, and $c_j = 1/2$. Combining these two sets of results then yields $a_i = a_j = 0$ and $c_i = c_j = 1/2$. That is, $b_i(v_i) = v_i/2$, as claimed earlier.

One might wonder whether there are other Bayesian Nash equilibria of this game, and also how equilibrium bidding changes as the distribution of the bidders' valuations changes. Neither of these questions can be answered using the technique just applied (of positing linear strategies and then deriving the coefficients that make the strategies an equilibrium): it is fruitless to try to guess all the functional forms other equilibria of this game might have, and a linear equilibrium does not exist for any other distribution of valuations. In the Appendix, we derive a symmetric Bayesian Nash equilibrium,[3] again for the case of uniformly distributed valuations. Under the assumption that the players' strategies are strictly increasing and differentiable, we show that the unique symmetric Bayesian Nash equilibrium is the linear equilibrium already derived. The technique we use can easily be extended to a broad class of valuation distributions, as well as the case of n bidders.[4]

Appendix 3.2.B

Suppose player j adopts the strategy $b(\cdot)$, and assume that $b(\cdot)$ is strictly increasing and differentiable. Then for a given value of v_i, player i's optimal bid solves

$$\max_{b_i} (v_i - b_i)\text{Prob}\{b_i > b(v_j)\}.$$

Let $b^{-1}(b_j)$ denote the valuation that bidder j must have in order to bid b_j. That is, $b^{-1}(b_j) = v_j$ if $b_j = b(v_j)$. Since v_j is uniformly distributed on $[0, 1]$, $\text{Prob}\{b_i > b(v_j)\} = \text{Prob}\{b^{-1}(b_i) > v_j\} = b^{-1}(b_i)$. The first-order condition for player i's optimization problem is therefore

$$-b^{-1}(b_i) + (v_i - b_i)\frac{d}{db_i}b^{-1}(b_i) = 0.$$

---

[3]A Bayesian Nash equilibrium is called symmetric if the players' strategies are identical. That is, in a symmetric Bayesian Nash equilibrium, there is a single function $b(v_i)$ such that player 1's strategy $b_1(v_1)$ is $b(v_1)$ and player 2's strategy $b_2(v_2)$ is $b(v_2)$, and this single strategy is a best response to itself. Of course, since the players' valuations typically will be different, their bids typically will be different, even if both use the same strategy.

[4]Skipping this appendix will not hamper one's understanding of what follows.

This first-order condition is an implicit equation for bidder i's best response to the strategy $b(\cdot)$ played by bidder j, given that bidder i's valuation is v_i. If the strategy $b(\cdot)$ is to be a symmetric Bayesian Nash equilibrium, we require that the solution to the first-order condition be $b(v_i)$: that is, for each of bidder i's possible valuations, bidder i does not wish to deviate from the strategy $b(\cdot)$, given that bidder j plays this strategy. To impose this requirement, we substitute $b_i = b(v_i)$ into the first-order condition, yielding:

$$-b^{-1}(b(v_i)) + (v_i - b(v_i))\frac{d}{db_i}b^{-1}(b(v_i)) = 0.$$

Of course, $b^{-1}(b(v_i))$ is simply v_i. Furthermore, $d\{b^{-1}(b(v_i))\}/db_i = 1/b'(v_i)$. That is, $d\{b^{-1}(b_i)\}/db_i$ measures how much bidder i's valuation must change to produce a unit change in the bid, whereas $b'(v_i)$ measures how much the bid changes in response to a unit change in the valuation. Thus, $b(\cdot)$ must satisfy the first-order differential equation

$$-v_i + (v_i - b(v_i))\frac{1}{b'(v_i)} = 0,$$

which is more conveniently expressed as $b'(v_i)v_i + b(v_i) = v_i$. The left-hand side of this differential equation is precisely $d\{b(v_i)v_i\}/dv_i$. Integrating both sides of the equation therefore yields

$$b(v_i)v_i = \frac{1}{2}v_i^2 + k,$$

where k is a constant of integration. To eliminate k, we need a boundary condition. Fortunately, simple economic reasoning provides one: no player should bid more than his or her valuation. Thus, we require $b(v_i) \leq v_i$ for every v_i. In particular, we require $b(0) \leq 0$. Since bids are constrained to be nonnegative, this implies that $b(0) = 0$, so $k = 0$ and $b(v_i) = v_i/2$, as claimed.

3.2.C   A Double Auction

We next consider the case in which a buyer and a seller each have private information about their valuations, as in Chatterjee and Samuelson (1983). (In Hall and Lazear [1984], the buyer is a firm and the seller is a worker. The firm knows the worker's marginal product and the worker knows his or her outside opportunity. See Problem 3.8.) We analyze a trading game called a double auction. The seller names an asking price, p_s, and the buyer simultaneously names an offer price, p_b. If $p_b \geq p_s$, then trade occurs at price $p = (p_b + p_s)/2$; if $p_b < p_s$, then no trade occurs.

The buyer's valuation for the seller's good is v_b, the seller's is v_s. These valuations are private information and are drawn from independent uniform distributions on $[0, 1]$. If the buyer gets the good for price p, then the buyer's utility is $v_b - p$; if there is no trade, then the buyer's utility is zero. If the seller sells the good for price p, then the seller's utility is $p - v_s$; if there is no trade, then the seller's utility is zero. (Each of these utility functions measures the change in the party's utility. If there is no trade, then there is no change in utility. It would make no difference to define, say, the seller's utility to be p if there is trade at price p and v_s if there is no trade.)

In this static Bayesian game, a strategy for the buyer is a function $p_b(v_b)$ specifying the price the buyer will offer for each of the buyer's possible valuations. Likewise, a strategy for the seller is a function $p_s(v_s)$ specifying the price the seller will demand for each of the seller's valuations. A pair of strategies $\{p_b(v_b), p_s(v_s)\}$ is a Bayesian Nash equilibrium if the following two conditions hold. For each v_b in $[0, 1]$, $p_b(v_b)$ solves

$$\max_{p_b} \left[v_b - \frac{p_b + E[p_s(v_s) \mid p_b \geq p_s(v_s)]}{2} \right] \text{Prob} \{ p_b \geq p_s(v_s) \}, \quad (3.2.3)$$

where $E[p_s(v_s) \mid p_b \geq p_s(v_s)]$ is the expected price the seller will demand, conditional on the demand being less than the buyer's offer of p_b. For each v_s in $[0, 1]$, $p_s(v_s)$ solves

$$\max_{p_s} \left[\frac{p_s + E[p_b(v_b) \mid p_b(v_b) \geq p_s]}{2} - v_s \right] \text{Prob} \{ p_b(v_b) \geq p_s \}, \quad (3.2.4)$$

where $E[p_b(v_b) \mid p_b(v_b) \geq p_s]$ is the expected price the buyer will offer, conditional on the offer being greater than the seller's demand of p_s.

There are many, many Bayesian Nash equilibria of this game. Consider the following one-price equilibrium, for example, in which trade occurs at a single price if it occurs at all. For any value x in $[0, 1]$, let the buyer's strategy be to offer x if $v_b \geq x$ and

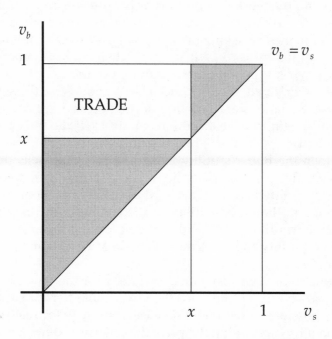

Figure 3.2.1.

to offer zero otherwise, and let the seller's strategy be to demand x if $v_s \leq x$ and to demand one otherwise. Given the buyer's strategy, the seller's choices amount to trading at x or not trading, so the seller's strategy is a best response to the buyer's because the seller-types who prefer trading at x to not trading do so, and vice versa. The analogous argument shows that the buyer's strategy is a best response to the seller's, so these strategies are indeed a Bayesian Nash equilibrium. In this equilibrium, trade occurs for the (v_s, v_b) pairs indicated in Figure 3.2.1; trade would be efficient for all (v_s, v_b) pairs such that $v_b \geq v_s$, but does not occur in the two shaded regions of the figure.

We now derive a linear Bayesian Nash equilibrium of the double auction. As in the previous section, we are *not* restricting the players' strategy spaces to include only linear strategies. Rather, we allow the players to choose arbitrary strategies but ask whether there is an equilibrium that is linear. Many other equilibria exist besides the one-price equilibria and the linear equilibrium, but the linear equilibrium has interesting efficiency properties, which we describe later.

Suppose the seller's strategy is $p_s(v_s) = a_s + c_s v_s$. Then p_s is uniformly distributed on $[a_s, a_s + c_s]$, so (3.2.3) becomes

$$\max_{p_b} \left[v_b - \frac{1}{2} \left\{ p_b + \frac{a_s + p_b}{2} \right\} \right] \frac{p_b - a_s}{c_s} ,$$

the first-order condition for which yields

$$p_b = \frac{2}{3} v_b + \frac{1}{3} a_s. \tag{3.2.5}$$

Thus, if the seller plays a linear strategy, then the buyer's best response is also linear. Analogously, suppose the buyer's strategy is $p_b(v_b) = a_b + c_b v_b$. Then p_b is uniformly distributed on $[a_b, a_b + c_b]$, so (3.2.4) becomes

$$\max_{p_s} \left[\frac{1}{2} \left\{ p_s + \frac{p_s + a_b + c_b}{2} \right\} - v_s \right] \frac{a_b + c_b - p_s}{c_b} ,$$

the first-order condition for which yields

$$p_s = \frac{2}{3} v_s + \frac{1}{3} (a_b + c_b). \tag{3.2.6}$$

Thus, if the buyer plays a linear strategy, then the seller's best response is also linear. If the players' linear strategies are to be best responses to each other, (3.2.5) implies that $c_b = 2/3$ and $a_b = a_s/3$, and (3.2.6) implies that $c_s = 2/3$ and $a_s = (a_b + c_b)/3$. Therefore, the linear equilibrium strategies are

$$p_b(v_b) = \frac{2}{3} v_b + \frac{1}{12} \tag{3.2.7}$$

and

$$p_s(v_s) = \frac{2}{3} v_s + \frac{1}{4}, \tag{3.2.8}$$

as shown in Figure 3.2.2.

Recall that trade occurs in the double auction if and only if $p_b \geq p_s$. Manipulating (3.2.7) and (3.2.8) shows that trade occurs in the linear equilibrium if and only if $v_b \geq v_s + (1/4)$, as shown in Figure 3.2.3. (Consistent with this, Figure 3.2.2 reveals that seller-types above 3/4 make demands above the buyer's highest offer,

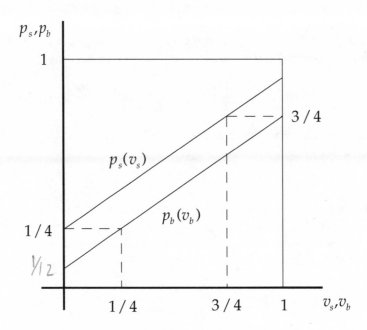

Figure 3.2.2.

$p_b(1) = 3/4$, and buyer-types below $1/4$ make offers below the seller's lowest offer, $p_s(0) = 1/4$.)

Compare Figures 3.2.1 and 3.2.3—the depictions of which valuation pairs trade in the one-price and linear equilibria, respectively. In both cases, the most valuable possible trade (namely, $v_s = 0$ and $v_b = 1$) does occur. But the one-price equilibrium misses some valuable trades (such as $v_s = 0$ and $v_b = x - \varepsilon$, where ε is small) and achieves some trades that are worth next to nothing (such as $v_s = x - \varepsilon$ and $v_b = x + \varepsilon$). The linear equilibrium, in contrast, misses all trades worth next to nothing but achieves all trades worth at least $1/4$. This suggests that the linear equilibrium may dominate the one-price equilibria, in terms of the expected gains the players receive, but also raises the possibility that the players might do even better in an alternative equilibrium.

Myerson and Satterthwaite (1983) show that, for the uniform valuation distributions considered here, the linear equilibrium yields higher expected gains for the players than any other Bayes-

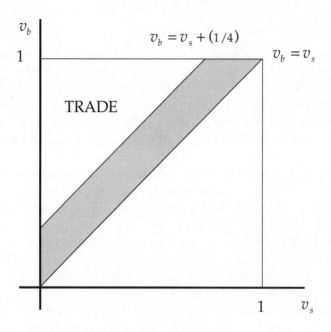

Figure 3.2.3.

ian Nash equilibria of the double auction (including but far from limited to the one-price equilibria). This implies that there is no Bayesian Nash equilibrium of the double auction in which trade occurs if and only if it is efficient (i.e., if and only if $v_b \geq v_s$). They also show that this latter result is very general: if v_b is continuously distributed on $[x_b, y_b]$ and v_s is continuously distributed on $[x_s, y_s]$, where $y_s > x_b$ and $y_b > x_s$, then there is no bargaining game the buyer and seller would willingly play that has a Bayesian Nash equilibrium in which trade occurs if and only if it is efficient. In the next section we sketch how the Revelation Principle can be used to prove this general result. We conclude this section by translating the result into Hall and Lazear's employment model: if the firm has private information about the worker's marginal product (m) and the worker has private information about his or her outside opportunity (v), then there is no bargaining game that the firm and the worker would willingly play that produces employment if and only if it is efficient (i.e., $m \geq v$).

3.3   The Revelation Principle

The Revelation Principle, due to Myerson (1979) in the context of Bayesian games (and to others in related contexts), is an important tool for designing games when the players have private information. It can be applied in the auction and bilateral-trading problems described in the previous two sections, as well as in a wide variety of other problems. In this section we state and prove the Revelation Principle for static Bayesian games. (Extending the proof to cover dynamic Bayesian games is straightforward.) Before doing so, however, we sketch the way the Revelation Principle is used in the auction and bilateral-trading problems.

Consider a seller who wishes to design an auction to maximize his or her expected revenue. Specifying the many different auctions the seller should consider could be an enormous task. In the auction in Section 3.2.B, for example, the highest bidder paid money to the seller and received the good, but there are many other possibilities. The bidders might have to pay an entry fee. More generally, some of the losing bidders might have to pay money, perhaps in amounts that depend on their own and others' bids. Also, the seller might set a reservation price—a floor below which bids will not be accepted. More generally, the good might stay with the seller with some probability, and might not always go to the highest bidder when the seller does release it.

Fortunately, the seller can use the Revelation Principle to simplify this problem dramatically, in two ways. First, the seller can restrict attention to the following class of games:

1. The bidders simultaneously make (possibly dishonest) claims about their types (i.e., their valuations). Bidder i can claim to be any type τ_i from i's set of feasible types T_i, no matter what i's true type, t_i.

2. Given the bidders' claims $(\tau_1, \ldots, \tau_n)$, bidder i pays $x_i(\tau_1, \ldots, \tau_n)$ and receives the good with probability $q_i(\tau_1, \ldots, \tau_n)$. For each possible combination of claims $(\tau_1, \ldots, \tau_n)$, the sum of the probabilities $q_1(\tau_1, \ldots, \tau_n) + \cdots + q_n(\tau_1, \ldots, \tau_n)$ must be less than or equal to one.

Games of this kind (i.e., static Bayesian games in which each player's only action is to submit a claim about his or her type) are called *direct mechanisms*.

The second way the seller can use the Revelation Principle is to restrict attention to those direct mechanisms in which it is a Bayesian Nash equilibrium for each bidder to tell the truth—that is, payment and probability functions $\{x_1(\tau_1,\ldots,\tau_n),\ldots,x_n(\tau_1,\ldots,\tau_n); q_1(\tau_1,\ldots,\tau_n),\ldots,q_n(\tau_1,\ldots,\tau_n)\}$ such that each player i's equilibrium strategy is to claim $\tau_i(t_i) = t_i$ for each t_i in T_i. A direct mechanism in which truth-telling is a Bayesian Nash equilibrium is called *incentive-compatible*.

Outside the context of auction design, the Revelation Principle can again be used in these two ways. Any Bayesian Nash equilibrium of any Bayesian game can be represented by a new Bayesian Nash equilibrium in an appropriately chosen new Bayesian game, where by "represented" we mean that for each possible combination of the players' types $(t_1,\ldots,t_n)$, the players' actions and payoffs in the new equilibrium are identical to those in the old equilibrium. No matter what the original game, the new Bayesian game is always a direct mechanism; no matter what the original equilibrium, the new equilibrium in the new game is always truth-telling. More formally:

Theorem (The Revelation Principle) *Any Bayesian Nash equilibrium of any Bayesian game can be represented by an incentive-compatible direct mechanism.*

In the auction analyzed in Section 3.2.B we assumed that the bidders' valuations are independent of each other. We also assumed (implicitly, in the definition of the bidders' valuations) that knowing bidder j's valuation would not change bidder i's valuation (although such knowledge typically would change i's bid). We characterize these two assumptions by saying that the bidders have independent, private values. For this case, Myerson (1981) determines which direct mechanisms have a truth-telling equilibrium, and which of these equilibria maximizes the seller's expected payoff. The Revelation Principle then guarantees that no other auction has a Bayesian Nash equilibrium that yields the seller a higher expected payoff, because such an equilibrium of such an auction would have been represented by a truth-telling equilibrium of a direct mechanism, and all such incentive-compatible direct mechanisms were considered. Myerson also shows that the symmetric Bayesian Nash equilibrium of the auction analyzed in Section 3.2.B is equivalent to this payoff-maxi-mizing truth-telling equilibrium (as are the symmetric equilibria of several other well-known auctions).

As a second example of the Revelation Principle in action, con-sider the bilateral trading problem described in Section 3.2.C. We analyzed one possible trading game the buyer and seller could play—the double auction. In that game, if there is trade then the buyer pays something to the seller, while if there is no trade then there is no payment, but there are again many other possibili-ties. There could be payments (from the buyer to the seller, or vice versa) even if there is no trade, and the probability of trade could be strictly between zero and one. Also, the rule for deter-mining whether trade is to occur could require that the buyer's offer exceed the seller's demand by a certain (positive or negative) amount; this amount could even vary depending on the prices the parties name.

We can capture these possibilities by considering the follow-ing class of direct mechanisms: the buyer and the seller simul-taneously make claims about their types, τ_b and τ_s, after which the buyer pays the seller $x(\tau_b, \tau_s)$, which could be positive or neg-ative, and the buyer receives the good with probability $q(\tau_b, \tau_s)$. Myerson and Satterthwaite determine which direct mechanisms have a truth-telling equilibrium. They then impose the constraint that each type of each party be willing to play the game (i.e., that each type of each party have an equilibrium expected payoff no less than the payoff that type could achieve by refusing to play—namely, zero for each buyer type and t_s for the seller type t_s). Finally, they show that none of these incentive-compatible direct mechanisms have trade with probability one if and only if trade is efficient. The Revelation Principle then guarantees that there is no bargaining game the buyer and seller would willingly play that has a Bayesian Nash equilibrium in which trade occurs if and only if it is efficient.

To give a formal statement and proof of the Revelation Princi-ple, consider the Bayesian Nash equilibrium $s^* = (s_1^*, \ldots, s_n^*)$ in the static Bayesian game $G = \{A_1, \ldots, A_n; T_1, \ldots, T_n; p_1, \ldots, p_n; u_1, \ldots, u_n\}$. We will construct a direct mechanism with a truth-telling equilibrium that represents s^*. The appropriate direct mechanism is a static Bayesian game with the same type spaces and beliefs as G but with new action spaces and new payoff functions. The new action spaces are simple. Player i's feasible actions in the direct mechanism are (possibly dishonest) claims about i's possible types. That is, player i's action space is T_i. The new payoff functions are more complicated. They depend not only on the original game, G, but also on the original equilibrium in that game, s^*. The crucial idea is to use the fact that s^* is an equilibrium in G to ensure that truth-telling is an equilibrium of the direct mechanism, as follows.

Saying that s^* is a Bayesian Nash equilibrium of G means that for each player i, s_i^* is i's best response to the other players' strategies $(s_1^*, \ldots, s_{i-1}^*, s_{i+1}^*, \ldots, s_n^*)$. More specifically, for each of i's types t_i in T_i, $s_i^*(t_i)$ is the best action for i to choose from A_i, given that the other players' strategies are $(s_1^*, \ldots, s_{i-1}^*, s_{i+1}^*, \ldots, s_n^*)$. Thus, if i's type is t_i and we allow i to choose an action from a subset of A_i that includes $s_i^*(t_i)$, then i's optimal choice remains $s_i^*(t_i)$, again assuming that the other players' strategies are $(s_1^*, \ldots, s_{i-1}^*, s_{i+1}^*, \ldots, s_n^*)$. The payoff functions in the direct mechanism are chosen so as to confront each player with a choice of exactly this kind.

We define the payoffs in the direct mechanism by substituting the players' type reports in the new game, $\tau = (\tau_1, \ldots, \tau_n)$, into their equilibrium strategies from the old game, s^*, and then substituting the resulting actions in the old game, $s^*(\tau) = (s_1^*(\tau_1), \ldots, s_n^*(\tau_n))$, into the payoff functions from the old game. Formally, i's payoff function is

$$v_i(\tau, t) = u_i[s^*(\tau), t],$$

where $t = (t_1, \ldots, t_n)$. One could imagine these payoffs occurring because a neutral outsider approaches the players and makes the following speech:

> I know you already know your types and were about to play the equilibrium s^* in the game G. Here is a new game to play—a direct mechanism. First, each of you will sign a contract that allows me to dictate the action you will take when we later play G. Second, each of you will write down a claim about your type, τ_i, and submit it to me. Third, I will use each player's type report in the new game, τ_i, together with the player's equilibrium strategy from the old game, s_i^*, to compute the action the player would have taken in

the equilibrium s^* if the player's type really were τ_i—namely, $s_i^*(\tau_i)$. Finally, I will dictate that each of you to take the action I have computed for you, and you will receive the resulting payoffs (which will depend on these actions and your true types).

We conclude this section (and the proof of the Revelation Principle) by showing that truth-telling is a Bayesian Nash equilibrium of this direct mechanism. By claiming to be type τ_i from T_i, player i is in effect choosing to take the action $s_i^*(\tau_i)$ from A_i. If all the other players tell the truth, then they are in effect playing the strategies $(s_1^*, \ldots, s_{i-1}^*, s_{i+1}^*, \ldots, s_n^*)$. But we argued earlier that if they play these strategies, then when i's type is t_i the best action for i to choose is $s_i^*(t_i)$. Thus, if the other players tell the truth, then when i's type is t_i the best type to claim to be is t_i. That is, truth-telling is an equilibrium. More formally, it is a Bayesian Nash equilibrium of the static Bayesian game $\{T_1, \ldots, T_n; T_1, \ldots, T_n; p_1, \ldots, p_n; v_1, \ldots, v_n\}$ for each player i to play the truth-telling strategy $\tau_i(t_i) = t_i$ for every t_i in T_i.

3.4   Further Reading

Myerson (1985) offers a more detailed introduction to Bayesian games, Bayesian Nash equilibrium, and the Revelation Principle. See McAfee and McMillan (1987) for a survey of the literature on auctions, including an introduction to the winner's curse. Bulow and Klemperer (1991) extend the auction model in Section 3.2.B to produce an appealing explanation of rational frenzies and crashes in (say) securities markets. On employment under asymmetric information, see Deere (1988), who analyzes a dynamic model in which the worker encounters a sequence of firms over time, each with its own privately known marginal product. For applications of the Revelation Principle, see Baron and Myerson (1982) on regulating a monopolist with unknown costs, Hart (1983) on implicit contracts and involuntary unemployment, and Sappington (1983) on agency theory.

3.5 Problems

Section 3.1

3.1. What is a static Bayesian game? What is a (pure) strategy in such a game? What is a (pure-strategy) Bayesian Nash equilibrium in such a game?

3.2. Consider a Cournot duopoly operating in a market with inverse demand $P(Q) = a - Q$, where $Q = q_1 + q_2$ is the aggregate quantity on the market. Both firms have total costs $c_i(q_i) = cq_i$, but demand is uncertain: it is high $(a = a_H)$ with probability θ and low $(a = a_L)$ with probability $1 - \theta$. Furthermore, information is asymmetric: firm 1 knows whether demand is high or low, but firm 2 does not. All of this is common knowledge. The two firms simultaneously choose quantities. What are the strategy spaces for the two firms? Make assumptions concerning a_H, a_L, θ, and c such that all equilibrium quantities are positive. What is the Bayesian Nash equilibrium of this game?

3.3. Consider the following asymmetric-information model of Bertrand duopoly with differentiated products. Demand for firm i is $q_i(p_i, p_j) = a - p_i - b_i \cdot p_j$. Costs are zero for both firms. The sensitivity of firm i's demand to firm j's price is either high or low. That is, b_i is either b_H or b_L, where $b_H > b_L > 0$. For each firm, $b_i = b_H$ with probability θ and $b_i = b_L$ with probability $1 - \theta$, independent of the realization of b_j. Each firm knows its own b_i but not its competitor's. All of this is common knowledge. What are the action spaces, type spaces, beliefs, and utility functions in this game? What are the strategy spaces? What conditions define a symmetric pure-strategy Bayesian Nash equilibrium of this game? Solve for such an equilibrium.

3.4. Find all the pure-strategy Bayesian Nash equilibria in the following static Bayesian game:

1. Nature determines whether the payoffs are as in Game 1 or as in Game 2, each game being equally likely.

2. Player 1 learns whether nature has drawn Game 1 or Game 2, but player 2 does not.

3. Player 1 chooses either T or B; player 2 simultaneously chooses either L or R.

4. Payoffs are given by the game drawn by nature.

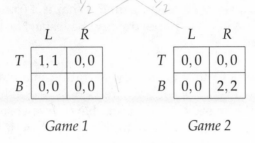

nature

$\frac{1}{2}$ $\frac{1}{2}$

	L	R
T	1,1	0,0
B	0,0	0,0

	L	R
T	0,0	0,0
B	0,0	2,2

Game 1   *Game 2*

Section 3.2

3.5. Recall from Section 1.3 that Matching Pennies (a static game of complete information) has no pure-strategy Nash equilibrium but has one mixed-strategy Nash equilibrium: each player plays H with probability $1/2$.

Player 2

		H	T
	H	1, −1	−1, 1
Player 1	T	−1, 1	1, −1

Provide a pure-strategy Bayesian Nash equilibrium of a corresponding game of incomplete information such that as the incomplete information disappears, the players' behavior in the Bayesian Nash equilibrium approaches their behavior in the mixed-strategy Nash equilibrium in the original game of complete information.

3.6. Consider a first-price, sealed-bid auction in which the bidders' valuations are independently and uniformly distributed on $[0, 1]$. Show that if there are n bidders, then the strategy of bidding $(n-1)/n$ times one's valuation is a symmetric Bayesian Nash equilibrium of this auction.

3.7. Consider a first-price, sealed-bid auction in which the bidders' valuations are independently and identically distributed ac-

↳ chris notes, also Appendix 3.2.B.

cording to the strictly positive density $f(v_i)$ on $[0, 1]$. Compute a symmetric Bayesian Nash equilibrium for the two-bidder case.

3.8. Reinterpret the buyer and seller in the double auction analyzed in Section 3.2.C as a firm that knows a worker's marginal product (m) and a worker who knows his or her outside opportunity (v), respectively, as in Hall and Lazear (1984). In this context, trade means that the worker is employed by the firm, and the price at which the parties trade is the worker's wage, w. If there is trade, then the firm's payoff is $m - w$ and the worker's is w; if there is no trade then the firm's payoff is zero and the worker's is v.

Suppose that m and v are independent draws from a uniform distribution on $[0, 1]$, as in the text. For purposes of comparison, compute the players' expected payoffs in the linear equilibrium of the double auction. Now consider the following two trading games as alternatives to the double auction.

Game I: Before the parties learn their private information, they sign a contract specifying that if the worker is employed by the firm then the worker's wage will be w, but also that either side can escape from the employment relationship at no cost. After the parties learn the values of their respective pieces of private information, they simultaneously announce either that they Accept the wage w or that they Reject that wage. If both announce Accept, then trade occurs; otherwise it does not. Given an arbitrary value of w from $[0, 1]$, what is the Bayesian Nash equilibrium of this game? Draw a diagram analogous to Figure 3.2.3 showing the type-pairs that trade. Find the value of w that maximizes the sum of the players' expected payoffs and compute this maximized sum.

Game II: Before the parties learn their private information, they sign a contract specifying that the following dynamic game will be used to determine whether the worker joins the firm and if so at what wage. (Strictly speaking, this game belongs in Chapter 4. We will anticipate the spirit of Chapter 4 by arguing that this game can be solved by combining the lessons of this chapter with those of Chapter 2.) After the parties learn the values of their respective pieces of private information, the firm chooses a wage w to offer the worker, which the worker then accepts or rejects. Try to analyze this game using backwards induction, as we did for the analogous complete-information games in Section 2.1.A, as follows. Given w and v, what will the worker do? If the firm anticipates what the worker will do, then given m what will the firm do? What is the sum of the players' expected payoffs?

3.6 References

Baron, D., and R. Myerson. 1982. "Regulating a Monopolist with Unknown Costs." *Econometrica* 50:911–30.

Bulow, J., and P. Klemperer. 1991. "Rational Frenzies and Crashes." Stanford University Graduate School of Business Research Paper #1150.

Chatterjee, K., and W. Samuelson. 1983. "Bargaining under Incomplete Information." *Operations Research* 31:835–51.

Deere, D. 1988. "Bilateral Trading as an Efficient Auction over Time." *Journal of Political Economy* 96:100–15.

Hall, R., and E. Lazear. 1984. "The Excess Sensitivity of Layoffs and Quits to Demand." *Journal of Labor Economics* 2:233–57.

Harsanyi, J. 1967. "Games with Incomplete Information Played by Bayesian Players Parts I II and III." *Management Science* 14:159–82, 320–34, 486–502.

_____. 1973. "Games with Randomly Disturbed Payoffs: A New Rationale for Mixed Strategy Equilibrium Points." *International Journal of Game Theory* 2:1–23.

Hart, O. 1983. "Optimal Labour Contracts under Asymmetric Information." *Review of Economic Studies* 50:3–35.

McAfee, P., and J. McMillan. 1987. "Auctions and Bidding." *Journal of Economic Literature* 25:699–738.

Myerson, R. 1979. "Incentive Compatability and the Bargaining Problem." *Econometrica* 47:61–73.

_____. 1981. "Optimal Auction Design." *Mathematics of Operations Research* 6:58–73.

_____. 1985. "Bayesian Equilibrium and Incentive Compatibility: An Introduction." In *Social Goals and Social Organization*. L. Hurwicz, D. Schmeidler, and H. Sonnenschein, eds. Cambridge: Cambridge University Press.

Myerson, R., and M. Satterthwaite. 1983. "Efficient Mechanisms for Bilateral Trading." *Journal of Economic Theory* 28:265–81.

Sappington, D. 1983. "Limited Liability Contracts between Principal and Agent." *Journal of Economic Theory* 29:1–21.

Chapter 4

Dynamic Games of Incomplete Information

In this chapter we introduce yet another equilibrium concept—
perfect Bayesian equilibrium. This makes four equilibrium concepts
in four chapters: Nash equilibrium in static games of complete information, subgame-perfect Nash equilibrium in dynamic games
of complete information, Bayesian Nash equilibrium in static games
of incomplete information, and perfect Bayesian equilibrium in
dynamic games of incomplete information. It may seem that we
invent a brand new equilibrium concept for each class of games
we study, but in fact these equilibrium concepts are closely related. As we consider progressively richer games, we progressively strengthen the equilibrium concept, in order to rule out implausible equilibria in the richer games that would survive if we
applied equilibrium concepts suitable for simpler games. In each
case, the stronger equilibrium concept differs from the weaker concept only for the richer games, not for the simpler games. In particular, perfect Bayesian equilibrium is equivalent to Bayesian Nash
equilibrium in static games of incomplete information, equivalent
to subgame-perfect Nash equilibrium in dynamic games of complete and perfect information (and in many dynamic games of
complete but imperfect information, including those discussed in
Sections 2.2 and 2.3), and equivalent to Nash equilibrium in static
games of complete information.

Perfect Bayesian equilibrium was invented in order to refine
(i.e., strengthen the requirements of) Bayesian Nash equilibrium

in the same way that subgame-perfect Nash equilibrium refines Nash equilibrium. Just as we imposed subgame perfection in dynamic games of complete information because Nash equilibrium failed to capture the idea that threats and promises should be credible, we now restrict attention to perfect Bayesian equilibrium in dynamic games of incomplete information because Bayesian Nash equilibrium suffers from the same flaw. Recall that if the players' strategies are to be a subgame-perfect Nash equilibrium, they must not only be a Nash equilibrium for the entire game but must also constitute a Nash equilibrium in every subgame. In this chapter we replace the idea of a subgame with the more general idea of a continuation game—the latter can begin at any complete information set (whether singleton or not), rather than only at a singleton information set. We then proceed by analogy: if the players' strategies are to be a perfect Bayesian equilibrium, they must not only be a Bayesian Nash equilibrium for the entire game but must also constitute a Bayesian Nash equilibrium in every continuation game.

In Section 4.1 we informally introduce the main features of a perfect Bayesian equilibrium. To do so, we temporarily adopt a second (complementary) perspective that reverses the emphasis above: perfect Bayesian equilibrium strengthens the requirements of subgame-perfect Nash equilibrium by explicitly analyzing the players' beliefs, as in Bayesian Nash equilibrium. This second perspective arises because, following Harsanyi (1967), we describe a game of incomplete information as though it were a game of imperfect information—nature reveals player i's type to i but not to j, so player j does not know the complete history of the game. Thus, an equilibrium concept designed to strengthen Bayesian Nash equilibrium in dynamic games of incomplete information also can strengthen subgame-perfect Nash equilibrium in dynamic games of complete but imperfect information.

In Section 4.2 we analyze the most widely applied class of games of incomplete information: *signaling games*. Stated abstractly, a signaling game involves two players (one with private information, the other without) and two moves (first a signal sent by the informed player, then a response taken by the uninformed player). The key idea is that communication can occur if one type of the informed player is willing to send a signal that would be too expensive for another type to send. We first define perfect Bayesian equilibrium for signaling games and describe the various kinds of equilibria (corresponding to various degrees of communication, from zero to complete) that can exist. We then consider Spence's (1973) seminal model of job-market signaling, as well as Myers and Majluf's (1984) model of corporate investment and Vickers' (1986) model of monetary policy.

In Section 4.3 we describe other applications of perfect Bayesian equilibrium. We begin with Crawford and Sobel's (1982) analysis of *cheap-talk games* (i.e., signaling games in which all messages are free), applications of which include presidential veto threats, policy announcements by the Federal Reserve, and communication (or "voice") in organizations. In cheap-talk games, the extent of communication is determined by the commonality of the players' interests, rather than by the costs of signals for different types. We then study Sobel and Takahashi's (1983) sequential bargaining model, in which a firm must tolerate a strike in order to demonstrate that it cannot afford to pay high wages (cf., Rubinstein's complete-information bargaining model in Section 2.1.D, in which strikes do not occur in equilibrium). Finally, we explore Kreps, Milgrom, Roberts, and Wilson's (1982) landmark account of the role of *reputation* in achieving rational cooperation in the finitely repeated Prisoners' Dilemma (cf., the Proposition in Section 2.3.A concerning the unique subgame-perfect Nash equilibrium of a finitely repeated game based on a stage game with a unique Nash equilibrium).

In Section 4.4 we return to theory. Although this is the final section in the book, it serves more as an indication of what might come next than as the culmination of the material we have covered. We describe and illustrate two (successive) refinements of perfect Bayesian equilibrium, the second of which is Cho and Kreps' (1987) *Intuitive Criterion*.

4.1 Introduction to Perfect Bayesian Equilibrium

Consider the following dynamic game of complete but imperfect information. First, player 1 chooses among three actions—L, M, and R. If player 1 chooses R then the game ends without a move by player 2. If player 1 chooses either L or M then player 2 learns that R was not chosen (but not which of L or M was chosen) and

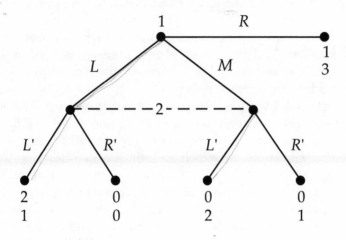

Figure 4.1.1.

Player 2

		L′	R′
	L	2,1	0,0
Player 1	M	0,2	0,1
	R	1,3	1,3

Figure 4.1.2.

then chooses between two actions, L' and R', after which the game ends. Payoffs are given in the extensive form in Figure 4.1.1.

Using the normal-form representation of this game given in Figure 4.1.2, we see that there are two pure-strategy Nash equilibria—(L, L') and (R, R'). To determine whether these Nash equilibria are subgame-perfect, we use the extensive-form representation to define the game's subgames. Because a subgame is defined to begin at a decision node that is a singleton information set (but is not the game's first decision node), the game in Figure 4.1.1 has no subgames. If a game has no subgames then the requirement of subgame-perfection (namely, that the players' strategies constitute a Nash equilibrium on every subgame) is trivially satisfied. Thus, in any game that has no subgames, the definition of subgame-perfect Nash equilibrium is equivalent to the definition of Nash equilibrium, so in Figure 4.1.1 both (L, L') and (R, R') are subgame-perfect Nash equilibria. Nonetheless, (R, R') clearly depends on a noncredible threat: if player 2 gets the move, then playing L' dominates playing R', so player 1 should not be induced to play R by 2's threat to play R' if given the move.

One way to strengthen the equilibrium concept so as to rule out the subgame-perfect Nash equilibrium (R, R') in Figure 4.1.1 is to impose the following two requirements.

Requirement 1 *At each information set, the player with the move must have a **belief** about which node in the information set has been reached by the play of the game. For a nonsingleton information set, a belief is a probability distribution over the nodes in the information set; for a singleton information set, the player's belief puts probability one on the single decision node.*

Requirement 2 *Given their beliefs, the players' strategies must be **sequentially rational**. That is, at each information set the action taken by the player with the move (and the player's subsequent strategy) must be optimal given the player's belief at that information set and the other players' subsequent strategies (where a "subsequent strategy" is a complete plan of action covering every contingency that might arise after the given information set has been reached).*

In Figure 4.1.1, Requirement 1 implies that if the play of the game reaches player 2's nonsingleton information set then player 2 must have a belief about which node has been reached (or, equivalently, about whether player 1 has played L or M). This belief is represented by the probabilities p and $1 - p$ attached to the relevant nodes in the tree, as shown in Figure 4.1.3.

Given player 2's belief, the expected payoff from playing R' is $p \cdot 0 + (1 - p) \cdot 1 = 1 - p$, while the expected payoff from playing L' is $p \cdot 1 + (1 - p) \cdot 2 = 2 - p$. Since $2 - p > 1 - p$ for any value of p, Requirement 2 prevents player 2 from choosing R'. Thus, simply requiring that each player have a belief and act optimally given this belief suffices to eliminate the implausible equilibrium (R, R') in this example.

Requirements 1 and 2 insist that the players have beliefs and act optimally given these beliefs, but not that these beliefs be rea-

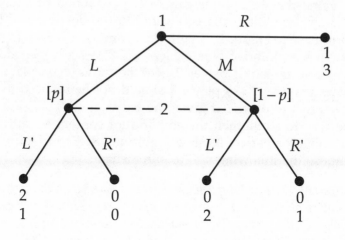

Figure 4.1.3.

sonable. In order to impose further requirements on the players' beliefs, we distinguish between information sets that are on the equilibrium path and those that are off the equilibrium path.

Definition *For a given equilibrium in a given extensive-form game, an information set is **on the equilibrium path** if it will be reached with positive probability if the game is played according to the equilibrium strategies, and is **off the equilibrium path** if it is certain not to be reached if the game is played according to the equilibrium strategies (where "equilibrium" can mean Nash, subgame-perfect, Bayesian, or perfect Bayesian equilibrium).*

Requirement 3 *At information sets on the equilibrium path, beliefs are determined by Bayes' rule and the players' equilibrium strategies.*

In the subgame-perfect Nash equilibrium (L, L') in Figure 4.1.3, for example, player 2's belief must be $p = 1$: given player 1's equilibrium strategy (namely, L), player 2 knows which node in the information set has been reached. As a second (hypothetical) illustration of Requirement 3, suppose that in Figure 4.1.3 there were a mixed-strategy equilibrium in which player 1 plays L with probability q_1, M with probability q_2, and R with probability $1 -$

$q_1 - q_2$. Then Requirement 3 would force player 2's belief to be $p = q_1/(q_1 + q_2)$.

Requirements 1 through 3 capture the spirit of a perfect Bayesian equilibrium. The crucial new feature of this equilibrium concept is due to Kreps and Wilson (1982): beliefs are elevated to the level of importance of strategies in the definition of equilibrium. Formally, an equilibrium no longer consists of just a strategy for each player but now also includes a belief for each player at each information set at which the player has the move.[1] The advantage of making the players' beliefs explicit in this way is that, just as in earlier chapters we insisted that the players choose credible strategies, we can now also insist that they hold reasonable beliefs, both on the equilibrium path (in Requirement 3) and off the equilibrium path (in Requirement 4, which follows, and in others in Section 4.4).

In simple economic applications—including the signaling game in Section 4.2.A and the cheap-talk game in Section 4.3.A—Requirements 1 through 3 not only capture the spirit but also constitute the definition of perfect Bayesian equilibrium. In richer economic applications, however, more requirements need to be imposed to eliminate implausible equilibria. Different authors have used different definitions of perfect Bayesian equilibrium. All definitions include Requirements 1 through 3; most also include Requirement 4; some impose further requirements.[2] In this chapter,

---

[1]Kreps and Wilson formalize this perspective on equilibrium by defining *sequential equilibrium*, an equilibrium concept that is equivalent to perfect Bayesian equilibrium in many economic applications but in some cases is slightly stronger. Sequential equilibrium is more complicated to define and apply than perfect Bayesian equilibrium, so most authors now use the latter. Some who do so (imprecisely) refer to the equilibrium concept they apply as sequential equilibrium. Kreps and Wilson show that in any finite game (i.e., any game with a finite number of players, types, and possible moves) there exists a sequential equilibrium; this implies that in any finite game there exists a perfect Bayesian equilibrium.

[2]To give a sense of the issues not addressed by Requirements 1 through 4, suppose players 2 and 3 have observed the same events and then both observe a deviation from the equilibrium by player 1. In a game of incomplete information in which player 1 has private information, should players 2 and 3 hold the same belief about player 1's type; in a game of complete information, should players 2 and 3 hold the same belief about earlier unobserved moves by player 1? Similarly, if players 2 and 3 have observed the same events and then player 2 deviates from the equilibrium, should player 3 change his or her belief about player 1's type, or about 1's unobserved moves?

we take Requirements 1 through 4 to be the definition of perfect Bayesian equilibrium.[3]

Requirement 4 *At information sets off the equilibrium path, beliefs are determined by Bayes' rule and the players' equilibrium strategies where possible.*

Definition *A **perfect Bayesian equilibrium** consists of strategies and beliefs satisfying Requirements 1 through 4.*

It would of course be useful to give a more precise statement of Requirement 4—one that avoids the vague instruction "where possible." We will do so in each of the economic applications analyzed in subsequent sections. For now, we use the three-player games in Figures 4.1.4 and 4.1.5 to illustrate and motivate Requirement 4. (The top, middle, and bottom payoffs are for players 1, 2, and 3, respectively.)

This game has one subgame: it begins at player 2's singleton information set. The unique Nash equilibrium in this subgame between players 2 and 3 is (L, R'), so the unique subgame-perfect Nash equilibrium of the entire game is (D, L, R'). These strategies and the belief $p = 1$ for player 3 satisfy Requirements 1 through 3. They also trivially satisfy Requirement 4, since there is no information set off this equilibrium path, and so constitute a perfect Bayesian equilibrium.

Now consider the strategies (A, L, L'), together with the belief $p = 0$. These strategies are a Nash equilibrium—no player wants to deviate unilaterally. These strategies and belief also satisfy Requirements 1 through 3—player 3 has a belief and acts optimally given it, and players 1 and 2 act optimally given the subsequent strategies of the other players. But this Nash equilibrium is not subgame-perfect, because the unique Nash equilibrium of the game's only subgame is (L, R'). Thus, Requirements 1 through 3 do not guarantee that the player's strategies are a subgame-perfect Nash equilibrium. The problem is that player 3's belief $(p = 0)$

---

[3]Fudenberg and Tirole (1991) give a formal definition of perfect Bayesian equilibrium for a broad class of dynamic games of incomplete information. Their definition addresses issues like those raised in footnote 2. In the simple games analyzed in this chapter, however, such issues do not arise, so their definition is equivalent to Requirements 1 through 4. Fudenberg and Tirole provide conditions under which their perfect Bayesian equilibrium is equivalent to Kreps and Wilson's sequential equilibrium.

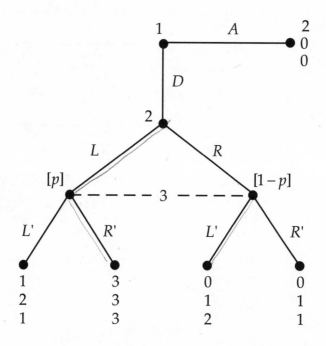

Figure 4.1.4.

is inconsistent with player 2's strategy (L), but Requirements 1 through 3 impose no restrictions on 3's belief because 3's information set is not reached if the game is played according to the specified strategies. Requirement 4, however, forces player 3's belief to be determined by player 2's strategy: if 2's strategy is L then 3's belief must be $p = 1$; if 2's strategy is R then 3's belief must be $p = 0$. But if 3's belief is $p = 1$ then Requirement 2 forces 3's strategy to be R', so the strategies (A, L, L') and the belief $p = 0$ do not satisfy Requirements 1 through 4.

As a second illustration of Requirement 4, suppose Figure 4.1.4 is modified as shown in Figure 4.1.5: player 2 now has a third possible action, A', which ends the game. (For simplicity, we ignore the payoffs in this game.) As before, if player 1's equilibrium strategy is A then player 3's information set is off the equilibrium path, but now Requirement 4 may not determine 3's belief from 2's strategy. If 2's strategy is A' then Requirement 4 puts no restrictions on 3's belief, but if 2's strategy is to play L with

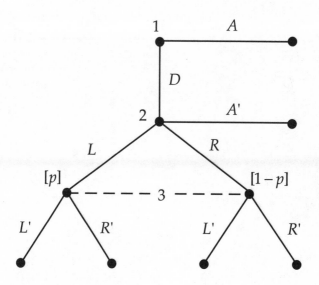

Figure 4.1.5.

probability q_1, R with probability q_2, and A' with probability $1 - q_1 - q_2$, where $q_1 + q_2 > 0$, then Requirement 4 dictates that 3's belief be $p = q_1/(q_1 + q_2)$.

To conclude this section, we informally relate perfect Bayesian equilibrium to the equilibrium concepts introduced in earlier chapters. In a Nash equilibrium, each player's strategy must be a best response to the other players' strategies, so no player chooses a strictly dominated strategy. In a perfect Bayesian equilibrium, Requirements 1 and 2 are equivalent to insisting that no player's strategy be strictly dominated beginning at any information set. (See Section 4.4 for a formal definition of strict dominance beginning at an information set.) Nash and Bayesian Nash equilibrium do not share this feature at information sets off the equilibrium path; even subgame-perfect Nash equilibrium does not share this feature at some information sets off the equilibrium path, such as information sets that are not contained in any subgame. Perfect Bayesian equilibrium closes these loopholes: players cannot threaten to play strategies that are strictly dominated beginning at any information set off the equilibrium path.

As noted earlier, one of the virtues of the perfect Bayesian equilibrium concept is that it makes the players' beliefs explicit and so allows us to impose not only Requirements 3 and 4 but also further requirements (on beliefs off the equilibrium path). Since perfect Bayesian equilibrium prevents player i from playing a strategy that is strictly dominated beginning at an information set off the equilibrium path, perhaps it is not reasonable for player j to believe that player i would play such a strategy. Because perfect Bayesian equilibrium makes the players' beliefs explicit, however, such an equilibrium often cannot be constructed by working backwards through the game tree, as we did to construct a subgame-perfect Nash equilibrium. Requirement 2 determines a player's action at a given information set based in part on the player's belief at that information set. If either Requirement 3 or 4 applies at this information set, then it determines the player's belief from the players' actions higher up the game tree. But Requirement 2 determines these actions higher up the game tree based in part on the players' subsequent strategies, including the action at the original information set. This circularity implies that a single pass working backwards through the tree (typically) will not suffice to compute a perfect Bayesian equilibrium.

4.2 Signaling Games

4.2.A Perfect Bayesian Equilibrium in Signaling Games

A signaling game is a dynamic game of incomplete information involving two players: a Sender (S) and a Receiver (R). The timing of the game is as follows:

1. Nature draws a type t_i for the Sender from a set of feasible types $T = \{t_1, \ldots, t_I\}$ according to a probability distribution $p(t_i)$, where $p(t_i) > 0$ for every i and $p(t_1) + \cdots + p(t_I) = 1$.

2. The Sender observes t_i and then chooses a message m_j from a set of feasible messages $M = \{m_1, \ldots, m_J\}$.

3. The Receiver observes m_j (but not t_i) and then chooses an action a_k from a set of feasible actions $A = \{a_1, \ldots, a_K\}$.

4. Payoffs are given by $U_S(t_i, m_j, a_k)$ and $U_R(t_i, m_j, a_k)$.

In many applications, the sets T, M, and A are intervals on the real line, rather than the finite sets considered here. It is straightforward to allow the set of feasible messages to depend on the type nature draws, and the set of feasible actions to depend on the message the Sender chooses.

Signaling models have been applied extremely widely in economics. To suggest the breadth of possible applications, we briefly interpret the formal structure in 1–4 in terms of the three applications to be analyzed in Sections 4.2.B through 4.2.D.

In Spence's (1973) model of job-market signaling, the Sender is a worker, the Receiver is the market of prospective employers, the type is the worker's productive ability, the message is the worker's education choice, and the action is the wage paid by the market.

In Myers and Majluf's (1984) model of corporate investment and capital structure, the Sender is a firm needing capital to finance a new project, the Receiver is a potential investor, the type is the profitability of the firm's existing assets, the message is the firm's offer of an equity stake in return for financing, and the action is the investor's decision about whether to invest.

In some applications, a signaling game is embedded within a richer game. For example, there could be an action by the Receiver before the Sender chooses the message in step 2, and there could be an action by the Sender after (or while) the Receiver chooses the action in step 3.

In Vickers's (1986) model of monetary policy, the Federal Reserve has private information about its willingness to accept inflation in order to increase employment, but the model is otherwise a two-period version of the complete-information repeated game analyzed in Section 2.3.E. Thus, the Sender is the Federal Reserve, the Receiver is the market of employers, the type is the Fed's willingness to accept inflation in order to increase employment, the message is the Fed's choice of first-period inflation, and the action is the employers'

expectation of second-period inflation. The employers' expectation of first-period inflation precedes the
signaling game, and the Fed's choice of second-period
inflation follows it.

For the rest of this section, we analyze the abstract signaling
game given in 1–4, rather than these applications. Figure 4.2.1
gives an extensive-form representation (without payoffs) of a sim-
ple case: $T = \{t_1, t_2\}$, $M = \{m_1, m_2\}$, $A = \{a_1, a_2\}$, and Prob$\{t_1\} =$
p. Note that the play of the game does not flow from an initial
node at the top of the tree to terminal nodes at the bottom, but
rather from an initial move by nature in the middle of the tree to
terminal nodes at the left and right edges.

Recall that (in any game) a player's strategy is a complete
plan of action—a strategy specifies a feasible action in every contingency in which the player might be called upon to act. In a signaling game, therefore, a pure strategy for the Sender is a function
$m(t_i)$ specifying which message will be chosen for each type that
nature might draw, and a pure strategy for the Receiver is a function $a(m_j)$ specifying which action will be chosen for each message

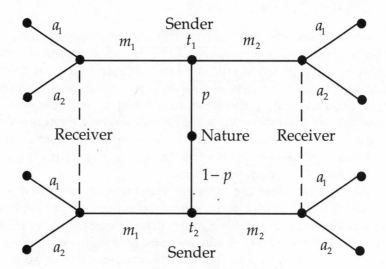

Figure 4.2.1.

that the Sender might send. In the simple game in Figure 4.2.1, the Sender and the Receiver both have four pure strategies.

> *Sender Strategy 1*: Play m_1 if nature draws t_1 and play m_1 if nature draws t_2.

> *Sender Strategy 2*: Play m_1 if nature draws t_1 and play m_2 if nature draws t_2.

> *Sender Strategy 3*: Play m_2 if nature draws t_1 and play m_1 if nature draws t_2.

> *Sender Strategy 4*: Play m_2 if nature draws t_1 and play m_2 if nature draws t_2.

> *Receiver Strategy 1*: Play a_1 if the Sender chooses m_1 and play a_1 if the Sender chooses m_2.

> *Receiver Strategy 2*: Play a_1 if the Sender chooses m_1 and play a_2 if the Sender chooses m_2.

> *Receiver Strategy 3*: Play a_2 if the Sender chooses m_1 and play a_1 if the Sender chooses m_2.

> *Receiver Strategy 4*: Play a_2 if the Sender chooses m_1 and play a_2 if the Sender chooses m_2.

We call the Sender's first and fourth strategies *pooling* because each type sends the same message, and the second and third *separating* because each type sends a different message. In a model with more than two types there are also *partially pooling* (or *semi-separating*) strategies in which all the types in a given set of types send the same message but different sets of types send different messages. In the two-type game in Figure 4.2.1 there are analogous mixed strategies, called *hybrid* strategies, in which (say) t_1 plays m_1 but t_2 randomizes between m_1 and m_2.

We now translate the informal statements of Requirements 1 through 3 in Section 4.1 into a formal definition of a perfect Bayesian equilibrium in a signaling game. (The discussion of Figure 4.1.5 implies that Requirement 4 is vacuous in a signaling game.) To keep things simple, we restrict attention to pure strategies; hybrid strategies are briefly discussed in the analysis of job-market signaling in the next section. We leave it as an exercise to define a Bayesian Nash equilibrium in a signaling game; see Problem 4.6.

Because the Sender knows the full history of the game when choosing a message, this choice occurs at a singleton information set. (There is one such information set for each type nature might draw.) Thus, Requirement 1 is trivial when applied to the Sender. The Receiver, in contrast, chooses an action after observing the Sender's message but without knowing the Sender's type, so the Receiver's choice occurs at a nonsingleton information set. (There is one such information set for each message the Sender might choose, and each such information set has one node for each type nature might have drawn.) Applying Requirement 1 to the Receiver yields:

Signaling Requirement 1 *After observing any message m_j from M, the Receiver must have a belief about which types could have sent m_j. Denote this belief by the probability distribution $\mu(t_i \mid m_j)$, where $\mu(t_i \mid m_j) \geq 0$ for each t_i in T, and*

$$\sum_{t_i \in T} \mu(t_i \mid m_j) = 1.$$

Given the Sender's message and the Receiver's belief, it is straightforward to characterize the Receiver's optimal action. Applying Requirement 2 to the Receiver therefore yields:

Signaling Requirement 2R *For each m_j in M, the Receiver's action $a^*(m_j)$ must maximize the Receiver's expected utility, given the belief $\mu(t_i \mid m_j)$ about which types could have sent m_j. That is, $a^*(m_j)$ solves*

$$\max_{a_k \in A} \sum_{t_i \in T} \mu(t_i \mid m_j) U_R(t_i, m_j, a_k).$$

Requirement 2 also applies to the Sender, but the Sender has complete information (and hence a trivial belief) and also moves only at the beginning of the game, so Requirement 2 is simply that the Sender's strategy be optimal given the Receiver's strategy:

Signaling Requirement 2S *For each t_i in T, the Sender's message $m^*(t_i)$ must maximize the Sender's utility, given the Receiver's strategy $a^*(m_j)$. That is, $m^*(t_i)$ solves*

$$\max_{m_j \in M} U_S(t_i, m_j, a^*(m_j)).$$

Finally, given the Sender's strategy $m^*(t_i)$, let T_j denote the set of types that send the message m_j. That is, t_i is a member of the set T_j if $m^*(t_i) = m_j$. If T_j is nonempty then the information set corresponding to the message m_j is on the equilibrium path; otherwise, m_j is not sent by any type and so the corresponding information set is off the equilibrium path. For messages on the equilibrium path, applying Requirement 3 to the Receiver's beliefs yields:

Signaling Requirement 3 *For each m_j in M, if there exists t_i in T such that $m^*(t_i) = m_j$, then the Receiver's belief at the information set corresponding to m_j must follow from Bayes' rule and the Sender's strategy:*

$$\mu(t_i \mid m_j) = \frac{p(t_i)}{\displaystyle\sum_{t_i \in T_i} p(t_i)}.$$

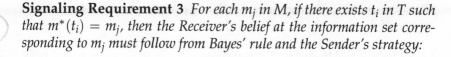

Definition *A pure-strategy **perfect Bayesian equilibrium** in a signaling game is a pair of strategies $m^*(t_i)$ and $a^*(m_j)$ and a belief $\mu(t_i \mid m_j)$ satisfying Signaling Requirements (1), (2R), (2S), and (3).*

If the Sender's strategy is pooling or separating then we call the equilibrium pooling or separating, respectively.

We conclude this section by computing the pure-strategy perfect Bayesian equilibria in the two-type example in Figure 4.2.2. Note that each type is equally likely to be drawn by nature; we use $(p, 1-p)$ and $(q, 1-q)$ to denote the Receiver's beliefs at his or her two information sets.

The four possible pure-strategy perfect Bayesian equilibria in this two-type, two-message game are: (1) pooling on L; (2) pooling on R; (3) separation with t_1 playing L and t_2 playing R; and (4) separation with t_1 playing R and t_2 playing L. We analyze these possibilities in turn.

1. Pooling on L: Suppose there is an equilibrium in which the Sender's strategy is (L, L), where (m', m'') means that type t_1 chooses m' and type t_2 chooses m''. Then the Receiver's information set corresponding to L is on the equilibrium path, so the Receiver's belief $(p, 1-p)$ at this information set is determined by Bayes' rule and the Sender's strategy: $p = .5$, the prior distribution. Given this belief (or any other belief, in fact), the Receiver's

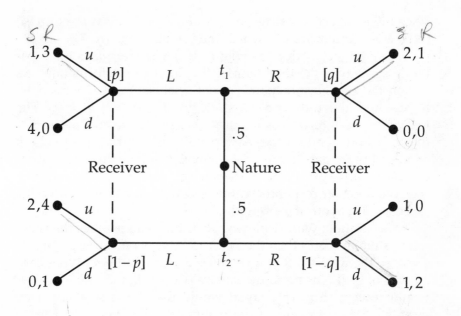

Figure 4.2.2.

best response following L is to play u, so the Sender types t_1 and t_2 earn payoffs of 1 and 2, respectively. To determine whether both Sender types are willing to choose L, we need to specify how the Receiver would react to R. If the Receiver's response to R is u, then type t_1's payoff from playing R is 2, which exceeds t_1's payoff of 1 from playing L. But if the Receiver's response to R is d then t_1 and t_2 earn payoffs of zero and 1 (respectively) from playing R, whereas they earn 1 and 2 (respectively) from playing L. Thus, if there is an equilibrium in which the Sender's strategy is (L, L) then the Receiver's response to R must be d, so the Receiver's strategy must be (u, d), where (a', a'') means that the Receiver plays a' following L and a'' following R. It remains to consider the Receiver's belief at the information set corresponding to R, and the optimality of playing d given this belief. Since playing d is optimal for the Receiver for any $q \leq 2/3$, we have that the $[(L, L), (u, d), p = .5, q]$ is a pooling perfect Bayesian equilibrium for any $q \leq 2/3$.

2. Pooling on R: Next suppose the Sender's strategy is (R, R). Then $q = .5$, so the Receiver's best response to R is d, yielding payoffs of 0 for t_1 and 1 for t_2. But t_1 can earn 1 by playing L,

since the Receiver's best response to L is u for any value of p, so there is no equilibrium in which the Sender plays (R, R).

3. *Separation, with t_1 playing L:* If the Sender plays the separating strategy (L, R) then both of the Receiver's information sets are on the equilibrium path, so both beliefs are determined by Bayes' rule and the Sender's strategy: $p = 1$ and $q = 0$. The Receiver's best responses to these beliefs are u and d, respectively, so both Sender types earn payoffs of 1. It remains to check whether the Sender's strategy is optimal given the Receiver's strategy (u, d). It is not: if type t_2 deviates by playing L rather than R, then the Receiver responds with u, earning t_2 a payoff of 2, which exceeds t_2's payoff of 1 from playing R.

4. *Separation, with t_1 playing R:* If the Sender plays the separating strategy (R, L) then the Receiver's beliefs must be $p = 0$ and $q = 1$, so the Receiver's best response is (u, u) and both types earn payoffs of 2. If t_1 were to deviate by playing L, then the Receiver would react with u; t_1's payoff would then be 1, so there is no incentive for t_1 to deviate from playing R. Likewise, if t_2 were to deviate by playing R, then the Receiver would react with u; t_2's payoff would then be 1, so there is no incentive for t_2 to deviate from playing L. Thus, $[(R, L), (u, u), p = 0, q = 1]$ is a separating perfect Bayesian equilibrium.

4.2.B Job-Market Signaling

The enormous literature on signaling games begins with Spence's (1973) model, which preceded both the widespread use of extensive-form games to describe economic problems and the definition of equilibrium concepts such as perfect Bayesian equilibrium. In this section we restate Spence's model as an extensive-form game and then describe some of its perfect Bayesian equilibria; in Section 4.4 we apply a refinement of perfect Bayesian equilibrium to this game. The timing is as follows:

1. Nature determines a worker's productive ability, η, which can be either high (H) or low (L). The probability that $\eta = H$ is q.

2. The worker learns his or her ability and then chooses a level of education, $e \geq 0$.

3. Two firms observe the worker's education (but not the worker's ability) and then simultaneously make wage offers to the worker.[4]

4. The worker accepts the higher of the two wage offers, flipping a coin in case of a tie. Let w denote the wage the worker accepts.

The payoffs are: $w - c(\eta, e)$ to the worker, where $c(\eta, e)$ is the cost to a worker with ability η of obtaining education e; $y(\eta, e) - w$ to the firm that employs the worker, where $y(\eta, e)$ is the output of a worker with ability η who has obtained education e; and zero to the firm that does not employ the worker.

We will focus (to some extent here and more so in Section 4.4) on a perfect Bayesian equilibrium in which firms interpret education as a signal of ability and so offer a higher wage to a worker with more education. The irony of Spence's (1973) paper was that wages may increase with education in this way even if education has *no* effect on productivity (i.e., even if the output of a worker with ability η is $y(\eta)$, independent of e). Spence's (1974) paper generalizes the argument to allow for the possibility that output increases not only with ability but also with education; the analogous conclusion is then that wages increase with education more than can be explained by the effect of education on productivity. We follow this more general approach.[5]

It is a well-established fact that wages are higher (on average) for workers with more years of schooling (see Mincer [1974], for example). This fact makes it tempting to interpret the variable e as years of schooling. In a separating equilibrium we might think of a low-ability worker as getting a high school education and a high-ability worker a college education. Unfortunately, interpreting e as years of schooling raises dynamic issues not addressed in the simple game in 1–4, such as the possibility that a firm will make a wage offer after a worker's freshman year in college (i.e.,

---

[4]The presence of two firms in the Receiver's role puts this game slightly outside the class of games analyzed in the previous section, but see the discussion preceding equation (4.2.1).

[5]Formally, we assume that high-ability workers are more productive (i.e., $y(H, e) > y(L, e)$ for every e), and that education does not reduce productivity (i.e., $y_e(\eta, e) \geq 0$ for every η and every e, where $y_e(\eta, e)$ is the marginal productivity of education for a worker of ability η at education e).

after a low-ability worker is supposed to have left school but before a high-ability worker is supposed to have done so). In a richer game, the worker might choose each year whether to accept the best current offer or to return to school for another year. Noldeke and van Damme (1990) analyze a richer game along these lines and show that: (i) there are many perfect Bayesian equilibria; (ii) after applying a refinement that is closely related to the refinement we will apply in Section 4.4, only one of these equilibria survives; and (iii) this surviving equilibrium is identical to the only equilibrium of the simple game in 1–4 that survives after we apply the refinement in Section 4.4. Thus, we could loosely interpret e as years of schooling in the simple game in 1–4, because the results are the same in the richer game.

Instead, we will sidestep these dynamic issues by interpreting differences in e as differences in the quality of a student's performance, *not* as differences in the duration of the student's schooling. Thus, the game in 1–4 could apply to a cohort of high school graduates (i.e., workers with exactly 12 years of education), or to a cohort of college graduates or MBAs. Under this interpretation, e measures the number and kind of courses taken and the caliber of grades and distinctions earned during an academic program of fixed length. Tuition costs (if they exist at all) are then independent of e, so the cost function $c(\eta, e)$ measures nonmonetary (or psychic) costs: students of lower ability find it more difficult to achieve high grades at a given school, and also more difficult to achieve the same grades at a more competitive school. Firms' use of education as a signal thus reflects the fact that firms hire and pay more to the best graduates of a given school and to the graduates of the best schools.

The crucial assumption in Spence's model is that low-ability workers find signaling more costly than do high-ability workers. More precisely, the marginal cost of education is higher for low- than for high-ability workers: for every e,

$$c_e(L, e) > c_e(H, e),$$

where $c_e(\eta, e)$ denotes the marginal cost of education for a worker of ability η at education e. To interpret this assumption, consider a worker with education e_1 who is paid wage w_1, as depicted in Figure 4.2.3, and calculate the increase in wages that would be necessary to compensate this worker for an increase in education

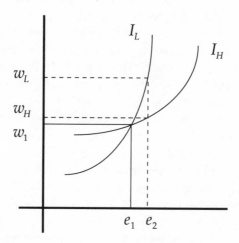

Figure 4.2.3.

from e_1 to e_2. The answer depends on the worker's ability: low-ability workers find it more difficult to acquire the extra education and so require a larger increase in wages (to w_L, rather than only to w_H) to compensate them for it. The graphical statement of this assumption is that low-ability workers have steeper indifference curves than do high-ability workers—compare I_L to I_H in the figure.

Spence also assumes that competition among firms will drive expected profits to zero. One way to build this assumption into our model would be to replace the two firms in stage (3) with a single player called the market that makes a single wage offer w and has the payoff $-[y(\eta, e) - w]^2$. (Doing so would make the model belong to the class of one-Receiver signaling games defined in the previous section.) To maximize its expected payoff, as required by Signaling Requirement 2R, the market would offer a wage equal to the expected output of a worker with education e, given the market's belief about the worker's ability after observing e:

$$w(e) = \mu(H \mid e) \cdot y(H, e) + [1 - \mu(H \mid e)] \cdot y(L, e), \qquad (4.2.1)$$

where $\mu(H \mid e)$ is the market's assessment of the probability that the worker's ability is H. The purpose of having two firms bidding against each other in stage (3) is to achieve the same result without resorting to a fictitious player called the market. To guarantee that the firms will always offer a wage equal to the worker's expected output, however, we need to impose another assumption: after observing education choice e, both firms hold the same belief about the worker's ability, again denoted by $\mu(H \mid e)$. Since Signaling Requirement 3 determines the belief that both firms must hold after observing a choice of e that is on the equilibrium path, our assumption really is that the firms also share a common belief after observing a choice of e that is off the equilibrium path. Given this assumption, it follows that in any perfect Bayesian equilibrium the firms both offer the wage $w(e)$ given in (4.2.1)—just as in the Bertrand model in Section 1.2.B the firms both offer a price equal to the marginal cost of output. Thus, (4.2.1) replaces Signaling Requirement 2R for this section's two-Receiver model.

To prepare for the analysis of the perfect Bayesian equilibria of this signaling game, we first consider the complete-information analog of the game. That is, we temporarily assume that the. worker's ability is common knowledge among all the players, rather than privately known by the worker. In this case, competition between the two firms in stage (3) implies that a worker of ability η with education e earns the wage $w(e) = y(\eta, e)$. A worker with ability η therefore chooses e to solve

$$\max_e \; y(\eta, e) - c(\eta, e).$$

Denote the solution by $e^*(\eta)$, as shown in Figure 4.2.4, and let $w^*(\eta) = y[\eta, e^*(\eta)]$.

We now return (permanently) to the assumption that the worker's ability is private information. This opens the possibility that a low-ability worker could try to masquerade as a high-ability worker. Two cases can arise. Figure 4.2.5 depicts the case in which it is too expensive for a low-ability worker to acquire education $e^*(H)$, even if doing so would trick the firms into believing that the worker has high ability and so cause them to pay the wage $w^*(H)$. That is, in Figure 4.2.5, $w^*(L) - c[L, e^*(L)] > w^*(H) - c[L, e^*(H)]$.

Figure 4.2.6 depicts the opposite case, in which the low-ability worker could be said to envy the high-ability worker's complete-information wage and education level—that is, $w^*(L) - c[L, e^*(L)] < w^*(H) - c[L, e^*(H)]$. The latter case is both more realistic and (as we will see) more interesting. In a model with more than two

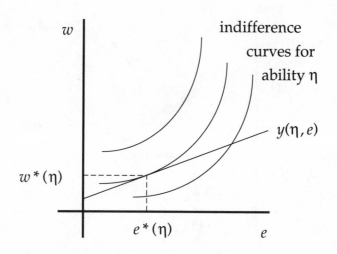

Figure 4.2.4.

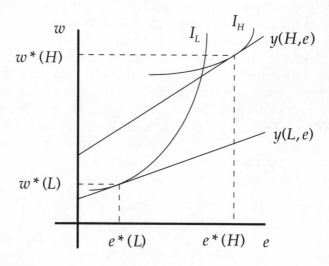

Figure 4.2.5.

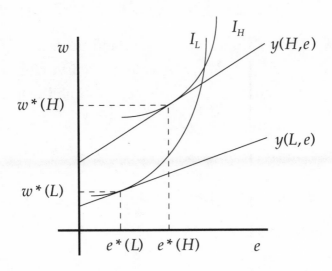

Figure 4.2.6.

values of the worker's ability, the former case arises only if each possible value of ability is sufficiently different from the adjacent possible values. If ability is a continuous variable, for example, then the latter case applies.

As described in the previous section, three kinds of perfect Bayesian equilibria can exist in this model: pooling, separating, and hybrid. Each kind of equilibrium typically exists in profusion; we restrict attention to a few examples. In a pooling equilibrium both worker-types choose a single level of education, say e_p. Signaling Requirement 3 then implies that the firms' belief after observing e_p must be the prior belief, $\mu(H \mid e_p) = q$, which in turn implies that the wage offered after observing e_p must be

$$w_p = q \cdot y(H, e_p) + (1 - q) \cdot y(L, e_p). \qquad (4.2.2)$$

To complete the description of a pooling perfect Bayesian equilibrium, it remains (i) to specify the firms' belief $\mu(H \mid e)$ for out-of-equilibrium education choices $e \neq e_p$, which then determines the rest of the firms' strategy $w(e)$ through (4.2.1), and (ii) to show that both worker-types' best response to the firms' strategy $w(e)$ is to choose $e = e_p$. These two steps represent Signaling Requirements 1 and 2S, respectively; as noted earlier, (4.2.1) replaces Signaling Requirement 2R in this two-Receiver model.

One possibility is that the firms believe that any education level other than e_p implies that the worker has low ability: $\mu(H \mid e) = 0$ for all $e \neq e_p$. Although this belief may seem strange, nothing in the definition of perfect Bayesian equilibrium rules it out, because Requirements 1 through 3 put no restrictions on beliefs off the equilibrium path and Requirement 4 is vacuous in a signaling game. The refinement we apply in Section 4.4 does restrict the Receiver's belief off the equilibrium path in a signaling game; indeed, it rules out the belief analyzed here. In this analysis of pooling equilibria we focus on this belief for expositional simplicity, but also briefly consider alternative beliefs.

If the firms' belief is

$$\mu(H \mid e) = \begin{cases} 0 & \text{for } e \neq e_p \\ q & \text{for } e = e_p \end{cases} \qquad (4.2.3)$$

then (4.2.1) implies that the firms' strategy is

$$w(e) = \begin{cases} y(L, e) & \text{for } e \neq e_p \\ w_p & \text{for } e = e_p. \end{cases} \qquad (4.2.4)$$

A worker of ability η therefore chooses e to solve

$$\max_e \ w(e) - c(\eta, e). \qquad (4.2.5)$$

The solution to (4.2.5) is simple: a worker of ability η chooses either e_p or the level of education that maximizes $y(L, e) - c(\eta, e)$. (The latter is precisely $e^*(L)$ for the low-ability worker.) In the example depicted in Figure 4.2.7, the former is optimal for both worker types: the low-ability worker's indifference curve through the point $[e^*(L), w^*(L)]$ lies below that type's indifference curve through (e_p, w_p), and the high-ability worker's indifference curve through the point (e_p, w_p) lies above the wage function $w = y(L, e)$.

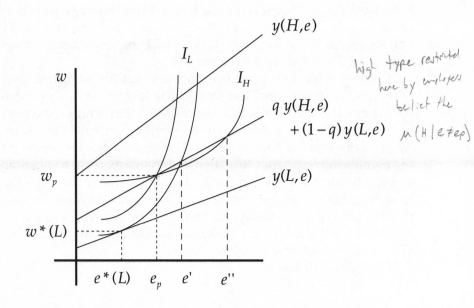

Figure 4.2.7.

In summary, given the indifference curves, production functions, and value of e_p in Figure 4.2.7, the strategy $[e(L) = e_p, e(H) = e_p]$ for the worker and the belief $\mu(H \mid e)$ in (4.2.3) and the strategy $w(e)$ in (4.2.4) for the firms are a pooling perfect Bayesian equilibrium.

Many other pooling perfect Bayesian equilibria exist in the example defined by the indifference curves and production functions in Figure 4.2.7. Some of these equilibria involve a different education choice by the worker (i.e., a value of e_p other than the one in the figure); others involve the same education choice but differ off the equilibrium path. As an example of the former, let $\hat{e}$ denote a level of education between e_p and e', where e' in Figure 4.2.7 is the level of education at which the low-ability worker's indifference curve through $(e^*(L), w^*(L))$ crosses the wage function $w = q \cdot y(H, e) + (1 - q) \cdot y(L, e)$. If we substitute $\hat{e}$ for e_p in (4.2.3) and (4.2.4) then the resulting belief and strategy for the firms together with the strategy $[e(L) = \hat{e}, e(H) = \hat{e}]$ for the worker are another pooling perfect Bayesian equilibrium. As an example of the latter, suppose the firms' belief is as in (4.2.3) except that any level of education above e'' is taken to mean that the worker is a random draw from the ability distribution:

$$\mu(H \mid e) = \begin{cases} 0 & \text{for } e \le e'' \text{ except for } e = e_p \\ q & \text{for } e = e_p \\ q & \text{for } e > e'', \end{cases}$$

where e'' in Figure 4.2.7 is the level of education at which the high-ability worker's indifference curve through the point (e_p, w_p) crosses the wage function $w = q \cdot y(H, e) + (1 - q) \cdot y(L, e)$. The firms' strategy is then

$$w(e) = \begin{cases} y(L, e) & \text{for } e \le e'' \text{ except for } e = e_p \\ w_p & \text{for } e = e_p \\ w_p & \text{for } e > e''. \end{cases}$$

This belief and strategy for the firms and the strategy $(e(L) = e_p, e(H) = e_p)$ for the worker are a third pooling perfect Bayesian equilibrium.

We now turn to separating equilibria. In Figure 4.2.5 (the no-envy case), the natural separating perfect Bayesian equilibrium involves the strategy $[e(L) = e^*(L), e(H) = e^*(H)]$ for the worker. Signaling Requirement 3 then determines the firms' belief after observing either of these two education levels (namely, $\mu[H \mid e^*(L)] = 0$ and $\mu[H \mid e^*(H)] = 1$), so (4.2.1) implies that $w[e^*(L)] = w^*(L)$ and $w[e^*(H)] = w^*(H)$. As in the discussion of pooling equilibria, to complete the description of this separating perfect Bayesian equilibrium it remains: (i) to specify the firms' belief $\mu(H \mid e)$ for out-of-equilibrium education choices (i.e., values of e other than $e^*(L)$ or $e^*(H)$), which then determines the rest of the firms' strategy $w(e)$ from (4.2.1); and (ii) to show that the best response for a worker of ability η to the firms' strategy $w(e)$ is to choose $e = e^*(\eta)$.

One belief that fulfills these conditions is that the worker has high ability if e is at least $e^*(H)$ but has low ability otherwise:

$$\mu(H \mid e) = \begin{cases} 0 & \text{for } e < e^*(H) \\ 1 & \text{for } e \ge e^*(H). \end{cases} \tag{4.2.6}$$

The firms' strategy is then

$$w(e) = \begin{cases} y(L,e) & \text{for } e < e^*(H) \\ y(H,e) & \text{for } e \geq e^*(H). \end{cases} \qquad (4.2.7)$$

Since $e^*(H)$ is the high-ability worker's best response to the wage function $w = y(H,e)$, it is also the best response here. As for the low-ability worker, $e^*(L)$ is that worker's best response when the wage function is $w = y(L,e)$, so $w^*(L) - c[L, e^*(L)]$ is the highest payoff that worker can achieve here among all choices of $e < e^*(H)$. Since the low-ability worker's indifference curves are steeper than those of the high-ability worker, $w^*(H) - c[L, e^*(H)]$ is the highest payoff the low-ability worker can achieve here among all choices of $e \geq e^*(H)$. Thus, $e^*(L)$ is the low-ability worker's best response because $w^*(L) - c[L, e^*(L)] > w^*(H) - c[L, e^*(H)]$ in the no-envy case.

We hereafter ignore the no-envy case. As suggested previously, Figure 4.2.6 (the envy case) is more interesting. Now the high-ability worker cannot earn the high wage $w(e) = y(H,e)$ simply by choosing the education $e^*(H)$ that he or she would choose under complete information. Instead, to signal his or her ability the high-ability worker must choose $e_s > e^*(H)$, as shown in Figure 4.2.8, because the low-ability worker will mimic any value of e between $e^*(H)$ and e_s if doing so tricks the firms into believing that the worker has high ability. Formally, the natural separating perfect Bayesian equilibrium now involves the strategy $[e(L) = e^*(L), e(H) = e_s]$ for the worker and the equilibrium beliefs $\mu[H \mid e^*(L)] = 0$ and $\mu[H \mid e_s] = 1$ and equilibrium wages $w[e^*(L)] = w^*(L)$ and $w(e_s) = y(H, e_s)$ for the firms. This is the only equilibrium behavior that survives the refinement we will apply in Section 4.4.

One specification of the firms' out-of-equilibrium beliefs that supports this equilibrium behavior is that the worker has high ability if $e \geq e_s$ but has low ability otherwise:

$$\mu(H \mid e) = \begin{cases} 0 & \text{for } e < e_s \\ 1 & \text{for } e \geq e_s. \end{cases}$$

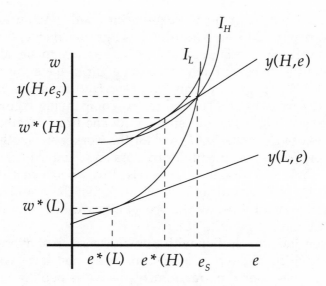

Figure 4.2.8.

The firms' strategy is then

$$w(e) = \begin{cases} y(L,e) & \text{for } e < e_s \\ y(H,e) & \text{for } e \geq e_s. \end{cases}$$

Given this wage function, the low-ability worker has two best responses: choosing $e^*(L)$ and earning $w^*(L)$, and choosing e_s and earning $y(H, e_s)$. We will assume that this indifference is resolved in favor of $e^*(L)$; alternatively, we could increase e_s by an arbitrarily small amount so that the low-ability worker would strictly prefer $e^*(L)$. As for the high-ability worker, since $e_s > e^*(H)$, choices of $e > e_s$ are inferior to e_s. Since the low-ability worker's indifference curves are steeper than the high-ability worker's, the latter's indifference curve through the point $(e_s, y(H, e_s))$ lies above the wage function $w = y(L, e)$ for $e < e_s$, so choices of $e < e_s$ are also inferior. Thus, the high-ability worker's best response to the firms' strategy $w(e)$ is e_s.

As with pooling equilibria, there are other separating equilibria that involve a different education choice by the high-ability worker (the low-ability worker always separates at $e^*(L)$; see below), and still other separating equilibria that involve the education choices

$e^*(L)$ and e_s but differ off the equilibrium path. As an example of the former, let $\hat{e}$ be an education level greater than e_s but sufficiently small that the high-ability worker prefers to signal his or her ability by choosing $\hat{e}$ than to be thought to have low ability: $y(H, \hat{e}) - c(H, \hat{e})$ is greater than $y(L, e) - c(H, e)$ for every e. If we substitute $\hat{e}$ for e_s in $\mu(H \mid e)$ and $w(e)$ accompanying Figure 4.2.8, then the resulting belief and strategy for the firms together with the strategy $[e(L) = e^*(L), e(H) = \hat{e}]$ for the worker are another separating perfect Bayesian equilibrium. As an example of the latter, let the firms' belief for education levels strictly between $e^*(H)$ and e_s be strictly positive but sufficiently small that the resulting strategy $w(e)$ lies strictly below the low-ability worker's indifference curve through the point $(e^*(L), w^*(L))$.

We conclude this section with a brief discussion of hybrid equilibria, in which one type chooses one education level with certainty but the other type randomizes between pooling with the first type (by choosing the first type's education level) and separating from the first type (by choosing a different education level). We analyze the case in which the low-ability worker randomizes; Problem 4.7 treats the complementary case. Suppose the high-ability worker chooses the education level e_h (where the subscript "h" connotes hybrid), but the low-ability worker randomizes between choosing e_h (with probability π) and choosing e_L (with probability $1 - \pi$). Signaling Requirement 3 (suitably extended to allow for mixed strategies) then determines the firms' belief after observing e_h or e_L: Bayes' rule yields[6]

$$\mu(H \mid e_h) = \frac{q}{q + (1 - q)\pi} , \qquad (4.2.8)$$

and the usual inference after separation yields $\mu(H \mid e_L) = 0$. Three observations may help interpret (4.2.8): first, since the high-ability worker always chooses e_h but the low-ability worker does so only with probability π, observing e_h makes it more likely that the worker has high ability so $\mu(H \mid e_h) > q$; second, as π approaches zero the low-ability worker almost never pools with the high-ability worker so $\mu(H \mid e_h)$ approaches one; third, as π approaches one the low-ability worker almost always pools with the high-ability worker so $\mu(H \mid e_h)$ approaches the prior belief q.

---

[6]Recall from footnote 2 in Chapter 3 that Bayes' rule states that $P(A \mid B) = P(A, B)/P(B)$. To derive (4.2.8), restate Bayes' rule as $P(A, B) = P(B \mid A) \cdot P(A)$ so that $P(A \mid B) = P(B \mid A) \cdot P(A)/P(B)$.

When the low-ability worker separates from the high-ability worker by choosing e_L, the belief $\mu(H \mid e_L) = 0$ implies the wage $w(e_L) = y(L, e_L)$. It follows that e_L must equal $e^*(L)$: the only education choice at which the low-ability worker can be induced to separate (whether probabilistically as here, or with certainty as in the separating equilibria discussed earlier) is that worker's complete-information education choice, $e^*(L)$. To see why this is so, suppose the low-ability worker separates by choosing some $e_L \neq e^*(L)$. Such separation yields the payoff $y(L, e_L) - c(L, e_L)$, but choosing $e^*(L)$ would yield a payoff of at least $y[L, e^*(L)] - c[L, e^*(L)]$ (or more if the firms' belief $\mu[H \mid e^*(L)]$ is greater than zero), and the definition of $e^*(L)$ implies that $y[L, e^*(L)] - c[L, e^*(L)] > y(L, e) - c(L, e)$ for every $e \neq e^*(L)$. Thus, there is no education choice $e_L \neq e^*(L)$ such that the low-ability worker can be induced to separate by choosing e_L.

For the low-ability worker to be willing to randomize between separating at $e^*(L)$ and pooling at e_h, the wage $w(e_h) = w_h$ must make that worker indifferent between the two:

$$w^*(L) - c[L, e^*(L)] = w_h - c(L, e_h). \qquad (4.2.9)$$

For w_h to be an equilibrium wage for the firms to pay, however, (4.2.1) and (4.2.8) imply

$$w_h = \frac{q}{q + (1-q)\pi} \cdot y(H, e_h) + \frac{(1-q)\pi}{q + (1-q)\pi} \cdot y(L, e_h). \qquad (4.2.10)$$

For a given value of e_h, if (4.2.9) yields $w_h < y(H, e_h)$, then (4.2.10) determines the unique value of π consistent with a hybrid equilibrium in which the low-ability worker randomizes between $e^*(L)$ and e_h, while if $w_h > y(H, e_h)$, then there does not exist a hybrid equilibrium involving e_h.

Figure 4.2.9 implicitly illustrates the value of π consistent with the indicated value of e_h. Given e_h, the wage w_h solves (4.2.9), so the point (e_h, w_h) is on the low-ability worker's indifference curve through the point $[e^*(L), w^*(L)]$. Given $w_h < y(H, e_h)$, the probability r solves $r \cdot y(H, e_h) + (1-r) \cdot y(L, e_h) = w_h$. This probability is the firms' equilibrium belief $\mu(H \mid e_h)$, so (4.2.8) implies $\pi = q(1-r)/r(1-q)$. The figure also illustrates that the constraint $w_h < y(H, e_h)$ is equivalent to $e_h < e_s$, where e_s is the education chosen by the high-ability worker in the separating equilibrium in Figure 4.2.8. Indeed, as e_h approaches e_s, r approaches one, so

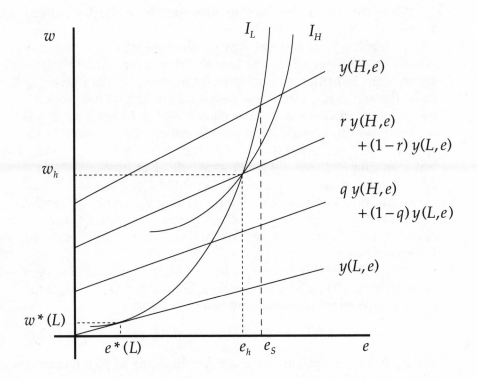

Figure 4.2.9.

π approaches zero. Thus, the separating equilibrium described in Figure 4.2.8 is the limit of the hybrid equilibria considered here.

To complete the description of the hybrid perfect Bayesian equilibrium in Figure 4.2.9, let the firms' belief be that the worker has low ability if $e < e_h$ but otherwise has high ability with probability r and low ability with probability $1 - r$:

$$\mu(H \mid e) = \begin{cases} 0 & \text{for } e < e_h \\ r & \text{for } e \geq e_h. \end{cases}$$

The firms' strategy is then

$$w(e) = \begin{cases} y(L, e) & \text{for } e < e_h \\ r \cdot y(H, e) + (1 - r) \cdot y(L, e) & \text{for } e \geq e_h. \end{cases}$$

It remains only to check that the worker's strategy $(e(L) = e_h$ with probability π, $e(L) = e^*(L)$ with probability $1 - \pi$; $e(H) = e_h)$ is a best response to the firms' strategy. For the low-ability worker, the optimal $e < e_h$ is $e^*(L)$ and the optimal $e \geq e_h$ is e_h. For the high-ability worker, e_h is superior to all alternatives.

4.2.C Corporate Investment and Capital Structure

Consider an entrepreneur who has started a company but needs outside financing to undertake an attractive new project. The entrepreneur has private information about the profitability of the existing company, but the payoff of the new project cannot be disentangled from the payoff of the existing company—all that can be observed is the aggregate profit of the firm. (We could allow the entrepreneur to have private information about the profitability of the new project, too, but this would be an unnecessary complication.) Suppose the entrepreneur offers a potential investor an equity stake in the firm in exchange for the necessary financing. Under what circumstances will the new project be undertaken, and what will the equity stake be?

To translate this problem into a signaling game, suppose that the profit of the existing company can be either high or low: $\pi = L$ or H, where $H > L > 0$. To capture the idea that the new project is attractive, suppose that the required investment is I, the payoff will be R, the potential investor's alternative rate of return is r, and $R > I(1 + r)$. The timing and payoffs of the game are then as follows:

1. Nature determines the profit of the existing company. The probability that $\pi = L$ is p.

2. The entrepreneur learns π and then offers the potential investor an equity stake s, where $0 \leq s \leq 1$.

3. The investor observes s (but not π) and then decides either to accept or to reject the offer.

4. If the investor rejects the offer then the investor's payoff is $I(1 + r)$ and the entrepreneur's payoff is π. If the investor

accepts s then the investor's payoff is $s(\pi + R)$ and the entrepreneur's is $(1 - s)(\pi + R)$.

Myers and Majluf (1984) analyze a model in this spirit, although they consider a large firm (with shareholders and a manager) rather than an entrepreneur (who is both the manager and the sole shareholder). They discuss different assumptions about how the shareholders' interests might affect the manager's utility; Dybvig and Zender (1991) derive the optimal contract for the shareholders to offer the manager.

This is a very simple signaling game, in two respects: the Receiver's set of feasible actions is extremely limited, and the Sender's set of feasible signals is larger but still rather ineffective (as we will see). Suppose that after receiving the offer s the investor believes that the probability that $\pi = L$ is q. Then the investor will accept s if and only if

$$s[qL + (1 - q)H + R] \geq I(1 + r). \tag{4.2.11}$$

As for the entrepreneur, suppose the profit of the existing company is π, and consider whether the entrepreneur prefers to receive the financing at the cost of an equity stake of s or to forego the project. The former is superior if and only if

$$s \leq \frac{R}{\pi + R} . \tag{4.2.12}$$

In a pooling perfect Bayesian equilibrium, the investor's belief must be $q = p$ after receiving the equilibrium offer. Since the participation constraint (4.2.12) is more difficult to satisfy for $\pi = H$ than for $\pi = L$, combining (4.2.11) and (4.2.12) implies that a pooling equilibrium exists only if

$$\frac{I(1 + r)}{pL + (1 - p)H + R} \leq \frac{R}{H + R} . \tag{4.2.13}$$

If p is close enough to zero, (4.2.13) holds because $R > I(1 + r)$. If p is close enough to one, however, then (4.2.13) holds only if

$$R - I(1 + r) \geq \frac{I(1 + r)H}{R} - L. \tag{4.2.14}$$

Intuitively, the difficulty with a pooling equilibrium is that the high-profit type must subsidize the low-profit type: setting $q = p$ in (4.2.11) yields $s \geq I(1 + r)/[pL + (1 - p)H + R]$, whereas if the investor were certain that $\pi = H$ (i.e., $q = 0$) then he or she would accept the smaller equity stake $s \geq I(1 + r)/(H + R)$. The larger equity stake required in a pooling equilibrium is very expensive for the high-profit firm—perhaps so expensive as to make the high-profit firm prefer to forego the new project. Our analysis shows that a pooling equilibrium exists if p is close to zero, so that the cost of subsidization is small, or if (4.2.14) holds, so that the profit from the new project outweighs the cost of subsidization.

If (4.2.13) fails then a pooling equilibrium does not exist. A separating equilibrium always exists, however. The low-profit type offers $s = I(1+r)/(L+R)$, which the investor accepts, and the high-profit type offers $s < I(1 + r)/(H + R)$, which the investor rejects. In such an equilibrium, investment is inefficiently low: the new project is certain to be profitable, but the high-profit type foregoes the investment. This equilibrium illustrates the sense in which the Sender's set of feasible signals is ineffective: there is no way for the high-profit type to distinguish itself; financing terms that are attractive to the high-profit type are even more attractive to the low-profit type. As Myers and Majluf observe, the forces in this model push firms toward either debt or internal sources of funds.

We conclude by briefly considering the possibility that the entrepreneur can offer debt as well as equity. Suppose the investor accepts the debt contract D. If the entrepreneur does not declare bankruptcy then the investor's payoff is D and the entrepreneur's is $\pi + R - D$; if the entrepreneur does declare bankruptcy then the investor's payoff is $\pi + R$ and the entrepreneur's is zero. Since $L > 0$, there is always a pooling equilibrium: both profit-types offer the debt contract $D = I(1 + r)$, which the investor accepts. If L were sufficiently negative that $R + L < I(1 + r)$, however, then the low-profit type could not repay this debt so the investor would not accept the contract. A similar argument would apply if L and H represented expected (rather than certain) profits. Suppose the type π means that the existing company's profit will be $\pi + K$ with probability $1/2$ and $\pi - K$ with probability $1/2$. Now if $L - K + R < I(1+r)$ then there is probability $1/2$ that the low-profit type will not be able to repay the debt $D = I(1 + r)$ so the investor will not accept the contract.

4.2.D   Monetary Policy

In this section we add private information to a two-period version
of the repeated monetary-policy game analyzed in Section 2.3.E.
As in Spence's model, there are many pooling, hybrid, and separating perfect Bayesian equilibria. Since we discussed such equilibria in detail in Section 4.2.B, we only sketch the main issues
here. See Vickers (1986) for the details of a similar two-period
analysis, and Barro (1986) for a multiperiod reputation model.

Recall from Section 2.3.E that the monetary authority's one-
period payoff is

$$W(\pi, \pi^e) = -c\pi^2 - [(b-1)y^* + d(\pi - \pi^e)]^2,$$

where π is actual inflation, π^e is employers' expectation of inflation, and y^* is the efficient level of output. For employers, the
one-period payoff is $-(\pi - \pi^e)^2$. In our two-period model, each
player's payoff is simply the sum of the player's one-period pay-
offs, $W(\pi_1, \pi_1^e) + W(\pi_2, \pi_2^e)$ and $-(\pi_1 - \pi_1^e)^2 - (\pi_2 - \pi_2^e)^2$, where π_t
is actual inflation in period t and π_t^e is employers' expectation (at
the beginning of period t) of inflation in period t.

The parameter c in the payoff function $W(\pi, \pi^e)$ reflects the
monetary authority's trade-off between the goals of zero inflation
and efficient output. In Section 2.3.E this parameter was common
knowledge. We now assume instead that this parameter is privately known by the monetary authority: $c = S$ or W (for "strong"
and "weak" at fighting inflation), where $S > W > 0$. The timing
of the two-period model is therefore as follows:

1. Nature draws the monetary authority's type, c. The probability that $c = W$ is p.

2. Employers form π_1^e, their expectation of first-period inflation.

3. The monetary authority observes π_1^e and then chooses actual
   first-period inflation, π_1.

4. Employers observe π_1 (but not c) and then form π_2^e, their
   expectation of second-period inflation.

5. The monetary authority observes π_2^e and then chooses actual
   second-period inflation, π_2.

As noted in Section 4.2.A, there is a one-period signaling game embedded in this two-period monetary-policy game. The Sender's message is the monetary authority's first-period choice of inflation, π_1, and the Receiver's action is employers' second-period expectation of inflation, π_2^e. Employers' first-period expectation of inflation and the monetary authority's second-period choice of inflation precede and follow the signaling game, respectively.

Recall that in the one-period problem (i.e., in the stage game of the repeated game analyzed in Section 2.3.E) the monetary authority's optimal choice of π given employers' expectation π^e is

$$\pi^*(\pi^e) = \frac{d}{c + d^2}[(1 - b)y^* + d\pi^e].$$

The same argument implies that if the monetary authority's type is c then its optimal choice of π_2 given the expectation π_2^e is

$$\frac{d}{c + d^2}[(1 - b)y^* + d\pi_2^e] \equiv \pi_2^*(\pi_2^e, c).$$

Anticipating this, if employers begin the second period believing that the probability that $c = W$ is q, then they will form the expectation $\pi_2^e(q)$ that maximizes

$$- q[\pi_2^*(\pi_2^e, W) - \pi_2^e]^2 - (1 - q)[\pi_2^*(\pi_2^e, S) - \pi_2^e]^2. \qquad (4.2.15)$$

In a pooling equilibrium, both types choose the same first-period inflation, say π^*, so employers' first-period expectation is $\pi_1^e = \pi^*$. On the equilibrium path, employers begin the second period believing that the probability that $c = W$ is p and so form the expectation $\pi_2^e(p)$. Then the monetary authority of type c chooses its optimal second-period inflation given this expectation, namely $\pi_2^*[\pi_2^e(p), c]$, thus ending the game. To complete the description of such an equilibrium, it remains (as usual) to define the Receiver's out-of-equilibrium beliefs, to compute the associated out-of-equilibrium actions using (4.2.15), and to check that these out-of-equilibrium actions do not create an incentive for any Sender-type to deviate from the equilibrium.

In a separating equilibrium, the two types choose different first-period inflation levels, say π_W and π_S, so employers' first-period expectation is $\pi_1^e = p\pi_W + (1 - p)\pi_S$. After observing π_W, employers begin the second period believing that $c = W$ and so form the expectation $\pi_2^e(1)$; likewise, observing π_S leads to $\pi_2^e(0)$. In equilibrium, the weak type then chooses $\pi_2^*[\pi_2^e(1), W]$ and the strong type $\pi_2^*[\pi_2^e(0), S]$, ending the game. To complete the description of such an equilibrium it remains not only to specify the Receiver's out-of-equilibrium beliefs and actions and to check that no Sender-type has an incentive to deviate, as above, but also to check that neither type has an incentive to mimic the other's equilibrium behavior. Here, for example, the weak type might be tempted to choose π_S in the first period, thereby inducing $\pi_2^e(0)$ as the employers' second-period expectation, but then choose $\pi_2^*[\pi_2^e(0), W]$ to end the game. That is, even if π_S is uncomfortably low for the weak type, the ensuing expectation $\pi_2^e(0)$ might be so low that the weak type receives a huge payoff from the unanticipated inflation $\pi_2^*[\pi_2^e(0), W] - \pi_2^e(0)$ in the second period. In a separating equilibrium, the strong type's first-period inflation must be low enough that the weak type is not tempted to mimic the strong type, in spite of the subsequent benefit from unanticipated second-period inflation. For many parameter values, this constraint causes π_S to be lower than the inflation level the strong type would choose under complete information, just as the high-ability worker overinvests in education in a separating equilibrium in Spence's model.

4.3   Other Applications of Perfect Bayesian Equilibrium

4.3.A   Cheap-Talk Games

Cheap-talk games are analogous to signaling games, but in cheap-talk games the Sender's messages are just talk—costless, non-binding, nonverifiable claims. Such talk cannot be informative in Spence's signaling game: a worker who simply announced "My ability is high" would not be believed. In other contexts, however, cheap talk can be informative. As a simple example, consider the likely interpretation of the phrase "Hey, look out for that bus!" In applications of greater economic interest, Stein (1989) shows that policy announcements by the Federal Reserve can be informative but cannot be too precise, and Matthews (1989) studies how a veto threat by the president can influence which bill gets through Congress. In addition to analyzing the effect of cheap talk in a fixed environment, one also can ask how to design environments to take advantage of cheap talk. In this vein, Austen-Smith (1990) shows that in some settings debate among self-interested legislators improves the social value of the eventual legislation, and Farrell and Gibbons (1991) show that in some settings unionization improves social welfare (in spite of the employment distortion described in Section 2.1.C) because it facilitates communication from the work force to management.

Cheap talk cannot be informative in Spence's model because all the Sender's types have the same preferences over the Receiver's possible actions: all workers prefer higher wages, independent of ability. To see why such uniformity of preferences across Sender-types vitiates cheap talk (both in Spence's model and more generally), suppose there were a pure-strategy equilibrium in which one subset of Sender-types, T_1, sends one message, m_1, while another subset of types, T_2, sends another message, m_2. (Each T_i could contain only one type, as in a separating equilibrium, or many types, as in a partially pooling equilibrium.) In equilibrium, the Receiver will interpret m_i as coming from T_i and so will take the optimal action given this belief; denote this action by a_i. Since all Sender-types have the same preferences over actions, if one type prefers (say) a_1 to a_2, then all types have this preference and will send m_1 rather than m_2, thereby destroying the putative equilibrium. In Spence's model, for example, if one cheap-talk message led to a high wage but another cheap-talk message led to a low wage, then workers of all ability levels would send the former message, so there cannot exist an equilibrium in which cheap talk affects wages.

Thus, for cheap talk to be informative, one necessary condition is that different Sender-types have different preferences over the Receiver's actions. A second necessary condition, of course, is that the Receiver prefer different actions depending on the Sender's type. (Both signaling and cheap talk are useless if the Receiver's preferences over actions are independent of the Sender's type.) A third necessary condition for cheap talk to be informative is that the Receiver's preferences over actions not be completely opposed to the Sender's. To anticipate a later example, suppose that the Receiver prefers low actions when the Sender's type is low and high actions when the Sender's type is high. If low Sender-types prefer low actions and high types high actions, then communication can occur, but if the Sender has the opposite preference then communication cannot occur because the Sender would like to mislead the Receiver. Crawford and Sobel (1982) analyze an abstract model that satisfies these three necessary conditions. They establish two intuitive results: loosely put, more communication can occur through cheap talk when the players' preferences are more closely aligned, but perfect communication cannot occur unless the players' preferences are perfectly aligned.

Each of the economic applications just described—cheap talk by the Fed, veto threats, information transmission in debate, and union voice—involves not only a simple cheap-talk game but also a more complicated model of an economic environment. Analyzing one of these applications would require us to describe not only the former game but also the latter model, which would divert attention from the basic forces at work in all cheap-talk games. In this section, therefore, we depart from the style of the rest of the book and analyze only abstract cheap-talk games, leaving the applications as further reading.

The timing of the simplest cheap-talk game is identical to the timing of the simplest signaling game; only the payoffs differ.

1. Nature draws a type t_i for the Sender from a set of feasible types $T = \{t_1, \ldots, t_I\}$ according to a probability distribution $p(t_i)$, where $p(t_i) > 0$ for every i and $p(t_1) + \cdots + p(t_I) = 1$.

2. The Sender observes t_i and then chooses a message m_j from a set of feasible messages $M = \{m_1, \ldots, m_J\}$.

3. The Receiver observes m_j (but not t_i) and then chooses an action a_k from a set of feasible actions $A = \{a_1, \ldots, a_K\}$.

4. Payoffs are given by $U_S(t_i, a_k)$ and $U_R(t_i, a_k)$.

The key feature of such a cheap-talk game is that the message has no *direct* effect on either the Sender's or the Receiver's payoff. The only way the message can matter is through its information content: by changing the Receiver's belief about the Sender's type, a message can change the Receiver's action, and thus indirectly affect both players' payoffs. Since the same information can be communicated in different languages, different message spaces can achieve the same results. The spirit of cheap talk is that anything can be said, but formalizing this would require M to be a very large set. Instead, we assume that M is (just) rich enough to say what needs to be said; that is, $M = T$. For the purposes of this section, this assumption is equivalent to allowing anything to be said; for the purposes of Section 4.4 (refinements of perfect Bayesian equilibrium), however, the assumption must be reconsidered.

Because the simplest cheap-talk and signaling games have the same timing, the definitions of perfect Bayesian equilibrium in the two games are identical as well: a pure-strategy perfect Bayesian equilibrium in a cheap-talk game is a pair of strategies $m^*(t_i)$ and $a^*(m_j)$ and a belief $\mu(t_i \mid m_j)$ satisfying Signaling Requirements (1), (2R), (2S), and (3), although the payoff functions $U_R(t_i, m_j, a_k)$ and $U_S(t_i, m_j, a_k)$ in Signaling Requirements (2R) and (2S) are now equivalent to $U_R(t_i, a_k)$ and $U_S(t_i, a_k)$, respectively. One difference between signaling and cheap-talk games, however, is that in the latter a pooling equilibrium always exists. Because messages have no direct effect on the Sender's payoff, if the Receiver will ignore all messages then pooling is a best response for the Sender; because messages have no direct effect on the Receiver's payoff, if the Sender is pooling then a best response for the Receiver is to ignore all messages. Formally, let a^* denote the Receiver's optimal action in a pooling equilibrium; that is, a^* solves

$$\max_{a_k \in A} \sum_{t_i \in T_i} p(t_i) U_R(t_i, a_k).$$

It is a pooling perfect Bayesian equilibrium for the Sender to play any pooling strategy, for the Receiver to maintain the prior belief $p(t_i)$ after all messages (on and off the equilibrium path), and for the Receiver to take the action a^* after all messages. The interesting question in a cheap-talk game therefore is whether nonpooling equilibria exist. The two abstract cheap-talk games discussed next illustrate separating and partially pooling equilibria, respectively.

We begin with a two-type, two-action example: $T = \{t_L, t_H\}$, $\text{Prob}(t_L) = p$, and $A = \{a_L, a_H\}$. We could use a two-type, two-message, two-action signaling game analogous to Figure 4.2.1 to describe the payoffs in this cheap-talk game, but the payoffs from the type-action pair (t_i, a_k) are independent of which message was chosen, so we instead describe the payoffs using Figure 4.3.1. The first payoff in each cell is the Sender's and the second the Receiver's, but this figure is *not* a normal-form game; rather, it simply lists the players' payoffs from each type-action pair. As in our earlier discussion of necessary conditions for cheap talk to be

	t_L	t_H
a_L	$x,1$	$y,0$
a_H	$z,0$	$w,1$

Figure 4.3.1.

informative, we have chosen the Receiver's payoffs so that the Receiver prefers the low action (a_L) when the Sender's type is low (t_L) and the high action when the type is high. To illustrate the first necessary condition, suppose both Sender-types have the same preferences over actions: $x > z$ and $y > w$, for example, so that both types prefer a_L to a_H. Then both types would like the Receiver to believe that $t = t_L$, so the Receiver cannot believe such a claim. To illustrate the third necessary condition, suppose the players' preferences are completely opposed: $z > x$ and $y > w$, so that the low Sender-type prefers the high action and the high type the low action. Then t_L would like the Receiver to believe that $t = t_H$ and t_H would like the Receiver to believe that $t = t_L$, so the Receiver cannot believe either of these claims. In this two-type, two-action game, the only case that satisfies both the first and the third necessary conditions is $x \geq z$ and $y \geq w$—the players' interests are perfectly aligned, in the sense that given the Sender's type the players agree on which action should be taken. Formally, in a separating perfect Bayesian equilibrium in this cheap-talk game, the Sender's strategy is $[m(t_L) = t_L, m(t_H) = t_H]$, the Receiver's beliefs are $\mu(t_L \mid t_L) = 1$ and $\mu(t_L \mid t_H) = 0$, and the Receiver's strategy is $[a(t_L) = a_L, a(t_H) = a_H]$. For these strategies and beliefs to be an equilibrium, each Sender-type t_i must prefer to announce the truth, thereby inducing the action a_i, rather than to lie, thereby inducing a_j. Thus, a separating equilibrium exists if and only if $x \geq z$ and $y \geq w$.

Our second example is a special case of Crawford and Sobel's model. Now the type, message, and action spaces are continuous: the Sender's type is uniformly distributed between zero and one (formally, $T = [0,1]$ and $p(t) = 1$ for all t in T); the message space is the type space ($M = T$); and the action space is the interval from zero to one ($A = [0,1]$). The Receiver's payoff function is $U_R(t,a) = -(a-t)^2$ and the Sender's is $U_S(t,a) = -[a - (t+b)]^2$, so when the Sender's type is t, the Receiver's optimal action is $a = t$ but the Sender's optimal action is $a = t + b$. Thus, different Sender-types have different preferences over the Receiver's actions (more specifically, higher types prefer higher actions), and the players' preferences are not completely opposed (more specifically, the parameter $b > 0$ measures the similarity of the players' preferences—when b is closer to zero, the players' interests are more closely aligned).

Crawford and Sobel show that all the perfect Bayesian equilibria of this model (and of a broad class of related models) are equivalent to a partially pooling equilibrium of the following form: the type space is divided into the n intervals $[0, x_1), [x_1, x_2), \ldots, [x_{n-1}, 1]$; all the types in a given interval send the same message, but types in different intervals send different messages. As noted earlier, a pooling equilibrium ($n = 1$) always exists. We will show that, given the value of the preference-similarity parameter b, there is a maximum number of intervals (or "steps") that can occur in equilibrium, denoted $n^*(b)$, and partially pooling equilibria exist for each $n = 1, 2, \ldots, n^*(b)$. A decrease in b increases $n^*(b)$—in this sense, more communication can occur through cheap talk when the players' preferences are more closely aligned. Also, $n^*(b)$ is finite for all $b > 0$ but approaches infinity as b approaches zero—perfect communication cannot occur unless the players' preferences are perfectly aligned.

We conclude this section by characterizing these partially pooling equilibria, starting with a two-step equilibrium ($n = 2$) as an illustration. Suppose all the types in the interval $[0, x_1)$ send one message while those in $[x_1, 1]$ send another. After receiving the message from the types in $[0, x_1)$, the Receiver will believe that the Sender's type is uniformly distributed on $[0, x_1)$, so the Receiver's optimal action will be $x_1/2$; likewise, after receiving the message from the types in $[x_1, 1]$, the Receiver's optimal action will be $(x_1 + 1)/2$. For the types in $[0, x_1)$ to be willing to send their message, it must be that all these types prefer the action $x_1/2$ to the action $(x_1 + 1)/2$; likewise, all the types above x_1 must prefer $(x_1 + 1)/2$ to $x_1/2$.

Because the Sender's preferences are symmetric around his or her optimal action, the Sender-type t prefers $x_1/2$ to $(x_1+1)/2$ if the midpoint between these two actions exceeds that type's optimal action, $t+b$ (as in Figure 4.3.2), but prefers $(x_1+1)/2$ to $x_1/2$ if $t+b$

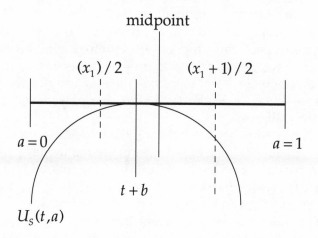

Figure 4.3.2.

exceeds the midpoint. Thus, for a two-step equilibrium to exist, x_1 must be the type t whose optimal action $t+b$ exactly equals the midpoint between the two actions:

$$x_1 + b = \frac{1}{2}\left[\frac{x_1}{2} + \frac{x_1 + 1}{2}\right],$$

or $x_1 = (1/2) - 2b$. Since the type space is $T = [0,1]$, x_1 must be positive, so a two-step equilibrium exists only if $b < 1/4$; for $b \geq 1/4$ the players' preferences are too dissimilar to allow even this limited communication.

To complete the discussion of this two-step equilibrium, we address the issue of messages that are off the equilibrium path. Crawford and Sobel specify the Sender's (mixed) strategy so that no such messages exist: all types $t < x_1$ choose a message randomly, according to a uniform distribution on $[0, x_1)$; all types $t \geq x_1$ choose a message randomly, according to a uniform distribution on $[x_1, 1]$. Since we assumed $M = T$, there are no messages that are sure not to be sent in equilibrium, so Signaling Requirement 3 determines the Receiver's belief after all possible messages: the Receiver's belief after observing any message from $[0, x_1)$ is

that t is uniformly distributed on $[0, x_1)$, and the Receiver's belief after observing any message from $[x_1, 1]$ is that t is uniformly
distributed on $[x_1, 1]$. (The use of uniform distributions in the
Sender's mixed strategy is entirely separate from the assumption
of a uniform distribution of the Sender's type; the Sender's mixed
strategy could just as well use any other strictly positive probability density over the indicated intervals.) As an alternative to
Crawford and Sobel's approach, we could specify a pure strategy for the Sender but choose appropriate beliefs for the Receiver
off the equilibrium path. For example, let the Sender's strategy
be that all types $t < x_1$ send the message 0 and all types $t \geq x_1$
send the message x_1, and let the Receiver's out-of-equilibrium belief after observing any message from $(0, x_1)$ be that t is uniformly
distributed on $[0, x_1)$, and after observing any message from $(x_1, 1]$
be that t is uniformly distributed on $[x_1, 1]$.

To characterize an n-step equilibrium, we repeatedly apply the
following observation from the two-step equilibrium: the upper
step, $[x_1, 1]$, is $4b$ longer than the lower step, $[0, x_1)$. This observation follows from the fact that, given the Sender's type (t), the
Sender's optimal action $(t + b)$ exceeds the Receiver's optimal action (t) by b. Thus, if two adjacent steps were of equal length, the
boundary type between the steps (x_1 in the two-step equilibrium)
would strictly prefer to send the message associated with the upper step; indeed, the types slightly below the boundary would
also prefer this. The only way to make the boundary type indifferent between the two steps (and thereby make the types above
and below the boundary strictly prefer their respective steps) is to
make the upper step appropriately longer than the lower step, as
follows.

If the step $[x_{k-1}, x_k)$ is of length c (i.e., $x_k - x_{k-1} = c$), then
the Receiver's optimal action associated with this step—namely,
$(x_k + x_{k-1})/2$—is $(c/2) + b$ below the optimal action for the boundary
type x_k—namely, $x_k + b$. To make the boundary type x_k indifferent
between the steps $[x_{k-1}, x_k)$ and $[x_k, x_{k+1})$, the Receiver's action
associated with the latter step must be $(c/2) + b$ above the optimal
action for x_k:

$$\frac{x_{k+1} + x_k}{2} - (x_k + b) = \frac{c}{2} + b,$$

or

$$x_{k+1} - x_k = c + 4b.$$

Thus, each step must be $4b$ longer than the last.

In an n-step equilibrium, if the first step is of length d, then the second must be of length $d + 4b$, the third of length $d + 8b$, and so on. The nth step must end exactly at $t = 1$, so we must have

$$d + (d + 4b) + \cdots + [d + (n - 1)4b] = 1.$$

Using the fact that $1 + 2 + \cdots + (n - 1) = n(n - 1)/2$, we have

$$n \cdot d + n(n - 1) \cdot 2b = 1. \tag{4.3.1}$$

Given any n such that $n(n-1) \cdot 2b < 1$, there exists a value of d that solves (4.3.1). That is, for any n such that $n(n - 1) \cdot 2b < 1$, there exists an n-step partially pooling equilibrium, and the length of its first step is the value of d that solves (4.3.1). Since the length of the first step must be positive, the largest possible number of steps in such an equilibrium, $n^*(b)$, is the largest value of n such that $n(n - 1) \cdot 2b < 1$. Applying the quadratic formula shows that $n^*(b)$ is the largest integer less than

$$\frac{1}{2}\left[1 + \sqrt{1 + (2/b)}\right].$$

Consistent with the derivation of the two-step equilibrium, $n^*(b) = 1$ for $b \geq 1/4$: no communication is possible if the players' preferences are too dissimilar. Also, as claimed earlier, $n^*(b)$ decreases in b but approaches infinity only as b approaches zero: more communication can occur through cheap talk when the players' preferences are more closely aligned, but perfect communication cannot occur unless the players' preferences are perfectly aligned.

4.3.B   Sequential Bargaining under Asymmetric Information

Consider a firm and a union bargaining over wages. For simplicity, assume that employment is fixed. The union's reservation wage (i.e., the amount that union members earn if not employed by the firm) is w_r. The firm's profit, denoted by π, is uniformly distributed on $[\pi_L, \pi_H]$, but the true value of π is privately known by the firm. Such private information might reflect the firm's superior knowledge concerning new products in the planning stage, for example. We simplify the analysis by assuming that $w_r = \pi_L = 0$.

The bargaining game lasts at most two periods. In the first period, the union makes a wage offer, w_1. If the firm accepts this offer then the game ends: the union's payoff is w_1 and the firm's is $\pi - w_1$. (These payoffs are the present values of the wage and (net) profit streams that accrue to the players over the life of the contract being negotiated—typically three years.) If the firm rejects this offer then the game proceeds to the second period. The union makes a second wage offer, w_2. If the firm accepts this offer then the present values of the players' payoffs (as measured in the first period) are δw_2 for the union and $\delta(\pi - w_2)$ for the firm, where δ reflects both discounting and the reduced life of the contract remaining after the first period. If the firm rejects the union's second offer then the game ends and payoffs are zero for both players. A more realistic model might allow the bargaining to continue until an offer is accepted, or might force the parties to submit to binding arbitration after a prolonged strike. Here we sacrifice realism for tractability; see Sobel and Takahashi (1983) and Problem 4.12 for an infinite-horizon analysis.

Defining and deriving a perfect Bayesian equilibrium is a bit complicated in this model, but the eventual answer is simple and intuitive. We therefore begin by sketching the unique perfect Bayesian equilibrium of this game.

- The union's first-period wage offer is

$$w_1^* = \frac{(2 - \delta)^2}{2(4 - 3\delta)}\pi_H.$$

- If the firm's profit, π, exceeds

$$\pi_1^* = \frac{2w_1}{2 - \delta} = \frac{2 - \delta}{4 - 3\delta}\pi_H$$

then the firm accepts w_1^*; otherwise, the firm rejects w_1^*.

- If its first-period offer is rejected, the union updates its belief about the firm's profit: the union believes that π is uniformly distributed on $[0, \pi_1^*]$.

- The union's second-period wage offer (conditional on w_1^* being rejected) is

$$w_2^* = \frac{\pi_1^*}{2} = \frac{2 - \delta}{2(4 - 3\delta)}\pi_H < w_1^*.$$

- If the firm's profit, π, exceeds w_2^* then the firm accepts the offer; otherwise, it rejects it.

Thus, in each period, high-profit firms accept the union's offer while low-profit firms reject it, and the union's second-period belief reflects the fact that high-profit firms accepted the first-period offer. (Note the slight change in usage here: we will refer interchangeably to one firm with many possible profit types and to many firms each with its own profit level.) In equilibrium, low-profit firms tolerate a one-period strike in order to convince the union that they are low-profit and so induce the union to offer a lower second-period wage. Firms with very low profits, however, find even the lower second-period offer intolerably high and so reject it, too.

We begin our analysis by describing the players' strategies and beliefs, after which we define a perfect Bayesian equilibrium. Figure 4.3.3 provides an extensive-form representation of a simplified version of the game: there are only two values of π (π_L and π_H), and the union has only two possible wage offers (w_L and w_H).

In this simplified game, the union has the move at three information sets, so the union's strategy consists of three wage offers: the first-period offer, w_1, and two second-period offers, w_2 after $w_1 = w_H$ is rejected and w_2 after $w_1 = w_L$ is rejected. These three moves occur at three nonsingleton information sets, at which the union's beliefs are denoted $(p, 1 - p)$, $(q, 1 - q)$, and $(r, 1 - r)$, respectively. In the full game (as opposed to the simplified game in Figure 4.3.3), a strategy for the union is a first-period offer w_1 and a second-period offer function $w_2(w_1)$ that specifies the offer w_2 to be made after each possible offer w_1 is rejected. Each of these moves occurs at a nonsingleton information set. There is one second-period information set for each different first-period wage offer the union might make (so there is a continuum of such information sets, rather than two as in Figure 4.3.3). Within both the lone first-period and the continuum of second-period information sets, there is one decision node for each possible value of π (so there is a continuum of such nodes, rather than two as in Figure 4.3.3). At each information set, the union's belief is a probability distribution over these nodes. In the full game, we denote the union's first-period belief by $\mu_1(\pi)$, and the union's second-period belief (after the first-period offer w_1 has been rejected) by $\mu_2(\pi \mid w_1)$.

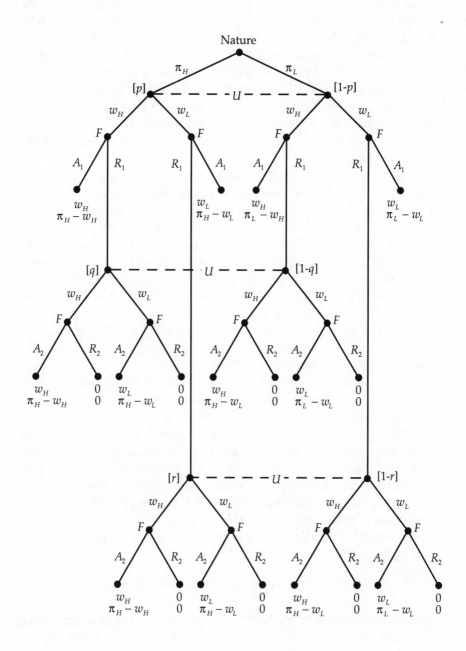

Figure 4.3.3.

A strategy for the firm involves two decisions (in either the simplified or the full game). Let $A_1(w_1 \mid \pi)$ equal one if the firm would accept the first-period offer w_1 when its profit is π, and zero if the firm would reject w_1 when its profit is π. Likewise, let $A_2(w_2 \mid \pi, w_1)$ equal one if the firm would accept the second-period offer w_2 when its profit is π and the first-period offer was w_1, and zero if the firm would reject w_2 under these circumstances. A strategy for the firm is a pair of functions $[A_1(w_1 \mid \pi), A_2(w_2 \mid \pi, w_1)]$. Since the firm has complete information throughout the game, its beliefs are trivial.

The strategies $[w_1, w_2(w_1)]$ and $[A_1(w_1 \mid \pi), A_2(w_2 \mid \pi, w_1)]$ and the beliefs $[\mu_1(\pi), \mu_2(\pi \mid w_1)]$ are a perfect Bayesian equilibrium if they satisfy Requirements 2, 3, and 4 given in Section 4.1. (Requirement 1 is satisfied by the mere existence of the union's beliefs.) We will show that there is a unique perfect Bayesian equilibrium. The simplest step of the argument is to apply Requirement 2 to the firm's second-period decision $A_2(w_2 \mid \pi, w_1)$: since this is the last move of the game, the optimal decision for the firm is to accept w_2 if and only if $\pi \geq w_2$; w_1 is irrelevant. Given this part of the firm's strategy, it is also straightforward to apply Requirement 2 to the union's second-period choice of a wage offer: w_2 should maximize the union's expected payoff, given the union's belief $\mu_2(\pi \mid w_1)$ and the firm's subsequent strategy $A_2(w_2 \mid \pi, w_1)$. The tricky part of the argument is to determine the belief $\mu_2(\pi \mid w_1)$, as follows.

We begin by temporarily considering the following one-period bargaining problem. (We will later use the results of this problem as the solution to the second period of the two-period problem.) In the one-period problem, suppose the union believes that the firm's profit is uniformly distributed on $[0, \pi_1]$, where for the moment π_1 is arbitrary. If the union offers w then the firm's best response is clear: accept w if and only if $\pi \geq w$. Thus, the union's problem can be stated as:

$$\max_{w} \ w \cdot \text{Prob}\{\text{firm accepts } w\} + 0 \cdot \text{Prob}\{\text{firm rejects } w\},$$

where $\text{Prob}\{\text{firm accepts } w\} = (\pi_1 - w)/\pi_1$ for the relevant range of wage offers (namely, $0 \leq w \leq \pi_1$). The optimal wage offer is therefore $w^*(\pi_1) = \pi_1/2$.

We now return (permanently) to the two-period problem. We show first that, for arbitrary values of w_1 and w_2, if the union offers

w_1 in the first period and the firm expects the union to offer w_2 in the second period, then all firms with sufficiently high profit will accept w_1 and all others will reject it. The firm's possible payoffs are $\pi - w_1$ from accepting w_1, $\delta(\pi - w_2)$ from rejecting w_1 and accepting w_2, and zero from rejecting both offers. The firm therefore prefers accepting w_1 to accepting w_2 if $\pi - w_1 > \delta(\pi - w_2)$, or

$$\pi > \frac{w_1 - \delta w_2}{1 - \delta} \equiv \pi^*(w_1, w_2),$$

and the firm prefers accepting w_1 to rejecting both offers if $\pi - w_1 > 0$. Thus, for arbitrary values of w_1 and w_2, firms with $\pi > \max\{\pi^*(w_1, w_2), w_1\}$ will accept w_1 and firms with $\pi < \max\{\pi^*(w_1, w_2), w_1\}$ will reject w_1. Since Requirement 2 dictates that the firm act optimally given the players' subsequent strategies, we can derive $A_1(w_1 \mid \pi)$ for an arbitrary value of w_1: firms with $\pi > \max\{\pi^*(w_1, w_2), w_1\}$ will accept w_1 and firms with $\pi < \max\{\pi^*(w_1, w_2), w_1\}$ will reject w_1, where w_2 is the union's second-period wage offer $w_2(w_1)$.

We can now derive $\mu_2(\pi \mid w_1)$, the union's second-period belief at the information set reached if the first-period offer w_1 is rejected. Requirement 4 implies that the correct belief is that π is uniformly distributed on $[0, \pi(w_1)]$, where $\pi(w_1)$ is the value of π such that the firm is indifferent between accepting w_1 and rejecting it but accepting the union's optimal second-period offer given this belief—namely $w^*(\pi(w_1)) = \pi(w_1)/2$, as computed in the one-period problem. To see this, recall that Requirement 4 dictates that the union's belief be determined by Bayes's rule and the firm's strategy. Thus, given the first part of the firm's strategy $A_1(w_1 \mid \pi)$ just derived, the union's belief must be that the types remaining in the second period are uniformly distributed on $[0, \pi_1]$, where $\pi_1 = \max\{\pi^*(w_1, w_2), w_1\}$ and w_2 is the union's second-period wage offer $w_2(w_1)$. Given this belief, the union's optimal second-period offer must be $w^*(\pi_1) = \pi_1/2$, which yields an implicit equation for π_1 as a function of w_1:

$$\pi_1 = \max\{\pi^*(w_1, \pi_1/2), w_1\}.$$

To solve this implicit equation, suppose $w_1 \geq \pi^*(w_1, \pi_1/2)$. Then

$\pi_1 = w_1$, but this contradicts $w_1 \geq \pi^*(w_1, \pi_1/2)$. Therefore, $w_1 < \pi^*(w_1, \pi_1/2)$, so $\pi_1 = \pi^*(w_1, \pi_1/2)$, or

$$\pi_1(w_1) = \frac{2w_1}{2 - \delta} \quad \text{and} \quad w_2(w_1) = \frac{w_1}{2 - \delta}.$$

We have now reduced the game to a single-period optimization problem for the union: given the union's first-period wage offer, w_1, we have specified the firm's optimal first-period response, the union's belief entering the second period, the union's optimal second-period offer, and the firm's optimal second-period response. Thus, the union's first-period wage offer should be chosen to solve

$$\max_{w_1} \ w_1 \cdot \text{Prob}\{\text{firm accepts } w_1\}$$

$$+ \ \delta w_2(w_1) \cdot \text{Prob}\{\text{firm rejects } w_1 \text{ but accepts } w_2\}$$

$$+ \ \delta \cdot 0 \cdot \text{Prob}\{\text{firm rejects both } w_1 \text{ and } w_2\}.$$

Note well that $\text{Prob}\{\text{firm accepts } w_1\}$ is *not* simply the probability that π exceeds w_1; rather, it is the probability that π exceeds $\pi_1(w_1)$:

$$\text{Prob}\{\text{firm accepts } w_1\} = \frac{\pi_H - \pi_1(w_1)}{\pi_H}.$$

The solution to this optimization problem is w_1^*, given at the beginning of the analysis, and π_1^* and w_2^* are then given by $\pi_1(w_1^*)$ and $w_2(w_1^*)$, respectively.

4.3.C   Reputation in the Finitely Repeated Prisoners' Dilemma

In the analysis of finitely repeated games of complete information in Section 2.3.A, we showed that if a stage game has a unique Nash equilibrium, then any finitely repeated game based on this stage game has a unique subgame-perfect Nash equilibrium: the Nash equilibrium of the stage game is played in every stage, after every history. In contrast to this theoretical result, a great deal of experimental evidence suggests that cooperation occurs frequently during finitely repeated Prisoners' Dilemmas, especially in stages that are not too close to the end; see Axelrod (1981) for references.

Kreps, Milgrom, Roberts, and Wilson (1982) show that a *reputation* model offers an explanation of this evidence.[7]

The simplest exposition of such a reputation equilibrium in the finitely repeated Prisoners' Dilemma involves a new way of modeling asymmetric information. Rather than assume that one player has private information about his or her payoffs, we will assume that the player has private information about his or her feasible strategies. In particular, we will assume that with probability p the Row player can play only the Tit-for-Tat strategy (which begins the repeated game by cooperating and thereafter mimics the opponent's previous play), while with probability $1 - p$ Row can play any of the strategies available in the complete-information repeated game (including Tit-for-Tat). Following common parlance, we will call the latter Row-type "rational." The expositional advantage of this formulation follows from the fact that if Row ever deviates from the Tit-for-Tat strategy then it becomes common knowledge that Row is rational.

The Tit-for-Tat strategy is simple and appealing. Also, it was the winning entry in Axelrod's prisoners' dilemma tournament. Nonetheless, some may find it unappealing to assume that a player may have only one strategy available, even if it is an attractive strategy. At the cost of some expositional simplicity, one could instead assume that both Row-types can play any strategy, but with probability p Row's payoffs are such that Tit-for-Tat strictly dominates every other strategy in the repeated game. (The exposition becomes more complicated under this assumption because a deviation from Tit-for-Tat does not make it common knowledge that Row is rational.) Such payoffs differ from those typically assumed in repeated games: to make it optimal to mimic the Column player's previous play, Row's payoffs in one stage must depend on Column's move in the previous stage. As a third possibility (again at the expense of expositional simplicity), one could allow a player to have private information about his or her stage-game payoffs, but insist that the payoff in a stage depend only on the

---

[7]We showed in Section 2.3.B that cooperation can occur in the infinitely repeated Prisoners' Dilemma. Some authors refer to such an equilibrium as a "reputation" equilibrium, even though both players' payoffs and opportunities are common knowledge. For clarity, one might instead describe such an equilibrium as based on "threats and promises," reserving the term "reputation" for games where at least one player has something to learn about another, as in this section.

moves in that stage, and that the total payoff for the repeated game be the sum of the payoffs in the stage games. In particular, one could assume that with probability p Row's best response to cooperation is cooperation. Kreps, Milgrom, Roberts, and Wilson (hereafter KMRW) show that one-sided asymmetric information of this kind is not sufficient to produce cooperation in equilibrium; rather, finking occurs in every stage, just as under complete information. They also show, however, that if there is two-sided asymmetric information of this kind (i.e., if there is also probability q that Column's best response to cooperation is cooperation) then there can exist an equilibrium in which both players cooperate until the last few stages of the game.

To reiterate, we will assume that with probability p Row can play only the Tit-for-Tat strategy. The spirit of KMRW's analysis is that even if p is very small (i.e., even if Column has only a tiny suspicion that Row might not be rational), this uncertainty can have a big effect, in the following sense. KMRW show that there is an upper bound on the number of stages in which either player finks in equilibrium. This upper bound depends on p and on the stage-game payoffs but not on the number of stages in the repeated game. Thus, in any equilibrium of a long enough repeated game, the fraction of stages in which both players cooperate is large. (KMRW state their result for sequential equilibria, but their arguments also apply to perfect Bayesian equilibria.) Two key steps in KMRW's argument are: (i) if Row ever deviates from Tit-for-Tat then it becomes common knowledge that Row is rational, so neither player cooperates thereafter, so the rational Row has an incentive to mimic Tit-for-Tat; and (ii) given an assumption on the stage-game payoffs to be imposed below, Column's best response against Tit-for-Tat would be to cooperate until the last stage of the game.

To provide a simple look at the forces at work in KMRW's model, we will consider the complement of their analysis: rather than assume that p is small and analyze long repeated games, we will assume that p is large enough that there exists an equilibrium in which both players cooperate in all but the last two stages of a short repeated game. We begin with the two-period case. The timing is:

1. Nature draws a type for the Row player. With probability p, Row has only the Tit-for-Tat strategy available; with proba-

bility $1 - p$, Row can play any strategy. Row learns his or her type, but Column does not learn Row's type.

2. Row and Column play the Prisoners' Dilemma. The players' choices in this stage game become common knowledge.

3. Row and Column play the Prisoners' Dilemma for a second and last time.

4. Payoffs are received. The payoffs to the rational Row and to Column are the (undiscounted) sums of their stage-game payoffs. The stage game is given in Figure 4.3.4.

To make this stage game a Prisoners' Dilemma, we assume that $a > 1$ and $b < 0$. KMRW also assume that $a + b < 2$, so that (as claimed in (ii) above) Column's best response against Tit-for-Tat would be to cooperate until the last stage of the game, rather than to alternate between cooperating and finking.

Column

		Cooperate	Fink
	Cooperate	$1, 1$	b, a
Row	Fink	a, b	$0, 0$

Figure 4.3.4.

As in the last period of a finitely repeated Prisoners' Dilemma under complete information, finking (F) strictly dominates cooperating (C) in the last stage of this two-period game of incomplete information, both for the rational Row and for Column. Since Column will surely fink in the last stage, there is no reason for the rational Row to cooperate in the first stage. Finally, Tit-for-Tat begins the game by cooperating. Thus, the only move to be determined is Column's first-period move (X), which is then mimicked by Tit-for-Tat in the second period, as shown in the equilibrium path in Figure 4.3.5.

By choosing $X = C$, Column receives the expected payoff $p \cdot 1 + (1 - p) \cdot b$ in the first period and $p \cdot a$ in the second period. (Since Tit-for-Tat and the rational Row choose different moves in the first period, Column will begin the second period knowing whether

	$t = 1$	$t = 2$
Tit-for-Tat	C	X
Rational Row	F	F
Column	X	F

Figure 4.3.5.

	$t = 1$	$t = 2$	$t = 3$
Tit-for-Tat	C	C	C
Rational Row	C	F	F
Column	C	C	F

Figure 4.3.6.

Row is Tit-for-Tat or rational. The expected second-period payoff $p \cdot a$ reflects Column's uncertainty about Row's type when deciding whether to cooperate or fink in the first period.) By choosing $X = F$, in contrast, Column receives $p \cdot a$ in the first period and zero in the second. Thus, Column will cooperate in the first period provided that

$$p + (1 - p)b \geq 0. \tag{4.3.2}$$

We hereafter assume that (4.3.2) holds.

Now consider the three-period case. Given (4.3.2), if Column and the rational Row both cooperate in the first period then the equilibrium path for the second and third periods will be given by Figure 4.3.5, with $X = C$ and the periods relabeled. We will derive sufficient conditions for Column and the rational Row to cooperate in the first period, as shown in the three-period equilibrium path in Figure 4.3.6.

In this equilibrium, the payoff to the rational Row is $1 + a$ and the expected payoff to Column is $1 + p + (1 - p)b + pa$. If the rational Row finks in the first period then it becomes common knowledge

	$t = 1$	$t = 2$	$t = 3$
Tit-for-Tat	C	F	F
Rational Row	C	F	F
Column	F	F	F

Figure 4.3.7.

that Row is rational, so both players fink in the second and third periods. Thus, the total payoff to the rational Row from finking in the first period is a, which is less than the equilibrium payoff of $1 + a$, so the rational Row has no incentive to deviate from the strategy implicit in Figure 4.3.6.

We next consider whether Column has an incentive to deviate. If Column finks in the first period then Tit-for-Tat will fink in the second period, and the rational Row will fink in the second period because Column is sure to fink in the last period. Having finked in the first period, Column must then decide whether to fink or cooperate in the second period. If Column finks in the second period, then Tit-for-Tat will fink in the third period, so play will be as shown in Figure 4.3.7. Column's payoff from this deviation is a, which is less than Column's equilibrium expected payoff provided that

$$1 + p + (1 - p)b + pa \geq a.$$

Given (4.3.2), a sufficient condition for Column not to play this deviation is

$$1 + pa \geq a. \tag{4.3.3}$$

Alternatively, Column could deviate by finking in the first period but cooperating in the second, in which case Tit-for-Tat would cooperate in the third period, so play would be as shown in Figure 4.3.8. Column's expected payoff from this deviation is $a+b+pa$, which is less than Column's equilibrium expected payoff provided that

$$1 + p + (1 - p)b + pa \geq a + b + pa.$$

	$t=1$	$t=2$	$t=3$
Tit-for-Tat	C	F	C
Rational Row	C	F	F
Column	F	C	F

Figure 4.3.8.

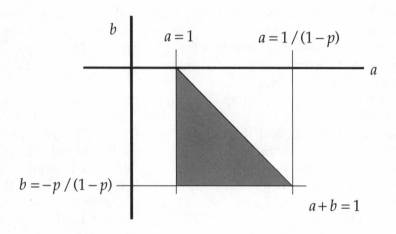

Figure 4.3.9.

Given (4.3.2), a sufficient condition for Column not to play this deviation is

$$a+b \leq 1. \tag{4.3.4}$$

We have now shown that if (4.3.2), (4.3.3), and (4.3.4) hold then the play described in Figure 4.3.6 is the equilibrium path of a perfect Bayesian equilibrium of the three-period Prisoners' Dilemma. For a given value of p, the payoffs a and b satisfy these three inequalities if they belong to the shaded region of Figure 4.3.9. As p approaches zero, this shaded region vanishes, consistent with the earlier observation that in this section we analyze equilibrium cooperation in short games with high values of p, whereas KMRW focus on long games with low values of p. On the other hand, if p is high enough to support cooperation in a short game, it certainly is high enough to do so in a long game. Formally, if a, b, and p satisfy (4.3.2), (4.3.3), and (4.3.4), then for any finite $T > 3$ there exists a perfect Bayesian equilibrium in the T-period repeated game in which the rational Row and Column both cooperate until period $T - 2$, after which periods $T - 1$ and T are as described in Figure 4.3.5. See Appendix 4.3.C for a proof of this claim.

Appendix 4.3.C

For brevity, we will refer to a perfect Bayesian equilibrium of a T-period repeated Prisoners' Dilemma as a *cooperative equilibrium* if the rational Row and Column both cooperate until period $T - 2$, after which periods $T - 1$ and T are as described in Figure 4.3.5. We will show that if a, b, and p satisfy (4.3.2), (4.3.3), and (4.3.4), then there exists a cooperative equilibrium for every finite $T > 3$. We argue by induction: given that for each $\tau = 2, 3, \ldots, T-1$ there exists a cooperative equilibrium in the τ-period game, we show there exists a cooperative equilibrium in the T-period game.

We first show that the rational Row has no incentive to deviate from a cooperative equilibrium in the T-period game. If Row were to fink in any period $t < T - 1$, it would become common knowledge that Row is rational, so Row would receive a payoff of a in period t and zero in each period thereafter. But Row's equilibrium payoff is one in periods t through $T - 2$ and a in period $T - 1$, or $(T - t - 1) + a$, so finking is not profitable for any $t < T - 1$. The argument concerning Figure 4.3.5 implies that the rational Row has no incentive to deviate in periods $T - 1$ or T.

We next show that Column has no incentive to deviate. The argument concerning Figure 4.3.5 implies that Column has no incentive to deviate by cooperating until period $T - 2$ and then finking in period $T - 1$; the argument concerning Figure 4.3.6 implies that Column has no incentive to deviate by cooperating until period $T - 3$ and then finking in period $T - 2$. We therefore need to show that Column has no incentive to deviate by cooperating until period $t - 1$ and then finking in period t, where $1 \le t \le T - 3$.

If Column finks in period t, Tit-for-Tat will fink in period $t + 1$, so the rational Row also will fink in period $t + 1$ (because finking strictly dominates cooperating in the $t + 1^{st}$ stage game, after which finking from $t + 2$ to T yields a payoff of at least zero, whereas cooperating at $t + 1$ would make it common knowledge that Row is rational, resulting in a payoff of exactly zero from $t + 2$ to T). Since Tit-for-Tat and the rational Row both cooperate until period t and then both fink in period $t + 1$, Column's belief at the beginning of period $t + 2$ is that the probability that Row is Tit-for-Tat is p. Therefore, if Column cooperates in period $t + 1$ then the continuation game beginning with period $t + 2$ will be identical to a τ-period game with $\tau = T - (t+2) + 1$. By the induction hypothesis, a cooperative equilibrium exists in this τ-period continuation game; assume it is played. Then Column's payoff in periods t through T from finking in period t and cooperating in period $t + 1$ is

$$a + b + [T - (t + 2) - 1] + p + (1 - p)b + pa,$$

which is less than Column's equilibrium payoff in periods t through T,

$$2 + [T - (t + 2) - 1] + p + (1 - p)b + pa. \tag{4.3.5}$$

We have so far shown that Column has no incentive to deviate by cooperating until period $t - 1$, finking in period t, and then cooperating in period $t+1$, given that the cooperative equilibrium will be played in the continuation game beginning with period $t + 2$. More generally, Column could cooperate until period $t - 1$, fink in periods t through $t + s$, and then cooperate in period $t + s + 1$. Three cases are trivial: (1) if $t + s = T$ (i.e., Column never cooperates after finking at t) then Column's payoff is a in period t and zero thereafter, which is less than (4.3.5); (2) if $t + s + 1 = T$ then Column's payoff from t through T is $a + b$, which is worse than in (1); and (3) if $t + s + 1 = T - 1$ then Column's payoff from t through T is $a + b + pa$, which is less than (4.3.5). It remains to consider values of s such that $t + s + 1 < T - 1$. As in the case of $s = 0$ above, there exists a cooperative equilibrium in the continuation game beginning in period $t+s+2$; assume it is played. Then Column's payoff in periods t through T from playing this deviation is

$$a + b + [T - (t + s + 2) - 1] + p + (1 - p)b + pa,$$

which is again less than (4.3.5).

4.4   Refinements of Perfect Bayesian Equilibrium

In Section 4.1 we defined a perfect Bayesian equilibrium to be strategies and beliefs satisfying Requirements 1 through 4, and we observed that in such an equilibrium no player's strategy can be strictly dominated beginning at any information set. We now consider two further requirements (on beliefs off the equilibrium path), the first of which formalizes the following idea: since perfect Bayesian equilibrium prevents player i from playing a strategy that is strictly dominated beginning at any information set, it is not reasonable for player j to believe that i would play such a strategy.

To make this idea more concrete, consider the game in Figure 4.4.1. There are two pure-strategy perfect Bayesian equilibria: $(L, L', p = 1)$, and $(R, R', p \leq 1/2)$.[8] The key feature of this example

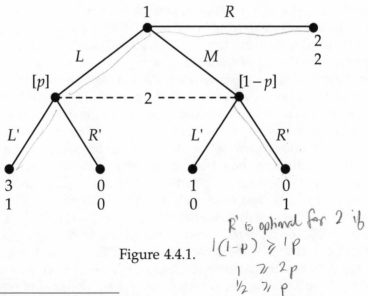

$$R' \text{ is optimal for } 2 \text{ if}$$
$$1(1-p) \geqslant 1p$$
$$1 \geqslant 2p$$
$$\tfrac{1}{2} \geqslant p$$

Figure 4.4.1.

---

[8]Deriving the normal-form representation reveals that there are two pure-strategy Nash equilibria in this game: (L, L') and (R, R'). Since there are no subgames in the extensive form, both Nash equilibria are subgame-perfect. In (L, L'), player 2's information set is on the equilibrium path, so Requirement 3 dictates that $p = 1$. In (R, R'), this information set is off the equilibrium path but Requirement 4 puts no restriction on p. We thus require only that 2's belief p make the action R' optimal—that is, $p \leq 1/2$.

is that M is a strictly dominated strategy for player 1: the payoff of 2 from R exceeds both of the payoffs that player 1 could receive from playing M—0 and 1. Thus, it is not reasonable for player 2 to believe that 1 might have played M; formally, it is not reasonable for $1 - p$ to be positive, so p must equal one. If the belief $1 - p > 0$ is not reasonable, then neither is the perfect Bayesian equilibrium $(R, R', p \leq 1/2)$, leaving $(L, L', p = 1)$ as the only perfect Bayesian equilibrium satisfying this requirement.

Two other features of this example deserve brief mention. First, although M is strictly dominated, L is not. If L were strictly dominated (as would be the case if player 1's payoff of 3 were, say, $3/2$) then the same argument would imply that it is not reasonable for p to be positive, implying that p must be zero, but this would contradict the earlier result that p must be one. In such a case, this requirement would not restrict player 2's out-of-equilibrium beliefs; see the formal definition below.

Second, the example does not precisely illustrate the requirement described initially, because M is not just strictly dominated beginning at an information set but also strictly dominated. To see the difference, recall from Section 1.1.B that the strategy s'_i is strictly dominated if there exists another strategy s_i such that, for each possible combination of the other players' strategies, i's payoff from playing s_i is strictly greater than the payoff from playing s'_i. Now consider an expanded version of the game in Figure 4.4.1, in which player 2 has a move preceding 1's move in the figure, and has two choices at this initial move: either end the game or give the move to 1 at 1's information set in the figure. In this expanded game, M is still strictly dominated beginning at 1's information set, but M is not strictly dominated because if 2 ends the game at the initial node then L, M, and R all yield the same payoff.

Since M is strictly dominated in Figure 4.4.1, it is certainly not reasonable for player 2 to believe that 1 might have played M, but strict dominance is too strong a test, and hence yields too weak a requirement. (Since more strategies are strictly dominated beginning at an information set than are strictly dominated, requiring that j not believe that i might have played one of the former strategies puts more restrictions on j's beliefs than would requiring that j not believe that i might have played one of the latter strategies.) In what follows, we adhere to the requirement as originally stated: player j should not believe that player i might have played a strategy that is strictly dominated beginning at any information set. We now state this requirement formally.

Definition *Consider an information set at which player i has the move. The strategy s'_i is **strictly dominated beginning at this information set** if there exists another strategy s_i such that, for every belief that i could hold at the given information set, and for each possible combination of the other players' subsequent strategies (where a "subsequent strategy" is a complete plan of action covering every contingency that might arise after the given information set has been reached), i's expected payoff from taking the action specified by s_i at the given information set and playing the subsequent strategy specified by s_i is strictly greater than the expected payoff from taking the action and playing the subsequent strategy specified by s'_i.*

Requirement 5 *If possible, each player's beliefs off the equilibrium path should place zero probability on nodes that are reached only if another player plays a strategy that is strictly dominated beginning at some information set.*

The qualification "If possible" in Requirement 5 covers the case that would arise in Figure 4.4.1 if R dominated both M and L, as would occur if player 1's payoff of 3 were $3/2$. In such a case, Requirement 1 dictates that player 2 have a belief, but it is not possible for this belief to place zero probability on the nodes following both M and L, so Requirement 5 would not apply.

As a second illustration of Requirement 5, consider the signaling game in Figure 4.4.2. As in Section 4.2.A, the Sender strategy (m', m'') means that type t_1 chooses message m' and type t_2 chooses m'', and the Receiver strategy (a', a'') means that the Receiver chooses action a' following L and a'' following R. It is straightforward to check that the strategies and beliefs $[(L, L), (u, d), p = .5, q]$ constitute a pooling perfect Bayesian equilibrium for any $q \geq 1/2$. The key feature of this signaling game, however, is that it makes no sense for t_1 to play R. Formally, the Sender's strategies (R, L) and (R, R)—that is, the strategies in which t_1 plays R—are strictly dominated beginning at the Sender's information set corresponding to t_1.[9] Thus, the t_1-node in the Receiver's information set following R can be reached only if the Sender plays a strategy that is

---

[9]Since the Sender's information set corresponding to t_1 is a singleton information set, the Sender's beliefs play no role in the definition of strict dominance beginning at this information set. Showing that (R, L) and (R, R) are strictly dominated beginning at this information set then amounts to exhibiting an alter-

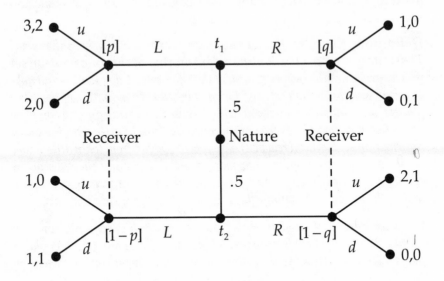

Figure 4.4.2.

strictly dominated beginning at an information set. Furthermore, the t_2-node in the Receiver's information set following R can be reached by a strategy that is not strictly dominated beginning at an information set, namely (L, R). Requirement 5 therefore dictates that $q = 0$. Since $[(L, L), (u, d), p = .5, q]$ is a perfect Bayesian equilibrium only if $q \geq 1/2$, such an equilibrium cannot satisfy Requirement 5.

An equivalent way to impose Requirement 5 on the perfect Bayesian equilibria of the signaling game defined in Section 4.2.A is as follows.

Definition *In a signaling game, the message m_j from M is* **dominated** *for type t_i from T if there exists another message $m_{j'}$ from M such that t_i's lowest possible payoff from $m_{j'}$ is greater than t_i's highest possible payoff from m_j:*

$$\min_{a_k \in A} U_S(t_i, m_{j'}, a_k) > \max_{a_k \in A} U_S(t_i, m_j, a_k).$$

native strategy for the Sender that yields a higher payoff for t_1 for each strategy the Receiver could play. (L, R) is such a strategy: it yields at worst 2 for t_1, whereas (R, L) and (R, R) yield at best 1.

Signaling Requirement 5 *If the information set following m_j is off the equilibrium path and m_j is dominated for type t_i then (if possible) the Receiver's belief $\mu(t_i \mid m_j)$ should place zero probability on type t_i. (This is possible provided m_j is not dominated for all the types in T.)*

In the game in Figure 4.4.2, the separating perfect Bayesian equilibrium $[(L, R), (u, u), p = 1, q = 0]$ satisfies Signaling Requirement 5 trivially (because there are no information sets off this equilibrium path). As an example of an equilibrium that satisfies Signaling Requirement 5 nontrivially, suppose that the Receiver's payoffs when type t_2 plays R are reversed: 1 from playing d and 0 from u, rather than 0 and 1 as in Figure 4.4.2. Now $[(L, L), (u, d), p = .5, q]$ is a pooling perfect Bayesian equilibrium for any value of q, so $[(L, L), (u, d), p = .5, q = 0]$ is a pooling perfect Bayesian equilibrium that satisfies Signaling Requirement 5.

In some games, there are perfect Bayesian equilibria that seem unreasonable but nonetheless satisfy Requirement 5. One of the most active areas of recent research in game theory has concerned the twin questions of (i) when a perfect Bayesian equilibrium is unreasonable and (ii) what further requirement can be added to the definition of equilibrium to eliminate such unreasonable perfect Bayesian equilibria. Cho and Kreps (1987) made an early and influential contribution to this area. We conclude this section by discussing three aspects of their paper: (1) the "Beer and Quiche" signaling game, which illustrates that unreasonable perfect Bayesian equilibria can satisfy Signaling Requirement 5; (2) a stronger (but by no means the strongest possible) version of Signaling Requirement 5, called the *Intuitive Criterion*; and (3) the application of the Intuitive Criterion to Spence's job-market signaling game.

In the "Beer and Quiche" signaling game, the Sender is one of two types: t_1 = "wimpy" (with probability .1) and t_2 = "surly" (with probability .9). The Sender's message is the choice of whether to have beer or quiche for breakfast; the Receiver's action is the choice of whether or not to duel with the Sender. The qualitative features of the payoffs are that the wimpy type would prefer to have quiche for breakfast, the surly type would prefer to have beer, both types would prefer not to duel with the Receiver (and care about this more than about which breakfast they have), and the Receiver would prefer to duel with the wimpy type but not to duel with the surly type. (Thus, with more conventional labels for the types, messages, and actions, this game could be a model

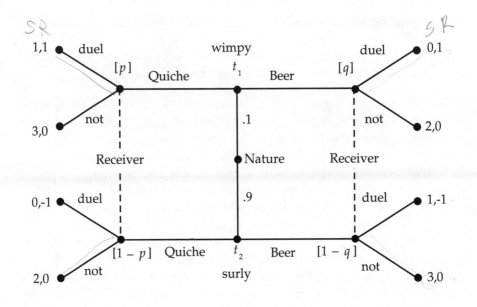

Figure 4.4.3.

of entry deterrence, much like Milgrom and Roberts [1982].) In the extensive-form representation in Figure 4.4.3, the payoff from having the preferred breakfast is 1 for both Sender types, the additional payoff from avoiding a duel is 2 for both Sender types, and the payoff from a duel with the wimpy (respectively, surly) type is 1 (respectively, −1) for the Receiver; all other payoffs are zero.

In this game, [(Quiche, Quiche), (not, duel), $p = .9, q$] is a pooling perfect Bayesian equilibrium for any $q \geq 1/2$. Furthermore, this equilibrium satisfies Signaling Requirement 5, because Beer is not dominated for either Sender type. In particular, the wimpy type is not guaranteed to do better by having Quiche (at worst a payoff of 1) than by having Beer (at best a payoff of 2). On the other hand, the Receiver's belief off the equilibrium path does seem suspicious: if the Receiver unexpectedly observes Beer then the Receiver concludes that the Sender is at least as likely to be wimpy as surly (i.e., $q \geq 1/2$), even though (a) the wimpy type cannot possibly improve on the equilibrium payoff of 3 by having Beer rather than Quiche, while (b) the surly type could improve on the equilibrium payoff of 2, by receiving the payoff of 3 that would follow if the Receiver held a belief $q < 1/2$. Given (a) and (b), one might expect the surly type to choose Beer and then make the following speech:

> Seeing me choose Beer should convince you that I am the surly type: choosing Beer could not possibly have improved the lot of the wimpy type, by (a); and if choosing Beer will convince you that I am the surly type then doing so will improve my lot, by (b).

If such a speech is believed, it dictates that $q = 0$, which is incompatible with this pooling perfect Bayesian equilibrium.

We can generalize this argument to the class of signaling games defined in Section 4.2.A; this yields Signaling Requirement 6.

Definition *Given a perfect Bayesian equilibrium in a signaling game, the message m_j from M is **equilibrium-dominated for type t_i** from T if t_i's equilibrium payoff, denoted $U^*(t_i)$, is greater than t_i's highest possible payoff from m_j:*

$$U^*(t_i) > \max_{a_k \in A} U_S(t_i, m_j, a_k).$$

Signaling Requirement 6 ("The Intuitive Criterion," Cho and Kreps 1987): *If the information set following m_j is off the equilibrium path and m_j is equilibrium-dominated for type t_i then (if possible) the Receiver's belief $\mu(t_i \mid m_j)$ should place zero probability on type t_i. (This is possible provided m_j is not equilibrium-dominated for all the types in T.)*

"Beer and Quiche" shows that a message m_j can be equilibrium-dominated for t_i without being dominated for t_i. If m_j is dominated for t_i, however, then m_j must be equilibrium-dominated for t_i, so imposing Signaling Requirement 6 makes Signaling Requirement 5 redundant. Cho and Kreps use a stronger result due to Kohlberg and Mertens (1986) to show that any signaling game from the class defined in Section 4.2.A has a perfect Bayesian equilibrium that satisfies Signaling Requirement 6. Arguments in this spirit are sometimes said to use *forward induction*, because in interpreting a deviation—that is, in forming the belief $\mu(t_i \mid m_j)$—the Receiver asks whether the Sender's past behavior could have been rational, whereas backwards induction assumes that future behavior will be rational.

To illustrate Signaling Requirement 6, we apply it to the envy case of the job-market signaling model analyzed in Section 4.2.B.

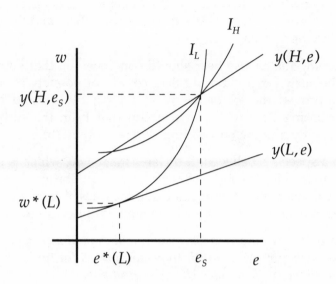

Figure 4.4.4.

Recall that there are enormous numbers of pooling, separating, and hybrid perfect Bayesian equilibria in this model. Strikingly, only one of these equilibria is consistent with Signaling Requirement 6—the separating equilibrium in which the low-ability worker chooses his or her complete-information level of education and the high-ability worker chooses just enough education to make the low-ability worker indifferent about mimicking the high-ability worker, as illustrated in Figure 4.4.4.

In any perfect Bayesian equilibrium, if the worker chooses education e and the firms subsequently believe that the probability that the worker has high ability is $\mu(H \mid e)$, then the worker's wage will be

$$w(e) = \mu(H \mid e) \cdot y(H,e) + [1 - \mu(H \mid e)] \cdot y(L,e).$$

Thus, the low-ability worker's utility from choosing $e^*(L)$ is at least $y[L, e^*(L)] - c[L, e^*(L)]$, which exceeds that worker's utility from choosing any $e > e_s$, no matter what the firms believe after observing e. That is, in terms of Signaling Requirement 5, any education level $e > e_s$ is dominated for the low-ability type.

Roughly speaking, Signaling Requirement 5 then implies that the firms' belief must be $\mu(H \mid e) = 1$ for $e > e_s$, which in turn implies that a separating equilibrium in which the high-ability worker chooses an education level $\hat{e} > e_s$ cannot satisfy Signaling Requirement 5, because in such an equilibrium the firms must believe that $\mu(H \mid e) < 1$ for education choices between e_s and $\hat{e}$. (A precise statement is: Signaling Requirement 5 implies that $\mu(H \mid e) = 1$ for $e > e_s$ provided that e is not dominated for the high-ability type, but if there exists a separating equilibrium in which the high-ability worker chooses an education level $\hat{e} > e_s$ then education choices between e_s and $\hat{e}$ are not dominated for the high-ability type, so the argument goes through.) Therefore, the only separating equilibrium that satisfies Signaling Requirement 5 is the equilibrium shown in Figure 4.4.4.

A second conclusion also follows from this argument: in any equilibrium that satisfies Signaling Requirement 5, the high-ability worker's utility must be at least $y(H, e_s) - c(H, e_s)$. We next show that this conclusion implies that some pooling and hybrid equilibria cannot satisfy Signaling Requirement 5. There are two cases, depending on whether the probability that the worker has high ability (q) is low enough that the wage function $w = q \cdot y(H, e) + (1 - q) \cdot y(L, e)$ lies below the high-ability worker's indifference curve through the point $[e_s, y(H, e_s)]$.

We first suppose that q is low, as shown in Figure 4.4.5. In this case, no pooling equilibrium satisfies Signaling Requirement 5, because the high-ability worker cannot achieve the utility $y(H, e_s) - c(H, e_s)$ in such an equilibrium. Likewise, no hybrid equilibrium in which the high-ability worker does the randomizing satisfies Signaling Requirement 5, because the (education, wage) point at which pooling occurs in such an equilibrium lies below the wage function $w = q \cdot y(H, e) + (1 - q) \cdot y(L, e)$. Finally, no hybrid equilibrium in which the low-ability worker does the randomizing satisfies Signaling Requirement 5, because the (education, wage) point at which pooling occurs in such an equilibrium must be on the low-ability worker's indifference curve through the point $[e^*(L), w^*(L)]$, as in Figure 4.2.9, and so lies below the high-ability worker's indifference curve through the point $[e_s, y(H, e_s)]$. Thus, in the case shown in Figure 4.4.5, the only perfect Bayesian equilibrium that satisfies Signaling Requirement 5 is the separating equilibrium shown in Figure 4.4.4.

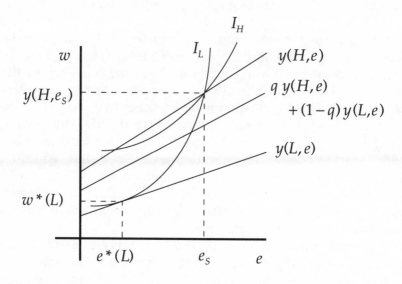

Figure 4.4.5.

We now suppose that q is high, as shown in Figure 4.4.6. As before, hybrid equilibria in which the low-ability type does the randomizing cannot satisfy Signaling Requirement 5, but now pooling equilibria and hybrid equilibria in which the high-type does the randomizing can satisfy this requirement if the pooling occurs at an (education, wage) point in the shaded region of the figure. Such equilibria cannot satisfy Signaling Requirement 6, however.

Consider the pooling equilibrium at e_p shown in Figure 4.4.7. Education choices $e > e'$ are equilibrium-dominated for the low-ability type, because even the highest wage that could be paid to a worker with education e, namely $y(H,e)$, yields an (education, wage) point below the low-ability worker's indifference curve through the equilibrium point (e_p, w_p). Education choices between e' and e'' are not equilibrium-dominated for the high-ability type, however: if such a choice convinces the firms that the worker has high ability, then the firms will offer the wage $y(H,e)$, which will make the high-ability worker better off than in the indicated pooling equilibrium. Thus, if $e' < e < e''$ then Signaling Requirement 6 implies that the firms' belief must be

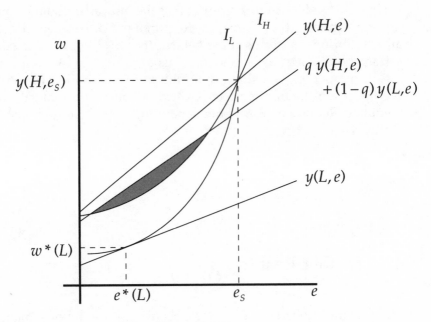

Figure 4.4.6.

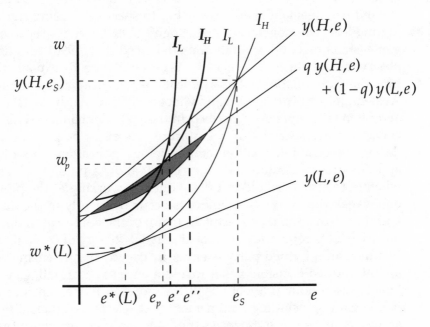

Figure 4.4.7.

$\mu(H \mid e) = 1$, which in turn implies that the indicated pooling equilibrium cannot satisfy Signaling Requirement 6, because in such an equilibrium the firms must believe that $\mu(H \mid e) < 1$ for education choices between e' and e''. This argument can be repeated for all the pooling and hybrid equilibria in the shaded region of the figure, so the only perfect Bayesian equilibrium that satisfies Signaling Requirement 6 is the separating equilibrium shown in Figure 4.4.4.

4.5 Further Reading

Milgrom and Roberts (1982) offer a classic application of signaling games in industrial organization. In financial economics, Bhattacharya (1979) and Leland and Pyle (1977) analyze dividend policy and management share ownership (respectively) using signaling models. On monetary policy, Rogoff (1989) reviews repeated-game, signaling, and reputation models, and Ball (1990) uses (unobservable) changes in the Fed's type over time to explain the time-path of inflation. For applications of cheap talk, see the Austen-Smith (1990), Farrell and Gibbons (1991), Matthews (1989), and Stein (1989) papers described in the text. Kennan and Wilson (1992) survey theoretical and empirical models of bargaining under asymmetric information, emphasizing applications to strikes and litigation. Cramton and Tracy (1992) allow a union to choose whether to strike or hold out (i.e., continue working at the previous wage); they show that holdouts occur frequently in the data, and that such a model can explain many of the empirical findings on strikes. On reputation, see Sobel's (1985) "theory of credibility," in which an informed party is either a "friend" or an "enemy" of an uninformed decision maker in a sequence of cheap-talk games. Finally, see Cho and Sobel (1990) for more on refinement in signaling games, including a refinement that selects the efficient separating equilibrium in Spence's model when there are more than two types.

4.6 Problems

Section 4.1

4.1. In the following extensive-form games, derive the normal-form game and find all the pure-strategy Nash, subgame-perfect, and perfect Bayesian equilibria.

a.

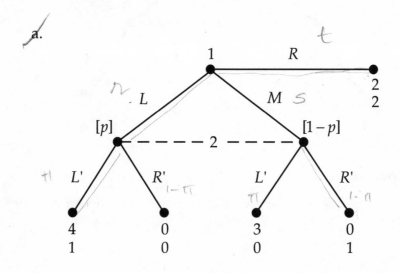

b.

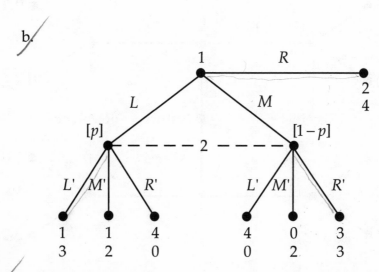

4.2. Show that there does not exist a pure-strategy perfect Bayesian equilibrium in the following extensive-form game. What is the mixed-strategy perfect Bayesian equilibrium? *minor question ?*

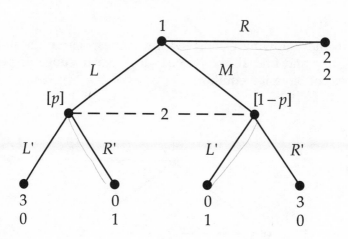

Section 4.2

4.3. a. Specify a pooling perfect Bayesian equilibrium in which both Sender types play *R* in the following signaling game.

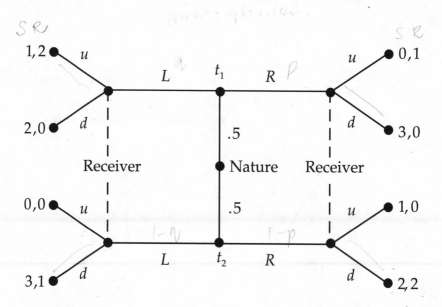

b. The following three-type signaling game begins with a move by nature, not shown in the tree, that yields one of the three types with equal probability. Specify a pooling perfect Bayesian equilibrium in which all three Sender types play *L*.

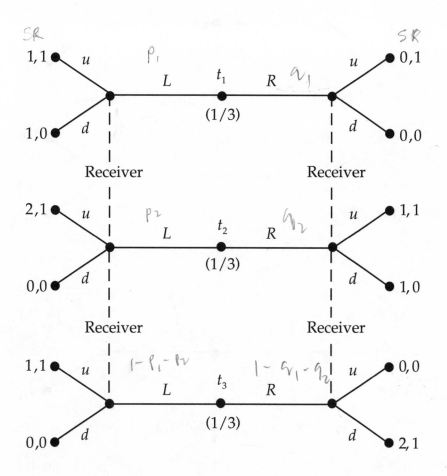

4.4. Describe all the pure-strategy pooling and separating perfect Bayesian equilibria in the following signaling games.

a.

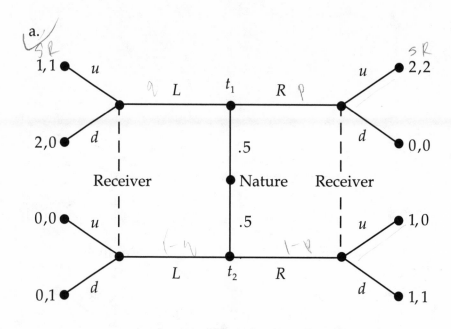

b.

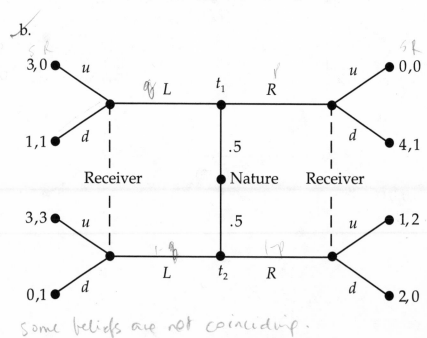

some beliefs are not coinciding.

4.5. Find all the pure-strategy perfect Bayesian equilibria in Problem 4.3 (a) and (b).

4.6. The following signaling game is analogous to the dynamic game of complete but imperfect information in Figure 4.1.1. (The types t_1 and t_2 are analogous to player 1's moves of L and M in Figure 4.1.1; if the Sender chooses R in the signaling game then the game effectively ends, analogous to player 1 choosing R in Figure 4.1.1.) Solve for (i) the pure-strategy Bayesian Nash equilibria, and (ii) the pure-strategy perfect Bayesian equilibria of this signaling game. Relate (i) to the Nash equilibria and (ii) to the perfect Bayesian equilibria in Figure 4.1.1.

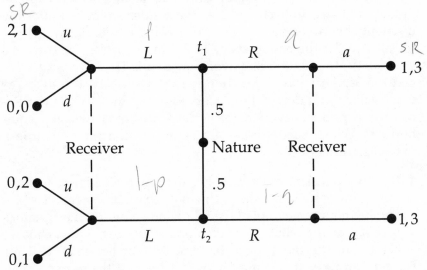

4.7. Draw indifference curves and production functions for a two-type job-market signaling model. Specify a hybrid perfect Bayesian equilibrium in which the high-ability worker randomizes.

Section 4.3

4.8. Solve for the pure-strategy perfect Bayesian equilibria in the following cheap-talk game. Each type is equally likely to be drawn by nature. As in Figure 4.3.1, the first payoff in each cell is the Sender's and the second is the Receiver's, but the figure is not a normal-form game; rather, it simply lists the players' payoffs from each type-action pair.

	t_1	t_2	t_3
a_1	0, 1	0, 0	0, 0
a_2	1, 0	1, 2	1, 0
a_3	0, 0	0, 0	2, 1

4.9.   Consider the example of Crawford and Sobel's cheap-talk model discussed in Section 4.3.A: the Sender's type is uniformly distributed between zero and one (formally, $T = [0, 1]$ and $p(t) = 1$ for all t in T); the action space is the interval from zero to one ($A = [0, 1]$); the Receiver's payoff function is $U_R(t, a) = -(a - t)^2$; and the Sender's payoff function is $U_S(t, a) = -[a - (t + b)]^2$. For what values of b does a three-step equilibrium exist? Is the Receiver's expected payoff higher in a three- or a two-step equilibrium? Which Sender-types are better off in a three- than in a two-step equilibrium?

4.10.   Two partners must dissolve their partnership. Partner 1 currently owns share s of the partnership, partner 2 owns share $1 - s$. The partners agree to play the following game: partner 1 names a price, p, for the whole partnership, and partner 2 then chooses either to buy 1's share for ps or to sell his or her share to 1 for $p(1 - s)$. Suppose it is common knowledge that the partners' valuations for owning the whole partnership are independently and uniformly distributed on $[0, 1]$, but that each partner's valuation is private information. What is the perfect Bayesian equilibrium?

4.11.   A buyer and a seller have valuations v_b and v_s. It is common knowledge that there are gains from trade (i.e., that $v_b > v_s$), but the size of the gains is private information, as follows: the seller's valuation is uniformly distributed on $[0, 1]$; the buyer's valuation $v_b = k \cdot v_s$, where $k > 1$ is common knowledge; the seller knows v_s (and hence v_b) but the buyer does not know v_b (or v_s). Suppose the buyer makes a single offer, p, which the seller either accepts or rejects. What is the perfect Bayesian equilibrium when $k < 2$? When $k > 2$? (See Samuelson 1984.)

4.12. This problem considers the infinite-horizon version of the two-period bargaining game analyzed in Section 4.3.B. As before, the firm has private information about its profit (π), which is uniformly distributed on $[0, \pi_0]$, and the union makes all the wage offers and has a reservation wage $w_r = 0$.

In the two-period game, the firm accepts the union's first offer (w_1) if $\pi > \pi_1$, where the profit-type π_1 is indifferent between (i) accepting w_1 and (ii) rejecting w_1 but accepting the union's second-period offer (w_2), and w_2 is the union's optimal offer given that the firm's profit is uniformly distributed on $[0, \pi_1]$ and that only one period of bargaining remains. In the infinite-horizon game, in contrast, w_2 will be the union's optimal offer given that the firm's profit is uniformly distributed on $[0, \pi_1]$ and that an infinite number of periods of (potential) bargaining remain. Although π_1 will again be the profit-type that is indifferent between options (i) and (ii), the change in w_2 will cause the value of π_1 to change.

The continuation game beginning in the second period of the infinite-horizon game is a rescaled version of the game as a whole: there are again an infinite number of periods of (potential) bargaining, and the firm's profit is again uniformly distributed from zero to an upper bound; the only difference is that the upper bound is now π_1 rather than π_0. Sobel and Takahashi (1983) show that the infinite-horizon game has a stationary perfect Bayesian equilibrium. In this equilibrium, if the firm's profit is uniformly distributed from zero to π^* then the union makes the wage offer $w(\pi^*) = b\pi^*$, so the first offer is $b\pi_0$, the second $b\pi_1$, and so on. If the union plays this stationary strategy, the firm's best response yields $\pi_1 = c\pi_0, \pi_2 = c\pi_1$, and so on, and the expected present value of the union's payoff when the firm's profit is uniformly distributed from zero to π^* is $V(\pi^*) = d\pi^*$. Show that $b = 2d, c = 1/[1 + \sqrt{1-\delta}]$, and $d = [\sqrt{1-\delta} - (1-\delta)]/2\delta$.

4.13. A firm and a union play the following two-period bargaining game. It is common knowledge that the firm's profit, π, is uniformly distributed between zero and one, that the union's reservation wage is w_r, and that only the firm knows the true value of π. Assume that $0 < w_r < 1/2$. Find the perfect Bayesian equilibrium of the following game:

1. At the beginning of period one, the union makes a wage offer to the firm, w_1.

2. The firm either accepts or rejects w_1. If the firm accepts w_1 then production occurs in both periods, so payoffs are $2w_1$ for the union and $2(\pi - w_1)$ for the firm. (There is no discounting.) If the firm rejects w_1 then there is no production in the first period, and payoffs for the first period are zero for both the firm and the union.

3. At the beginning of the second period (assuming that the firm rejected w_1), the firm makes a wage offer to the union, w_2. (Unlike in the Sobel-Takahashi model, the union does not make this offer.)

4. The union either accepts or rejects w_2. If the union accepts w_2 then production occurs in the second period, so second-period (and total) payoffs are w_2 for the union and $\pi - w_2$ for the firm. (Recall that first-period payoffs were zero.) If the union rejects w_2 then there is no production. The union then earns its alternative wage, w_r, for the second period and the firm shuts down and earns zero.

4.14. Nalebuff (1987) analyzes the following model of pre-trial bargaining between a plaintiff and a defendent. If the case goes to trial, the defendant will be forced to pay the plaintiff an amount d in damages. It is common knowledge that d is uniformly distributed on $[0, 1]$ and that only the defendant knows the true value of d. Going to trial costs the plaintiff $c < 1/2$ but (for simplicity) costs the defendant nothing.

The timing is as follows: (1) The plaintiff makes a settlement offer, s. (2) The defendant either settles (in which case the plaintiff's payoff is s and the defendant's is $-s$) or rejects the offer. (3) If the defendant rejects s then the plaintiff decides whether to go to trial, where the plaintiff's payoff will be $d - c$ and the defendant's $-d$, or to drop the charges, in which case the payoff to both players is zero.

In stage (3), if the plaintiff believes that there exists some d^* such that the defendant would have settled if and only if $d > d^*$, ' what is the plaintiff's optimal decision regarding trial? In stage (2), given an offer of s, if the defendant believes that the probability that the plaintiff will go to trial if s is rejected is p, what is the optimal settlement decision for the defendant of type d? Given an offer $s > 2c$, what is the perfect Bayesian equilibrium of the continuation game beginning at stage (2)? Given an offer $s < 2c$?

What is the perfect Bayesian equilibrium of the game as a whole if $c < 1/3$? If $1/3 < c < 1/2$?

4.15. Consider a legislative process in which the feasible policies vary continuously from $p = 0$ to $p = 1$. The ideal policy for the Congress is c, but the status quo is s, where $0 < c < s < 1$; that is, the ideal policy for Congress is to the left of the status quo. The ideal policy for the president is t, which is uniformly distributed on $[0, 1]$ but is privately known by the president. The timing is simple: Congress proposes a policy, p, which the president either signs or vetoes. If p is signed then the payoffs are $-(c - p)^2$ for the Congress and $-(t - p)^2$ for the president; if it is vetoed then they are $-(c - s)^2$ and $-(t - s)^2$. What is the perfect Bayesian equilibrium? Verify that $c < p < s$ in equilibrium.

Now suppose the president can engage in rhetoric (i.e., can send a cheap-talk message) before the Congress proposes a policy. Consider a two-step perfect Bayesian equilibrium in which the Congress proposes either p_L or p_H, depending on which message the president sends. Show that such an equilibrium cannot have $c < p_L < p_H < s$. Explain why it follows that there cannot be equilibria involving three or more proposals by Congress. Derive the details of the two-step equilibrium in which $c = p_L < p_H < s$: which types send which message, and what is the value of p_H? (See Matthews 1989.)

Section 4.4

4.16. Consider the pooling equilibria described in Problem 4.3 (a) and (b). For each equilibrium: (i) determine whether the equilibrium can be supported by beliefs that satisfy Signaling Requirement 5; (ii) determine whether the equilibrium can be supported by beliefs that satisfy Signaling Requirement 6 (The Intuitive Criterion).

4.7 References

Austen-Smith, D. 1990. "Information Transmission in Debate." *American Journal of Political Science* 34:124–52.

Axelrod, R. 1981. "The Emergence of Cooperation Among Egoists." *American Political Science Review* 75:306–18.

Ball, L. 1990. "Time-Consistent Policy and Persistent Changes in Inflation." National Bureau of Economic Research Working Paper #3529 (December).

Barro, R. 1986. "Reputation in a Model of Monetary Policy with Incomplete Information." *Journal of Monetary Economics* 17:3–20.

Bhattacharya, S. 1979. "Imperfect Information, Dividend Policy, and the 'Bird in the Hand' Fallacy." *Bell Journal of Economics* 10:259–70.

Cho, I.-K., and D. Kreps. 1987. "Signaling Games and Stable Equilibria." *Quarterly Journal of Economics* 102:179–222.

Cho, I.-K., and J. Sobel. 1990. "Strategic Stability and Uniqueness in Signaling Games." *Journal of Economic Theory* 50:381–413.

Cramton, P., and J. Tracy. 1992. "Strikes and Holdouts in Wage Bargaining: Theory and Data." *American Economic Review* 82: 100–21.

Crawford, V., and J. Sobel. 1982. "Strategic Information Transmission." *Econometrica* 50:1431–51.

Dybvig, P., and J. Zender. 1991. "Capital Structure and Dividend Irrelevance with Asymmetric Information." *Review of Financial Studies* 4:201–19.

Farrell, J., and R. Gibbons. 1991. "Union Voice." Mimeo, Cornell University.

Fudenberg, D., and J. Tirole. 1991. "Perfect Bayesian Equilibrium and Sequential Equilibrium." *Journal of Economic Theory* 53:236–60.

Harsanyi, J. 1967. "Games with Incomplete Information Played by Bayesian Players, Parts I, II, and III." *Management Science* 14:159–82, 320–34, 486–502.

Kennan, J., and R. Wilson. 1992. "Bargaining with Private Information." forthcoming in *Journal of Economic Literature*.

Kohlberg, E., and J.-F. Mertens. 1986. "On the Strategic Stability of Equilibria." *Econometrica.* 54:1003–38.

Kreps, D., and R. Wilson. 1982. "Sequential Equilibrium." *Econometrica* 50:863–94.

Kreps, D., P. Milgrom, J. Roberts, and R. Wilson. 1982. "Rational Cooperation in the Finitely Repeated Prisoners' Dilemma." *Journal of Economic Theory* 27:245–52.

Leland, H., and D. Pyle. 1977. "Informational Asymmetries, Financial Structure, and Financial Intermediation." *Journal of Fi-*

nance 32:371–87.

Matthews, S. 1989. "Veto Threats: Rhetoric in a Bargaining Game." *Quarterly Journal of Economics* 104:347–69.

Milgrom, P., and J. Roberts. 1982. "Limit Pricing and Entry under Incomplete Information: An Equilibrium Analysis." *Econometrica* 40:443–59.

Mincer, J. 1974. *Schooling, Experience, and Earnings.* New York: Columbia University Press for the NBER.

Myers, S., and N. Majluf. 1984. "Corporate Financing and Investment Decisions When Firms Have Information that Investors Do Not Have." *Journal of Financial Economics* 13:187–221.

Nalebuff, B. 1987. "Credible Pretrial Negotiation." *Rand Journal of Economics* 18:198–210.

Noldeke, G., and E. van Damme. 1990. "Signalling in a Dynamic Labour Market." *Review of Economic Studies* 57:1–23.

Rogoff, K. 1989. "Reputation, Coordination, and Monetary Policy." In *Modern Business Cycle Theory.* R. Barro, ed. Cambridge: Harvard University Press.

Samuelson, W. 1984. "Bargaining Under Asymmetric Information." *Econometrica* 52:995–1005.

———. 1985. "A Theory of Credibility." *Review of Economic Studies* 52:557–73.

Sobel, J., and I. Takahashi. 1983. "A Multistage Model of Bargaining." *Review of Economic Studies* 50:411–26.

Spence, A. M. 1973. "Job Market Signaling." *Quarterly Journal of Economics* 87:355–74.

———. 1974. "Competitive and Optimal Responses to Signaling: An Analysis of Efficiency and Distribution." *Journal of Economic Theory* 8:296–332.

Stein, J. 1989. "Cheap Talk and the Fed: A Theory of Imprecise Policy Announcements." *American Economic Review* 79:32–42.

Vickers, J. 1986. "Signalling in a Model of Monetary Policy with Incomplete Information." *Oxford Economic Papers* 38:443–55.

Index